Texas Country

*For you, Andrew,
with love,
Del Wenger*

Mr. Bart Oates, 1981.
Photograph by June Van Cleef.

Texas Country
The Changing Rural Scene

Edited by
GLEN E. LICH
and
DONA B. REEVES-MARQUARDT

Foreword by
JOE B. FRANTZ

Afterword by
JOHN J. MCDERMOTT

Texas A&M University Press
COLLEGE STATION

Copyright © 1986
by Glen E. Lich and
Dona B. Reeves-Marquardt
All rights reserved

Library of Congress Cataloging-in-Publication Data
Texas country.
   Bibliography: p.
   Includes index.
   Contents: The rural scene in Texas, half-created/
half-perceived / Glen E. Lich—Nature, the settler,
and the ecological perspective in rural Texas /
Del Weniger—From Eden to Uncertain / Al Lowman—
[etc.]
   1. Texas—Civilization.   2. Anthropo-geography—
Texas.   3. Texas—Popular culture.   4. Texas—Rural
conditions.   I. Lich, Glen E., 1948–   .
II. Reeves-Marquardt, Dona B., 1932–   .
F386.5.T47   1986   976.4   86-40216
ISBN 0-89096-247-2

Manufactured in
the United States of America
First Edition

To Katherine Anne Porter

"I want to live in a world capital

or the howling wilderness."

Contents

Foreword: "Thinking Country," Joe B. Frantz / ix
Preface, Glen E. Lich / xiii
Acknowledgments / xv

1

The Rural Scene in Texas:
Half-Created/Half-Perceived,
Glen E. Lich / 3

2

Nature, the Settler, and the Ecological
Perspective in Rural Texas, Del Weniger / 17

3

From Eden to Uncertain: Observations on
People and Place Names in Texas,
Al Lowman / 37

4

Cotton, Cattle, and Crude:
The Texas Economy, 1865–1980,
J. B. Smallwood, Jr. / 67

5

Whatever Happened to the Little Frame House
on the Prairie? Clarence C. Schultz / 93

Contents

viii

6

Women on the Land,
Martha Mitten Allen / 119

7

Texas Folk and Modern Country Music,
Francis Edward Abernethy / 137

8

The Landed Heritage of Texas Writing,
Betsy Colquitt / 171

9

**From the Other Side of the Furrow:
A Folk-Group Sampler,**
Dona B. Reeves-Marquardt, Karl Weigand,
Joe S. Graham, and Joseph Wilson / 191

Afterword, John J. McDermott / 243
The Contributors / 247
Index / 250

Foreword:
"Thinking Country"

This is either the saddest book I have read in a long time, or one of the happiest. Reaction is a study of self-perception. Of what was against what is. Of what was versus what might have been.

For poignancy, Del Weniger's "Nature, the Settler, and the Ecological Perspective in Rural Texas" is a compelling epic prose-poem that tears at the soul. It manages to be simultaneously joyous and mordant, without straining toward either viewpoint. What more lovely (the word fits here) portrait than his descriptions from contemporary travelers of a Texas tall-grass prairie stretching for miles and miles, the grass always horse-high, a rolling level six feet above the ground? But then you remember the drive from, say, Bastrop to Houston in the 1980s and you ask yourself, as you look about at roadside junkyards, honkytonks, town sprawl, and cut-up land where the grass seldom reaches above the ankle, "Is this what we have done to Texas?" Is the Texas tradition oil rigs with their clutter and spatter, whole copses of trees cut away so that the land could be put to the plow, the prairie fragmented until strangers can never know it existed and sentimentalists can only hurt as they look for something they will probably never see?

The inevitable question then arises: but how would we have nurtured fourteen million people, the round-number current population of the Texas sub-empire, if we had been careful with these precious resources? Did we *have* to accept destruction and waste of resources and, yes, avarice to bring this vast nation forward? Were those people that the environmentalists so decry necessary to bring us to the abundant life? That is an argument without end.

But the melancholy continues.

On the upbeat side the reader can pick up the chapter on place names by the ubiquitous Al Lowman and let soul soar. I have often expressed regret that most of our principal towns have such ordinary names as Austin, Houston, or Dallas. Fort Worth is borderline but doesn't really conjure. El Paso del Norte, now there's a name. Or San Antonio de Bexar. Too bad that in our Anglo-American haste we had to shorten the names, but the abbreviated versions still raise imaginative sights. Or Corpus Christi. I reveled in the controversy a couple of years ago when the Department of Defense tried to name one of its instruments of war after Corpus Christi and had to back off. You do not use Corpus Christi—translated, Body of Christ—to designate something that kills and maims. The name in this instance transcended national policy.

Let those names run off your tongue. Roots that are multilingual, roots that express hope and despair, roots that show people's roots. Names borrowed for whatever reasons from cities in other countries: Paris, Odessa, Naples, Roma, Florence, Panna Maria, Palo Pinto, Danevang, New Ulm, Sebastopol. Magnificent, and not a politician in the bunch, unless you want to designate the Virgin Mary—Panna Maria in Polish—as the first feminist.

Lest it seem that I favor foreign names, let me put in a plug for Paint Rock, for Turkey, for Salt Gap. Or give me Sweetwater, Agua Dulce, and Mobeetie on an equal basis—English, Spanish, and Indian—and each one meaning "sweet water." Or in English, how about Bee Caves for giving a picture? So I spent my formative years in ordinary-named towns like Weatherford, Temple, and Austin, when I could have sold my soul to list my permanent address as Mesquite, Chisholm, Atascosa, or Bosqueville. By quirk of fate I did not visit my favorite, Mesquite, until a few years ago, when to my horror I discovered it was now a continuation of Dallas with a listed population of sixty-seven thousand and still growing. A grove of mesquite trees in the town of Mesquite must be as rare as Betty Smith's tree that grew in Brooklyn. Now I'll have to pin my hopes on Red Oak or Mustang, though they too are in Dallas's path.

Texas has a name for every mood. I revel in driving through the state, calling out place names as I meet them, like a sophomore blooming with first love singing out his sweetheart's name as if Rosemary or Sally or whoever represents purest poetry. Meanwhile, I'll live on in Austin, a name with good history but no romance, unless I decide to move to Utopia or Lowman's favorite, Uncertain.

This foreword is becoming more personal than I intended, but that is the kind of response this book evokes. Every chapter sets the reader off in another direction, dreaming and speculating about the Texas whence and wherefore. Through it all runs the apt editorial hand of Glen Lich, who again engages to interpret Texas as a place where people and geography and spaciousness and background meet. He sets up each essay with deftness and conciseness, that rarest of qualities in an academic. He hints and points, rather than tells what the next author is going to expatiate on, so that you avoid that feeling of having read the same thing twice.

I want to borrow two quotes that must be shared. One is by Francis Abernethy, who has carved out a national reputation as a folklorist without ever leaving Nacogdoches. After detailing how our generation of Texans have left the country behind because even with its problems, the city promised more opportunity than bare subsistence on a long-gone topsoil, he opines that we and our kids are still there—in Houston, Dallas, and the Golden Triangle, "living city but thinking and singing country."

In one phrase Abernethy has encapsulated Texas in the 1980s. "Living city but thinking and singing country."

That statement has implications that reach to finance, politics, industry, the arts, education, style, and almost any other Texas abstraction. I will be plagiarizing Abernethy's pithiness until I die, or at least until the situation in Texas changes, which I do not foresee in my lifetime. "Living city but thinking and singing country."

The other quotation is lifted from Betsy Colquitt's essay, which in turn quotes from Frederick Law Olmsted, that reasonably objective and undeniably artistic and sensitive traveler through the South and Texas before the Civil War. Wrote Olmsted: "In the whole journey through Eastern Texas, we did not see one of the inhabitants look into . . . a book." A century and a quarter later he might could write the same thing, unless the book were about cowboys and desperados.

But if those Texans were going to read one book for understanding, I would recommend that they try this one. They might discover that they have been missing something, and that they are not nearly the understanding Texans they thought they were.

Enough. Tomorrow is Sunday, and I am trying to decide whether to visit the town of Dilley, Dimple, Divot, or Dobrowolski. Being one of those greedy native Texans, I will probably wind up in Dinero.

JOE B. FRANTZ

Austin (why not Austonio?)
February, 1984

Preface

The present volume, which grew out of an occasional Southwest Symposium Series, examines the character of a place and its history. The book asks readers to consider what the end of rural Texas means to modern citizens. Can nostalgia bind people to the past and prevent change for the better in the present?

This collection of essays looks at the whole of Texas, the meaning of a place and the lives that are lived there, just as an urbanizing Texas bids farewell to a colorful but not conclusive rural past. The careful reader may discover a kind of party line in the chapters. History is never finished. Each new generation must believe it into being. Likewise has Texas come a long way, but it is by no means at the end of its existence.

Texas Country: The Changing Rural Scene is dedicated to one of the legendary Texans, by her own making bigger than life, a study in contrasts: Katherine Anne Porter. There are some dichotomies that can never be resolved. When she said, "I want to live in a world capital or the howling wilderness," she was remembering Texas—both parts of it. She could love it and she could hate it. She never forgot it.

Glen E. Lich

Acknowledgments

During the long time that we have been working on this book, we have received help and encouragement from many friends. Foremost are the contributors—patient, painstaking, and thoughtful. Over the years they have helped keep this project alive, and they have our greatest appreciation.

Two university administrators must next be mentioned. Professor Clarence C. Schultz, then acting dean of the College of Liberal Arts of Southwest Texas State University, helped us to start the Southwest Symposium Series in 1977. Professor Raeburn Miller, head of the Department of English at the University of New Orleans, provided considerable clerical support to start this second volume of the series.

Several individuals have dedicated hours of support: Clare Bass and Tom Shelton of the Institute of Texan Cultures, June Van Cleef of Fort Worth, Kay Satchell of Kerrville, and Mike Barba, Laura Salley, Carole DeHart, Jeanne Crenshaw, Anabel Rivera, Sally Baulch and Mary Ann Parker of Schreiner College. Our native Texan spouses, Ed Reeves and Lera Patrick Tyler, read revisions, judged illustrations, and gave valuable advice. They supported this work with their endless patience, humor, and understanding.

Texas Country

To the extent that Texas thinks of itself as an alter ego of America, the myth of Texas is not merely nostalgia, but rather is an attempt by a community of believers to survive in the shadow of Yankee America. The product of a residual, intuitive America where assimilation has been slow, this state of mind is neither solely escapist nor solely reactionary—though in part it is both of those—but projects instead an America that was, and might have been. Its culture is like that of emerging nations—vernacular and visionary— and its people both contradict and congratulate themselves, bedeviled by almost endless possibilities. Visitors to the Southwest have sensed where these tendencies come together more clearly than those who live with them every day—from John Marin's and Marsden Hartley's and Georgia O'Keeffe's images of primeval origins to Frank Waters's construct in Masked Gods *of the greater Southwest as the offspring of Mother Mexico and Uncle Sam, from William Goyen's* Arcadio *with a central character who is half-man/half-woman, half-Texan/half-Mexican, to Whitley Strieber's and James Kunetka's more recent* Warday *with its nation of Aztlan, capital El Paso, surviving after nuclear holocaust has wiped out the United States. Texans like to think of themselves as survivors, and the semiarid landscape where they have survived has often tamed their romanticism and toughened their bodies. But if they kept their imagination, they found this land beautiful after a fashion. Fred Gipson was remembering Texas when he wrote that "generally in everyone's life there is a time when he is more himself than at any other time between birth and death." When Texans recollect that time, they think of the rural scene—the picture from which the myth of Texas springs.*

1
The Rural Scene in Texas: Half-Created/Half-Perceived
Glen E. Lich

Texas appeals to romantics. It seems always to have attracted more than its share of people looking back over their shoulders as they rode ahead into the future, sometimes refractory or recalcitrant, always ready to bolt the party and initiate an independent course. Texas has grown into America. The main current of American experience has likewise been romantic. Settlement of the country as a new world, the revolution, westward expansion, and the way America entered the world wars and embarked on space exploration embody the romantic experience. Not only our history but also our culture—with its emphasis on idealism, exploration, invention, youthfulness, and purpose—confirm the romantic pattern. The Texas of today claims descent from this view of the past, from an America that might have been.

The color of Texas is golden, and the face looks both ways—back to a legendary past, ahead to an adventurous future. From Hondo Crouch at Luckenbach, where "everybody's somebody," to the Dixie Dewdrops strumming "Down Home in the City," the scene is rural—a bigger state of mind, a style, a taproot that feeds a large crown and runs deep in the caliche soil.

Texans enjoy this history. They like to think of Texas as always different—as if it were a subcontinent of the United States, as if they could pick and choose what they like from mainstream America as once the colonies developed a critical attitude toward the mother country. Texans cultivate this attitude. They like to recall that they were once an independent republic. It is an old notion, thoroughly romantic, but its roots are more than political. The sense of isolation goes back beyond politics to the geography, to the landscapes of Texas, and to the mindscapes that these scenes have engendered in generations of Texans—native or not.

The general undesirability of the region protected its earliest historic inhabitants—from the man-eating Karankawas along its swampy,

He Sent Roses.
Photograph by June Van Cleef.

disease-infested coast to the stunted and slovenly Tonkawas in its hilly midlands and beyond to the Comanches and other taller, better-fed Plains Indians. Minor Spanish and French explorers passed briefly and intermittently through the region. They sought glory, gold, and converts for their God. Their expeditions slowed down in the eroded valleys and brushy toplands. They lost their way in the high plains. They stopped at the mountains. When they left, they seldom came back. The obstacles guarded no great treasures, but Texas now had a name.

The colorful ethos imagined in that name gradually drew settlers into the more habitable parts of Texas. Spanish speakers spotted at some of the largest watering holes, and English speakers broke the blacklands and felled the forests inland from the coast. They were romantics, and like all romantics everywhere they found only fragments of their dreams in Texas, all the while loving the land and hating the weather.

Then came the Germans, farmers mostly, who brought little of the necessary equipment for clothing and feeding their families on the frontier. Like romantics, they learned to love this new country, but only because they came in the spring and because they wanted to love it. They expressed their feelings in eloquent writings. In this way, other Germans still in the old homeland learned of a rolling and hilly land similar to Sicily, alternately forested and covered by grassy prairies. The constant breezes, almost always from the east, were gentle, and the climate was mild, like springtime in Germany. The soil needed no fertilizer. Wine grapes thrived, honey could be found in hollow trees, and "wild prey such as deer, bears, raccoons, wild turkeys, geese and partridges" filled the woodlands. Even the meadows were carpeted "with the most charming flowers." Of course, there were panthers and leopards and rattlesnakes, but every planter knew "safe means against them." Besides, passports were not necessary.[1]

The dream so appealed to one romantic refugee, who wrote in the New World under the assumed name of Charles Sealsfield, that he imagined Texas into a novel, having perhaps never gotten closer than New Orleans. From there Texas looked wonderful, and his novel about life in Texas, *The Cabin Book* (1841), became a best seller.[2] Texas for

1. Friedrich Ernst, letter written Feb. 1, 1832, from Mill Creek, Tex., is quoted in G. G. Benjamin, *The Germans in Texas: A Study in Immigration* (1910; rpt. Austin: Jenkins, 1974).
2. *Das Kajütenbuch* (1841) ran fourteen printings in German and English. Rpt. Stuttgart: Philipp Reclam, 1982, with an introduction by Alexander Ritter. *The Cabin Book,* trans. Sarah Powell (1852; rpt. Austin: Eakin, 1985), with an introduction by Glen E. Lich.

Sealsfield was a "boundless sea of green," an unspoiled Garden of Eden in "God's world immaculate." It was part of an immeasurably beautiful and rich land that stood "for the progress of all civilizations."[3] Every dream is thus nourished by myths and legends. The dream of Texas as a great, golden land was no exception.

Even in those days, however, the promise of Texas did not always sustain closer scrutiny. Frederick Law Olmsted, that zealous New Englander always eager to "answer the needs and give expression to the life of [an] immense and miscellaneous democracy," found the land less grand than the mythic state of mind pictured by Sealsfield a mere twelve years earlier.[4] During his six-month stay in 1853-54, Olmsted nosed out a number of good stories, gathered materials, and moved at a fast clip, stopping long enough here and there to observe with that close scrutiny which makes *A Journey through Texas* (1857) appear to sustain depth. In most parts of Texas he was shocked at the crudeness, squalor, anti-intellectualism, ineptitude, and chauvinism of the "natives." Yet in this or that community, Olmsted glimpsed unmistakable signs of industry (with prosperity just around the corner, if not already at hand), resourcefulness, and moral and ethical well-being. The promise of a free-soil agrarian utopia, which Henry Nash Smith says had haunted the American imagination since the time of Crèvecoeur,[5] seemed everywhere just waiting to take root, but Olmsted left the state uncertain whether Texans would rise above the indolence that their climate encouraged. Olmsted shared Sealsfield's observation that there was "indeed a lot of rabble in Texas," but he was not as confident as Sealsfield that the bones of this Texas rabble would "pave the way into a better tomorrow."[6]

The faith of Texans was not shaken by such doubts. They trusted the land, perhaps indolently trusted. It had given rise to their myth. It was their legacy. They had worn out the worlds they left behind, but

---

3. Charles Sealsfield is quoted in A. Leslie Willson, "Another Planet: Texas in German Literature," *Texas and Germany: Crosscurrents*, ed. Joseph Wilson, *Rice University Studies* 63, no. 3 (1977): 101-103. Compare Henry David Thoreau's essay "Walking."

4. Charles Eliot Norton quoted in Theodora Kimball Hubbard, "Frederick Law Olmsted," in *Dictionary of American Biography*, ed. Dumas Malone (New York: Scribner's, 1948), 14: 27.

5. Henry Nash Smith, *Virgin Land: The American West as Symbol and Myth* (Cambridge: Harvard University Press, 1950), p. 170.

6. Charles Sealsfield, *The Making of an American: An Adaptation of Memorable Tales by Charles Sealsfield*, trans. Ulrich S. Carrington (Dallas: Southern Methodist University Press, 1974), pp. 26, 77.

Texas they invested with the qualities of abundance and promise—as long as it rained. Texas offered a break from "the monotony of existence," in the words of an early Texas woman. She praised it as a land of "golden freedom." Another early woman described a strange, psychic landscape where fear of the unknown mingled with the temptation to see what lay ahead. "I find that as soon as one is here, one is overcome with an amazing change; the farther one comes, the more civilization ceases, but one transforms with the changes."[7]

But the climate also shaped the people, then as now. When early settlers dispersed up the fertile river valleys more than a century ago, they learned in hard ways that the weather as they moved westward was characterized by increasing irregularity, wider extremes, and more rapid changes. In the high plains settlers were troubled by constant and drying winds, but more commonly there and elsewhere the complaint was lack of water. Rainfall was erratic. Farmers and millers washed out one year could be scorched the next. If Texas was a land of too much sky, so was it a land of the unobscured face of the sun. Even windmills and deep wells and reservoirs have not erased the fear. Rather than leaving Texans indolent, the climate sometimes made them rapacious. The land still bears scars, but so do innumerable stunted towns and teenagers. Perhaps more than the landscape, the climate has given Texans a strong identity. Texas has been a land in search of rain for as long as any Texans can remember. Out of all that Texans have seen, felt, and heard in their lifetimes, it is images of weather that recur, charged with emotion, in their letters, novels, and movies—in their faces and fields. Olmsted recognized the inevitable stunting when he observed again and again the rarity of "symmetrical and glorious" live oaks in the southwestern landscape. Most trees were only "meagerly furnished with leaves."[8] The people, living symbols of the land, have acted as the land where they live has trained them to act. There is comfort, though, in the thought that biologists now observe that such relatively barren areas often become evolutionary crucibles.

Thus the heritage alternated—between Sealsfield and Olmsted, between landscape and climate, between promise and denial. The con-

---

7. Emma Murck Altgelt is quoted in Crystal Sasse Ragsdale, *The Golden Free Land: The Reminiscences and Letters of Women on an American Frontier* (Austin: Landmark, 1976), p. 134; Ida Kappell Kapp, letter written Jan. 15, 1850, from Comaltown, Tex.

8. Frederick Law Olmsted, *A Journey through Texas; or, a Saddle-Trip on the Southwestern Frontier* (New York: Dix, Edwards, 1857; rpt. Barker Texas History Center Series 2, Austin: University of Texas Press, 1978), p. 130.

flict between these contradictions and the necessity for resolving it is the great theme running through this book and through the myths of Texas. It unites a land that still today is a blend of convenience, a sprawling convergence of three major regions with diverse cultures, ethics, and aesthetics. It is not surprising that imagination picks up where reality leaves off. As William Blake, a preeminent romantic, wrote, "Without contraries there is no progression."

Over the past century since the closing of the frontier, Texas has passed through unprecedented social changes and major economic and intellectual crises, seemingly untouched and secure in its rural outlook, a life that derives from the home, the extended family, the livelihood of the men, and the landscape. These traditions continue to play a large part in Texas life, even though today the state has three of the nation's largest cities. What dominates the popular consciousness, however, is still the rural scene, nostalgic farmsteads that present a picture of uniformity, and open, rugged landscape imbued with the qualities of the early settlers, named after them and their hopes and their old ways. People like to recall a time when food, rather than house and clothing, was an important discriminator of status. A time when work and religion retained secondary social functions, and games of mimesis, pranks, and joking were highly developed. When life was picturesque and simple, though hard, and the land was the fixed point by which people knew their relationships to everyone and everything else. An atavistic, and sometimes animistic, island in a changing world. But nostalgia and romance are not cures for physical, political, and ethical illnesses. Texans today must not remember things that their ancestors never knew.

Yet for all its strength and wisdom, the rural environment does not seem to be weathering well. More and more rural Texans, sitting on family holdings worth in many instances far more than the villas of their oil-rich city cousins, find that they can hardly support themselves and pay taxes from the income that their land produces. The emerging rural scene shows increasing disparity of wealth. The "land wealthy" have not been able to keep their homesteads up. Yet, if today the best maintained ranches (some of them used to be farms) belong to city people, the farmers and ranchers of the traditional past are partly to blame. Land and water management have lagged behind other conservation programs—game, fish, oysters, and forests—that had more obvious dollar values. Wildlife conservation started with river stocking in the 1860s. By the turn of the century Texas had progressive wildlife and forest conservation programs. By the 1920s laws gave these programs

Photograph by Susan Woolfley Lich.

teeth. In the 1930s and 1940s Texas developed some of the most professional management programs in the nation, for forests, wildlife, wilderness, historic sites, and recreational facilities. Paying in part through a luxury tax on cigarettes, Texans smoked their way to better parks.

Water and soil conservation, however, lagged miserably, and agricultural innovation all but ceased over large parts of the state—first because of the easy boom years in the late 1930s and early 1940s, then because of the debilitating drought. A Board of Water Engineers was formed in 1913, but it soon became dormant. In 1926 the Texas Forest Service looked into water use. After noting that the main rivers in the state flowed from arid to rainy regions, the forest service glimpsed a legal nightmare of conflicting and inadequate laws, and proposed almost nothing about water ownership and use. Following a few more brief attempts to come back to life, a state water program finally got going in 1945 with the Texas Water Conservation Association, led by retailers and small-town bankers. Soil conservation likewise struggled into existence.

If not forlorn to the nineteenth-century romantics, rural Texas certainly had become so in the 1950s, when there were barely enough prickly pears to get livestock through the drought. Then, when it almost seemed too late, people saw the need for agricultural conservation. It was the businessmen in the towns who led the way. Not the farmers. The problems will worsen as growth accelerates. Had Texans started to deal with them in 1860, it would be much easier today, and the rural scene would not face increasing impoverishment.

Written on the land and on the faces of its guardians, some of the movements and forces that shape human destiny can be seen when people refuse or start too late to move with the times. Hence the need to study the way people perceive history—past, present, future. The problem is not exclusively rural; Texas entered the 1980s with the largest city in the nation that had neither a freeway nor a public transit system —Arlington. But it had Six Flags.

Without conflicts, though, there would be no progression. Certainly the picture of rural Texas is not as bleak as it was in the 1950s. As once the example for public education in the state came from a small group of migrant outsiders, so the leadership in conservation has been taken by those now a generation or two removed from the land. It is a cycle. "People impose themselves on land and land imposes itself on them," reminds John Graves, who has tried to give the region a literature that reflects its life;

ways of living and building and farming come in with settlers and then evolve into other ways in accordance not only with the ethos the people have brought and what happens to them there, but also with the land's possibilities and demands. Thus landscapes where man's presence is seen do have historic weight in Texas quite as certainly as in Tuscany or Scotland or along the castled Loire. Most of us Texans so far have been too absorbed with acting and doing and making meanings to have worried much about what those meanings are and to have read their lessons. . . . Some are proud meanings . . . and others need ferreting out; some affirm Manifest Destiny while others prophesy exhaustion and deserts and doom. But all have a part in the wide, varied, rather improbable place we call Texas, and have a part in us too, insofar as we are Texans.[9]

If romanticism lured people to Texas and then a century later compares it with gentled and grassy Europe, then it shall also preserve whatever is picturesque and country and wholesome. If nostalgia for a rural past sells beer—"It's no downstream beer, no city beer"—it can surely fertilize and irrigate some things, grassroots things, that are intimately connected with human life and meaning.

Preservation of the vernacular and indigenous past may be viewed in a broader national and international context. As more and more people move into the Sunbelt states, so too are the rural areas and small towns growing most rapidly—at a rate of 15 percent compared with 9 percent for the cities.[10] Depopulation of the countryside, lamented by Oliver Goldsmith eight generations ago in England in "The Deserted Village" (1770), has turned, but some of the old agrarians complain now of "rural slums." They are right, for the present. They are right when they say too that the cities are taking up more and more valuable, arable land, encroaching on rural ways and imposing city values on the countryside. They are right too when they recognize that before the turn of this century an area the size of two average East Texas counties may be stripped for the lignite deposits that lie beneath the soil. Not only the trees will then need to be replanted, but the rural world—the people and towns, churches, schools—will need to be landscaped anew. History has seen all these changes.

9. John Graves, foreword to *Landscapes of Texas* (College Station: Texas A&M University Press, 1980), p. 24.
10. Based on the U.S. Federal Census of 1980.

In *Dust Bowl* (1979) Donald Worster draws such a lesson from the great ecological disaster of the southern plains during the 1930s. "We speak of farmers and plows on the plains and the damage they did, but the language is inadequate," he asserts. "What brought them to the region was a social system, a set of values, an economic order. . . . Capitalism . . . has been the decisive factor in this nation's use of nature."[11]

The population shifts in the United States are not only to the South but also to the West. These modern westering Americans are not responding only to a sun tropism but seem to be moving in accordance with ideological shifts in Washington, London, Bonn, and Rome: a futuring, traditionalizing, coalescing trend in the West. We see a whole generation of Americans once again following lower land prices and lower energy needs, making jobs where none were, simplifying lifestyles and shaping a Nova West. This migration seems to be part of a survival strategy in the face of dramatic, rapid changes. Whether these changes show a civilization rallying its forces for a last battle or preparing for major advances remains to be seen. History has shown it both ways.

However modern Texans approach these changes, the new regionalism and the evolving rural scene are expressions of the need to belong, to look back into the past or to see into the future. The ascendance of grassroots and conservative values, along with the increased emphasis on cultural diversity, may suggest some disconcerting things about America, or the American dream, or nationalism, or whatever description one uses for the big picture left to us by the national consensus historians.[12] This idea of mainstream America was, of course, an oversimplification. More likely, the resurgence of these values points to some parts of the American self-portrait that people do not want to lose: a romanticizing of particularism, of the little man and small town, as more viable and more organic, warmer, than national culture.

If Texas became in the 1950s "the prime new political challenger to New York," as Theodore White writes in *America in Search of Itself* (1982), that was possible only because those traditional roots ran deep in America. Texans generally would agree with White that people who come to Texas seek older values, whereas people who go to California

---

11. Donald Worster, *Dust Bowl: The Southern Plains in the 1930s* (New York: Oxford University Press, 1979), p. 5.
12. William H. Goetzmann, "Time's American Adventures," *American Studies International* 19, no. 2 (Winter, 1981): 5–47.

Domino Hall.
Photograph by June Van Cleef.

divorce themselves from old values. He flatters Texans when he reminds them that San Antonio gave *maverick* to the English language, the word for grassroots rebels, as well as stray yearlings. Even that had deeper roots. "Texas politics," White concludes, "proclaimed the state as the last frontier of free American enterprise."[13]

Texas, with its dominant rural past, is a transition in the discussion of America. Joel Garreau's provocative *Nine Nations of North America* (1981) divides the state's 1850 boundaries by three of his nine major political and socioeconomic regions: Dixie (east of Interstate 45), The Breadbasket (west of Interstate 45 and north of Interstate 10), and Mexamerica (south of Interstate 10). Older Texans knew all along, when those highways were laid in, that they more or less marked the major perceptual and cultural regions of the state—half-created/half-perceived. Of course, they would agree with Garreau that Texas has long since passed New York in wealth and that governors of Texas conduct their own foreign policy.[14] How Texans employ that wealth, especially over the next several decades, will largely determine the state of life in the Southwest, for it is the lives that are lived that are a place and its history.

In this regard, one may recall a story of two Hill Country families, both from Europe, one from Prussia and one from the Alsace. Both men were about the same age and had vaguely similar backgrounds: while the one descended from a rich Baltic family and married a young lady-in-waiting of the Prussian queen, the other descended from a more modest military and gentry background. The Prussian came to Texas with all his money, a fortune perhaps the largest between Baton Rouge and the gold rush; the Alsatian came with little money but a good head. He borrowed from the Prussian, founded a store, a bank, an industry, a ranching empire, and endowed a county road system and a small college, and stole the county seat away from the town where the Prussian lived. All of that with money originally borrowed from the Prussian. The Prussian family, on the other hand, kept its investment intact, and they still have it. Enormous then, it is inconsequential today.

Texans may not make a shibboleth of the past, but they should enrich the present with it. After major changes during the 1960s and 1970s, the ethic of survival again dominates American thought, convincing

---

13. Theodore H. White, *America in Search of Itself: The Making of the President, 1956–1980* (New York: Harper & Row, 1982), pp. 55, 64, 62.
14. Joel Garreau, *The Nine Nations of North America* (Boston: Houghton Mifflin, 1981).

Americans of their humanity, their shared legacy with all people of the past. If the country now seems less authoritarian and less urban, that is because it has become more tribal. This look at the rural scene is not only a genre painting, but a way to construct the social fabric and to filter a changing reality. The state's isolation—first geographic, then political, and now almost self-congratulatory—from the rest of the United States has fostered a spirit of backward progress, an attitude that one first sees in the romantic posture of the migrant forebears.[15] All along the way since then, the region and the people have zigzagged into modernity, one eye toward the future and the other fixed on the past. In the rural scene, the style is called "primitive refurbished."

15. John Graves, *Hard Scrabble: Observations on a Patch of Land* (New York: Knopf, 1974), pp. 59, 263–67.

What is referred to as "Texas" is a vaguely unsettling blend of convenience—part terrain, part vegetation, part culture, part politics. If wars were fought here, this land would have been contested, oft divided. Its integrity as a self-defined region rests on an earlier set of circumstances. In the beginning, place and people were caught in a delicate, and sometimes not so delicate, balance. From that union the history comes forth. We late-born citizens melt down everything, lump everything together, describe the immense number of changes with one and the same term—Texas. And we suppose that we have achieved something unchanging, stable.

2
Nature, the Settler, and the Ecological Perspective In Rural Texas
Del Weniger

From the beginning Texas attracted settlers. They flocked here from many countries, and from other states in which they had often stopped only a generation or two. Certainly the buildup of populations and of social problems pushed them and the lure of the frontier pulled them out here, but Texas must have offered something special. What gave Texas a special lure to those hemmed in and frustrated and persecuted, wanting to settle and live the good life? How did this country pan out for them, and what did they, in turn, do to it?

First to draw them, of course, was space. Few places offered the amount of pure, open space that Texas has had to offer. It is hard for us to realize how the very size of Texas sparked the imaginations of those crushing each other in the crowded countries and little states of the world. They poured in, intoxicated with the vision of all that space, and heady with the idea of getting all of it they could.

Another drawing card was the Texas climate. To those worn out by the huge expenditures of resources and energy necessary for survival in the northern winters, the comparatively mild climate of Texas, requiring only simple houses, no huge barns, no big haying operations, and the smallest of woodpiles, called loudly.

But the third and strongest attraction to Texas was the fabulous prairie. Generally, there is today little conception either of the quantity of prairies in original Texas or of what they were like. Most of us have heard of the Grand Prairie and the Blackland Prairies, and as we move about Texas we come across countless communities with names like Prairie View, Prairie Creek, Prairie Hill, String Prairie, or Roans Prairie, but we don't see anything distinctive about these places today, and the meaning of the names is lost on us. Add to that the concept we get from stereotyped songs and stories of the lone prairie as a place where cowboys love to roam but don't want to be buried, and most of us have acquired an erroneous idea of what the prairies meant to the settlers and why these expanses drew them to Texas in such droves.

Explorers used the French term *prairie* for something they found in North America. In Europe the word meant an extensive meadow, different from the flat, treeless expanse indicated by the other French word, *plaine*.

Prairies might be any size. They could be flat, but they more often were not, and they could be included in very broken country. Prairies were described by Arthur Ikin in 1841 as ranging all the way from large areas with gentle swells to rough country with "every variety of hill and dale," to "beautiful meadows," locked between mountains and "communicating with each other by small romantic dells or passes." William Kennedy in 1839 explained the beautiful unevenness of the typical prairie, writing, "In the expressive language of the Western country, the surface of the prairies is termed 'rolling,' from its supposed resemblances to the long, heavy swell of the ocean, when its waves are subsiding after a storm."[1]

Both plains and prairies had grass-covered expanses, but the plains were treeless, while the prairies had trees. Nothing shows this better than the fact that Dr. Ferdinand Roemer, one of the most highly trained scientific observers of early Texas, could write of "the forests of the prairies."[2] Nor is it any mistake that the whole watershed of a San Augustine County watercourse called Prairie Creek lies within the present Angelina National Forest.

Erasing the image of the flat, treeless expanse called up in most of our modern minds by the word may be difficult, but if we are to know what the pioneers saw when they looked out across the primeval prairie, we must imagine what the great landscape architect, Frederick Law Olmsted, saw when in 1854 he stood in the new village of San Marcos. He described "very beautiful prairies rolling off far to the southward with the smooth grassed surface varied here and there by herds of cattle and little belts, mottes and groups of live oaks."[3]

---

1. Arthur Ikin, *Texas: Its History, Topography, Agriculture, Commerce and General Statistics* (London: Gilber & Piper, 1841), p. 20; William Kennedy, *Texas: The Rise, Progress, and Prospects of the Republic of Texas*, 2nd ed. (1841; rpt. Fort Worth: Molyneaux, 1925), p. 104.

2. Ferdinand von Roemer, *Texas: With Particular Reference to German Immigration and the Physical Appearance of the Country*, trans. Oswald Mueller (San Antonio: Standard, 1935), p. 76.

3. Frederick Law Olmsted, *A Journey through Texas* (1857; rpt. Austin: von Boeckmann-Jones, 1962), p. 69.

This blending of trees and grass as prairie land is clarified by further descriptions. Dr. Roemer expressed it most simply. Writing about present Harris County, he said that "after passing through the forest, I had my first view of a Texas prairie . . . . The oft-made comparison with an English park on a grand scale appeared very appropriate to me." Later, in present Colorado and Fayette counties, west of Columbus, he described what he saw in this way: "The open prairie began again beyond this house but the ground rose in higher undulations. Here and there a single live oak stood among the tall yellow grass, presenting a view which reminded me very vividly of regions in Southern Germany where fruit trees grow in the midst of ripening grain."[4]

These references are to parks and orchards, and they are echoed time and again by others. Even western stretches which we do not usually consider prairies at all were described in the same terms. Cora Montgomery's description of Maverick County in 1852 put it this way: "Our embryo town [Eagle Pass] lies on a sloping prairie, sprinkled with mesquite trees like a vast and venerable orchard." J. De Cordova, in 1858, found the country far northwest on the Little Wichita "a high rolling prairie, covered with a heavy growth of luxuriant and nutritious grasses, and dotted here and there with islands of timber." Col. Edward Stiff, at about the same time, called his whole third division of Texas that part "north and west of the mountains . . . extensive and verdant prairies sprinkled over with lovely islands of timber."[5]

William Kennedy quoted from an earlier, unnamed observer who wrote perhaps the most beautiful and complete description of a prairie surviving.

> If the prairie be small, its greatest beauty consists in the vicinity of the surrounding margin of woodland, which resembles the shore of a lake, indented with deep vistas, like bays and inlets, and throwing out long points, like capes and headlands; while occasionally these points approach so close on either hand, that the traveller passes through a narrow avenue, or strait, where the shadows of the woodland fall upon his path, and then again emerges into another prairie. Where the plain is large, the forest outline is seen in the far perspective, like the dim shore when beheld at a distance from the ocean. The eye sometimes

---

4. Roemer, *Texas*, pp. 57, 83.
5. Cora Montgomery, *Eagle Pass; or, Life on the Border* (New York: George P. Putnam, 1852), p. 92; Jacob De Cordova, *Texas: Her Resources and Her Public Men* (Philadelphia: J. B. Lippincott, 1858), p. 292; Edward Stiff, *The Texas Emigrant* (Waco: Texian, 1968), pp. 11–12.

roves over the green meadow without discovering a tree, a shrub, or any other object in the immense expanse but the wilderness of grass and flowers; while, at another time, the prospect is enlivened by the groves, which are seen interspersed like islands, or the solitary tree, which stands alone in the blooming desert.[6]

This combination of grass and trees, a fusion of the forest and the grassland, or rather, since it is probably more accurate to see them as antagonists, the no-man's-land between these major provinces where each held its outposts but neither could triumph any more than the sea and the land on the beach, was the Texas prairie.

And the settlers came seeking the prairies with an urgency bordering on frenzy. There must have been reasons for such a drive. Dr. Ferdinand von Herff wrote a beautiful word-picture of the 1850 Texas scene that gives some clues. He put it this way: "Let us compare a western woods farmer . . . with an inhabitant of the Texas prairie. . . . Here in Texas we find a simply-built frame house with open gallery, a well-cultivated, highly productive piece of land, in the foreground the beautiful green prairie with scattered clumps of trees on the placid hills, in the background cedar brakes or elms and a liveoak thicket."[7]

We see in this passage the simply built house with its openness that the wonderful climate not only allowed, but actually demanded. Then we see a clue in the high productivity of the prairie, another in the spaciousness of the scene in contrast to the closed-in homestead of the woods dweller, and another in the variety of natural resources available on this prairie farm, from wide meadows for the animals to timber for lumber and fuel. No wonder people swarmed into these rich prairies. There was convenience as nature seldom arranged it elsewhere.

This rich grassland interspersed with forests equally rich in their resources was reason enough for the pioneers to come. But apparently for a yet more subtle reason these scenes drew them.

The prairies constituted a belt where neither the forest province of the east nor the western grassland completely triumphed, but where each held its outposts and enclaves. This whole area was a unique mix-

---

6. Kennedy, *Texas*, pp. 104, 105.
7. Arthur L. Finck, "A Translation of *The Regulated Emigration of the German Proletariat with Special Reference to Texas*," by Ferdinand von Hoff (M.A. thesis, University of Texas, 1949), pp. 64, 65.

Nature, Settler, and Ecological Perspective

ture of the two. Such a zone of mixture where two such biomes meet is natural. Ecologists call it an ecotone. The prairies of Texas constituted one of the grandest, most extensive ecotones of the continent. It was often three hundred miles wide, from the scattered prairies included in the forests of East Texas, to the breaks of the Llano Estacado and the Pecos River Valley. Its presence had historical consequence.

There are those who tell us that the human being is by nature an ecotone dweller. They have pointed out that we most naturally choose to live on the edges of the forests, grasslands, deserts or swamps, instead of in the middle of any of them. In other words, the sites we prefer for our homes have always been in an ecotone such as that between a forest and a river, between the uplands and the marsh, or somewhere along the great ecotone between the land and the sea. Conversely, if for some reason we have to make our home in the forest or on the plain, we quickly make a clearing in the forest or set out trees around the house on the plain. As rapidly as possible we turn the area around an abode into ecotone. Only when this is accomplished have we mitigated the awesome closeness of the forest, or can we stand straight upon the plain without feeling lonesome and exposed and truly call it home. We turn our estates, campuses, and parks into alternating grassy vistas and groves—into tame prairies or artificial ecotones.

Corroboration of these feelings of having escaped the threat of wilderness and arrived instead at places welcoming them as though prepared for their living is not hard to find in the writings of the pioneers as they entered the prairies of Texas. For instance, from Kennedy,

> The gaiety of the prairie, its embellishments, and the absence of the gloom and savage wildness of the forest, all contribute to dispel the feeling of lonesomeness which usually creeps over the mind of the solitary traveller in the wilderness. Though he may see neither house nor human and though conscious that he is far from the habitation of man, he can scarcely divest himself of the idea that he is travelling through scenes embellished by the hand of art. The flowers, so fragile, so delicate, and so ornamental, seem to have been tastefully disposed to adorn the scene. The groves and clumps of trees appear to have been scattered over the lawn to beautify the landscape, and it is not easy to avoid that illusion of the fancy which persuades the beholder that such scenery has been created to gratify the refined taste of civilized man. Europeans are often reminded of the resemblance of this scene to that of the extensive parks of noblemen, which

they have been accustomed to admire in the old world; the lawn, the avenue, the grove, the copse, which are there produced by art, are here produced by nature—a splendid specimen of massy architecture, and the distant view of villages, are alone wanting to render the similitude complete.[8]

Who would not strive to live in such parks? Seldom did nature prepare sites more appealing to human homing instincts than the ones in these prairies. Roemer expressed it after his trip with Baron Meusebach to the uninhabited San Saba region in 1847: "I had grown to love the beautiful land of meadows, to which belongs a great future. . . . May its broad, green prairies become the habitation of a great and happy people."[9]

In these prairies of Texas the pioneers settled. Rarely did they stop in the middle of the forests and carve out clearings until all the prairies were filled up. In East Texas they settled on the natural clearings of the included prairies, placing their houses and villages at the edges of the woods. In the Hill Country they settled along what we call the alluvial plains, which were Ikin's "beautiful meadows" locked between mountains. And they did not move out onto the actual plains until later, when they had technologies with which they could turn bits of these into mock prairies.

They came in to fill up this land, but how did this fabulous country pan out for the settlers? Did it grant these frantic seekers all it promised? The answer is yes and no; since there were very definite limits to what it granted, some conditions had to be met before it gave. It could be a tricky environment to deal with.

The space and resources in Texas absorbed and provided for many pioneers, but, as those who got here a little late soon found out, the possibilities were far from infinite. In each part of the state in its turn the good prairies where settlers could live successfully were "filled up" within thirty years after the first push. Accounts are full of the pathetic ones who came too late and had the choice of settling out in inferior situations where their success could at best be marginal, remaining unlanded laborers, or going back to where they had started. The land speculations and the bitter fights over grants that occurred in those days make for interesting studies today, but it is too seldom pointed out

8. Kennedy, *Texas,* p. 106.
9. Ferdinand von Roemer, in "Samuel W. Geiser," *Naturalists of the Frontier* (Dallas: Southern Methodist University Press, 1948), p. 171.

Nature, Settler, and Ecological Perspective

that the shoddy, vicious, and often violent things that happened evidence not only the failures of human nature and human institutions but also the limitations of that vast and rich land.

The settlers also soon found out that this wonderful country gave up its resources grudgingly and only at the price of supreme effort. Living by the sweat of the brow was certainly enforced by the early Texas environment, and this discovery was an unkind surprise for many immigrants because almost all of the emigrant guides gave the impression that settlers could live here with a minimum of effort, watch their loose-running livestock multiply, plant corn practically in the prairie sod, spend most of their time being heroic hunters, and everything would somehow be supplied in abundance. Many tried it, and their failures were horrible. A central theme of the pioneer story was the everlasting struggle to survive and the bitterness or resignation it so often engendered in those who had hoped for better in this Eden. Only those who were prepared spiritually as well as materially for superhuman efforts succeeded here, and that is probably why we venerate them now.

We tend, however, to forget those who failed, and along with them the fact that the environment was actually harsh and demanding. Olmsted's account of the procession of pathetic settlers' shacks he visited on his 1854 trek across Texas, where the occupants were usually destitute and starved while the father was typically away hunting even though the stock pens were empty and the fields overgrown, is a picture of squalor. His account of one settler's consumptive son coughing away his life between a superheated fireplace and the windows through which an icy norther blasted over him because no one had ever bothered to cover them with anything, is a graphic lesson that this was no Eden.[10] Olmsted's euphoria at all he found at New Braunfels is not just the result of finding a culture akin to his own but his reaction to finding a society of people who had come here, taken the challenge of the environment squarely, and proved willing to expend enough effort in farming and building to reap the country's prizes. Texas offered fruits, but seldom just for the plucking.

Even for the sincerely struggling, the Texas environment could be so tricky as to seem almost devilish. The quirks of the climate illustrate this best.

Over and over again the climate was advertised as warm, languid,

10. Olmsted, *A Journey through Texas,* p. 54.

and salubrious. But there is another side to this climate. Although usually serene, it is at times a climate of sudden extremes: droughts, floods, hurricanes, and northers. Read the accounts of the droughts in the first years of Castroville, of the floods that routinely wiped out the mills built in the Hill Country, of the hurricanes that decimated Indianola and Galveston, and of the northers such as that which froze the water in Eliza Johnston's cup before she could drink it in North Texas in 1856[11] or the one that came as the 1863 snowstorm, which killed fourteen hundred sheep at Onion Creek, near Austin, and kept their bodies frozen for at least four days so that owners managed to shear all of them before they spoiled.[12] The Texas climate is deceptive; it can nurture well, only to deliver a deathblow diabolical in its suddenness. It is not an environment for the unwary.

Many settlers found places in this Texas, and did heroic deeds, and were resourceful and prospered mightily. But many found no places left for them, or were less heroic, not resourceful enough, or a little careless, and they failed, moved on, or just vanished—and we never think of them. The same goes on. There is still a Texas environment that offers space, resources, and promises of an affluent life, and it still attracts the world's peoples, perhaps as never before.

Yet another question now arises. What have these settlers done to this fabulous country? This question is crucial to any realistic ecological understanding of people in rural Texas.

The pioneers' first impact upon the country can hardly be seen as anything but a frenzied drive to tame it. Faced with an overpowering biomass in standing forests and in grasses that rose waist- or head-high each summer and then lay down to form entangling mats, only to be resurrected again each year, settlers resorted to whatever means at their disposal to bring this frightening, rampant prolificacy under control. Thousands of settlers embarked on one of the most intense slash-and-burn campaigns ever seen. The axe did its part, but the best weapon against the uncontrolled productivity of the prairies was fire.

All of the conflagrations described in scores of eyewitness accounts were credited to human beings, and the fires seem to have begun with the advent of the historical period. Friedrich von Wrede implied this when he wrote in 1838 of "great areas of land in Texas which were sud-

---

11. Eliza Johnston, "The Diary of Eliza (Mrs. Albert Sidney) Johnston," ed. Charles P. Roland and Richard C. Robbins, *Southwestern Historical Quarterly* 60 (1957): 486-87.
12. Rose Ann Harper, "Blizzard on Onion Creek," *Texana* 10 (1972): 46-50.

Nature, Settler, and Ecological Perspective

denly exposed to new meteorological influences after huge forest and prairie fires."[13]

Among the best evidence are the accounts from the early nineteenth-century mesquite prairies of stands of fire-killed trees that had obviously not been burned earlier. In 1849 Lieutenant Michler wrote, "On rising the bluffs of the main fork of the Brazos, we again found a continuation of the mezquite flats, over which we travelled until we reached the head of the Double Mountain fork of the Brazos.... The whole country was well timbered with mezquite, but most of it had been killed by prairie fires."[14] In his 1854 report Capt. John Pope stated, "The mezquite, a hard and durable wood, grows in extensive forests, is about thirty feet high, and from four to ten inches in diameter.... The yearly burning of the prairies has very seriously obstructed the growth of this timber, as was sufficiently apparent in the scorched and blackened forests west of the Colorado."[15] With as much grass as there was then, the fires must have been a more effective brush eradication tool than anything since devised, and the implication is that the face of the country was being changed by the extensive fires in a way new since the coming of the Anglo-American.

The almost universal extent of the burning in eastern Texas is also attested to by many eyewitnesses. All of Galveston Island was burnt over in 1831 under orders of Colonel Bradburn.[16] Thomas Drummond wrote in an 1834 letter, "I am sorry to say that I have found no insects, as they are very scarce in these and all prairie countries, owing to the frequent burning of these lands. The whole country, from the Rio Colorado to the Guadalupe, a distance of eighty or ninety miles, is as destitute of verdure as the streets of Glasgow, except some small patches along the creeks."[17] But the extent of the practice is made most graphic by some 1841 entries in the diary of Adolphus Sterne, a prominent

---

13. Friedrich W. von Wrede, *Sketches of Life in the United States of North America and Texas,* ed. Emil Drescher, Chester W. Geue (Waco: Texian Press, 1970; orig. 1844), p. 96.

14. Lt. N. Michler, "Report of January 28, 1850," *Senate Ex. Doc.* 64, 31st Cong. 1st sess., 1850, p. 35.

15. Capt. John Pope, "Report of Exploration of a Route for the Pacific Railroad, Near the Thirty-Second Parallel of North Latitude, from the Red River to the Rio Grande," *Senate Ex. Doc.* 78, 33rd Cong., 2nd sess., 1855, p. 28.

16. Robert S. Gray, ed., *A Visit to Texas in 1831,* 3rd ed. (Houston: Cordovan, 1975), p. 72.

17. Thomas Drummond, Letter to Sir William Jackson Hooker, Sept. 26, 1834, quoted in Samuel W. Geiser, *Naturalists of the Frontier* (Dallas: Southern Methodist University Press, 1948), p. 85.

businessman of early Nacogdoches: "Saturday [February] the 27th the whole Country is on fire so much so that the Sun has not, nor could not, make her appearance for several days past, and there has been so much Smoke, yet it will not rain, and I seriously believe it is going to end in Smoke alltogether.... The Smoke this Evening is so thick as to obscure the Sun completely, and is becoming very disagreeable to the Eyes. Sunday the 28th fine weather, smoke in abundance."[18]

The practice presented enough of a problem that the state legislature in 1848 made it illegal to burn prairies from July 1 to February 15, except on a person's own land, but this had so little effect that in 1852 two of the early sisters at San Antonio's Ursuline Convent wrote, "At this season [December 16] the prairies are all set on fire, to destroy the remains of the old grass, so that a fresh supply may spring up. They present a beautiful aspect at night—the fire is too distant to be seen, but the horizon is all illuminated. Many poor animals perish with hunger during the winter."[19]

The other agent of the settlers that early decimated the natural community was their domestic animals—if they could really be called that.

At the beginning of the historical period, the Talon brothers, who were with La Salle, reported in 1698, "There will be presently a quantity of runaway or wild pigs in all the country, the French having released some that had already marvelously reproduced by the time the Talons arrived there. And the savages do not eat them, saying that they are the dogs of the French."[20]

The Spanish turned their animals loose early and started the ranching system on the prairies of South Texas. The five mission ranches in the San Antonio area possessed a total of more than five thousand cattle and seventeen thousand sheep in the 1760s. The Mission Espíritu Santo near present Goliad was grazing sixteen thousand cattle on the countryside by 1768.[21] Many of these cows remained in the wilderness

---

18. Adolphus Sterne, "Diary of Adolphus Sterne," ed. Harriet Smither, pt. 6, *Southwestern Historical Quarterly* 31 (1928): 287.

19. Sr. Mary Patrick Joseph and Sr. Mary Augustine Joseph, *Letters from the Ursuline, 1852–1853*, ed. Catherine McDowell (San Antonio: Trinity University Press, 1977), p. 267.

20. Pierre and Jean Baptiste Talon, "Report of two Canadian Soldiers Who made the Trip with de la Salle to the Mississippi and Returned," dated Feb. 14, 1698 (Manuscript, trans. Sr. Ann Linda Bell).

21. Del Weniger, "Wilderness, Farm and Ranch," *San Antonio in the 18th Century,* ed. Frances K. Hendricks (San Antonio: San Antonio Bicentennial Heritage Committee, 1976), pp. 111–12.

and propagated beyond the time of the mission period. As Pierre Pages was traveling down the old San Antonio Road between present Houston and Bastrop counties in 1767, he reported, "We began to observe the traces of horned cattle, which were originally tame, but have long since become wild, and now roam in large herds all over the plains."[22] In 1821 Stephen F. Austin reported, "Near the mouth of the Brazos there are plenty of wild cattle . . . we saw abundance of cattle."[23] That these Spanish cattle had spread far to the north is made clear by W. B. Dewees's experience in 1822. "In May, some six or seven of us took a trip as high up as Little river by water. . . . On our way, we would amuse ourselves by going out and shooting wild cattle, which are in great abundance here. It was dangerous for us to encamp at night, on the east side of the river, on account of the cattle coming in for water, the night being the only time they go to water."[24]

By the 1840s the Americans were getting into the ranching business, and there was competition between cows, as pictured in 1848 by Viktor Bracht.

> Enormous herds of wild cattle, or cattle which have grown wild, range on the Sabinas and the upper Guadalupe, on the Rio Grande and on Peach Creek, as well as in several other regions, particularly along the Brazos. To chase them is a most difficult and dangerous undertaking. These animals, by their appearance, seem to be descendants of the Spanish cattle. At times they are so shy that one cannot get within a mile of them. At other times they charge angrily on man though some distance away. They are a great nuisance to owners of large herds of cattle, because they often cause the tame cattle to run away. For these reasons the border settlers continually hunt them as game, and therefore seldom have to butcher any of their domestic cattle.[25]

The nineteenth-century wave of pioneers expanded the numbers of animals swiftly. These were their harvesters to reap with the least of

---

22. Pierre Marie François de Pages, "Across Texas in 1767: The Travels of Captain Pages," ed. Marilyn McAdams Sibley, *Southwestern Historical Quarterly* 70 (1967): 612.

23. Stephen F. Austin, "Journal of Stephen F. Austin on His First Trip to Texas, 1821," *Southwestern Historical Quarterly* 7 (1904): 307.

24. W. B. Dewees, *Letters from an Early Settler of Texas* (Waco: Texian Press, 1968), p. 26.

25. Viktor Bracht, *Texas in 1848, 1849*, trans. Charles Frank Schmidt (San Antonio: Naylor, 1931), p. 42.

effort the riches of the prairies that they had not had to plant. Ranching was a passive agriculture. It was a transplantation and adaptation of the African herd-following and meant for these settlers an abandonment of the European tradition of enfolding, of essentially keeping the animals in or near the house. Numerous people wrote back to Europe about this wondrous country where one could start with a few cows, let them roam on the prairies, and watch them multiply until one was rich in herds. Nothing could be easier.

The effects of this ranching were seen in accounts of the towns of those days where the meat from both wild game and the semiwild cattle was cheap, while vegetables were almost unavailable, and sometimes corn could not even be bought for the traveler's horses. Olmsted's accounts are especially graphic in picturing semistarvation in the settlers' shacks, including disease occasioned by their persistence in trying to be glorified hunters and gatherers instead of buckling down to farming. This is what made the often-noted contrast between the typical settler's squalor and the wealth of the slaveholding plantations, early New Braunfels, and the South Texas *haciendas* so striking. Few besides Germans, slaves, and *peons* would work like that. It was all summed up the night that Olmsted considered himself fortunate to be able to barricade himself inside a significantly empty pig pen in order to keep safe from wild hogs in the forest[26] and by the fact that an ordinance had to be enacted in early San Antonio requiring those settlers who persisted in farming to fence their fields so livestock could continue to roam loose.[27]

But the practice continued with dire effects on the living community —both natural and introduced. The prairies around San Antonio, which Dewees had said were covered with thick grass three feet high in 1823, were only thirty years later devoid of grasses. "Cows give very little milk," one of the Ursuline sisters wrote, "as they get no care, and are exposed to all the wintry winds. Indeed I know not where they now find food, as not a spot of verdure could we discover for the last months in the broad tracts of prairie which bound us to the north."[28]

Soon newer, even more efficient harvesters of the natural lushness, and those that could better work the hills, were brought in. These were the sheep. They finished tidying up the landscape. A citizen, writing on Robertson County for the 1861 *Texas Almanac*, gives us the scope

---

26. Olmsted, *A Journey through Texas*, pp. 33, 37.
27. Del Weniger, "Wilderness, Farm and Ranch," p. 113.
28. Joseph and Joseph, *Letters from the Ursuline, 1852–1853*, p. 365.

of this new assault. "Sheep grazing has received a great deal of attention in this county, there being now some 30,000 head within its boundaries.... There are probably about the same number of hogs in the county."[29] Much of Texas was by that time similarly populated by sheep.

To his everlasting credit, in an 1860 letter, Jack Burrowes, a settler on Onion Creek in Hays County, recognized the problem. "I am getting a little afraid the sheep will take the mountains in four or five years more, for their is herds from 500 to 5000 passing every five or six weeks going up a little higher than I am, and once in a while a herd will stop within three or four miles of us. Sheep is mighty hard on the range. You can tell a sheep ranch before you get in two or three miles of the house, for they keep the grass eat plum in the ground, and cattle or horses cant get hold of it. And after they are on a place six months their haint no grass within a quarter of the pens. And that keeps off other stock."[30]

In one of the oldest colonies of the state the land endured first fire and then grazing, and then moved on to what, until strip-mining came to Texas, we thought was the final form of exploitation—tilling. J. H. Kuykendall wrote in the 1850s that

> in that portion of the State embraced within the limits of Austin's colony, the face of the country has greatly changed since its first settlement. In 1821 and for several years afterwards, wild oats and wild rye grew in great luxuriance in the bottoms of the Brazos and Colorado. These fine grasses have long since disappeared. In many localities in the same bottoms where dense and extensive cane brakes formerly existed, scarcely a cane can now be found. Many of the prairies on which, of old, the grass waved in rank luxuriance, have been grazed and trodden by stock until weeds and bushes are fast usurping their surface. Formerly the annual burning of the grass prevented the spread of forest vegetation in the prairies. Thirty years ago the currents of the small creeks in the hilly and undulating portion of the colony whispered along through tall reeds and flags and "flowing hair of green confervae," and, here and there were deep and limpid pools, on the surface of which floated the broad, disclike leaves of the water-lily. Innumerable perch, trout, and other

29. A Citizen, "Robertson County," *Texas Almanac for 1861*, p. 180.
30. Jack (John Taylor) Burrowes, letter quoted in Charles M. Snyder, "New Jersey Pioneers in Texas," *Southwestern Historical Quarterly* 64 (1961): 360.

scaly fry tenanted these pools undisturbed by the angler. *Now, how different is the aspect which these brooks present!* The reeds, the flags, the confervae, the lilies, and even the pools (and with them the fish) have disappeared, and in many instances, deep and unsightly ravines conduct the streams over muddy beds. The formation of these ravines is easily explained. The cattle grazed and trampled down the flags and other vegetation and sank into and destroyed the cohesion of the turf. Successive freshets did the rest. Greatly changed is also the appearance of the wooded bottoms of the larger creeks in the same section of the country. The small confluents of such streams, during freshets, carry down their tribute of earth washed from innumerable farms. This sediment is deposited over the length and breadth of the bottoms, covering from time to time the scanty winter-range that remains.[31]

"In twenty-one short years," according to one authority, "the range changed from a virgin grassland to a man-made desert. In 1873 the first buffalo hunters arrive; by 1894 domestic cattle were dying by the thousands on overgrazed ranges. The history of the ravaging of a vast grassland in so short a time is almost unbelievable. An entire biological community that had taken millennia to evolve was destroyed in less than a quarter of one century."[32]

The reduction of the trees of Texas followed rapidly. The spread of lumbering is better documented than the destruction of lesser-regarded trees. Mrs. S. G. Miller, for instance, relates that her father had built on his ranch in the Nueces Valley, soon after 1870, a *palisado* fence consisting of fifteen miles of mesquite posts set upright *against each other*, three feet into the ground and as high as a man.[33] Another person tells that a pasture of a million acres was fenced with cedar posts hauled from the Canadian brakes in 1886.[34]

As a result of fires, animals, and cutting—human effects—by the last twenty years of the nineteenth century Texas had less vegetation than before the settlers arrived. This is one reason why old-timers who

---

31. J. H. Kuykendall, "Miscellaneous Remarks.—By J.H.K.," *Southwestern Historical Quarterly* 7 (1903): 51–52.

32. Thadis W. Box, "Range Deterioration in West Texas," *Southwestern Historical Quarterly* 71 (1967): 37.

33. Mrs. S. G. Miller, *Sixty Years in the Nueces Valley, 1870–1930* (San Antonio: Naylor, 1930), p. 34.

34. D. B. Hiatt, *Ever the Wildebeest* (Kerrville, Tex.: D. B. Hiatt, 1978), p. 154.

were young then describe early Texas as so open and so different from what we know now was truly the original state. For descriptions of many parts of Texas in primeval condition, one must go to sources before the 1850s. Scientists have speculated on plant diseases and droughts in looking for natural causes for this late-nineteenth-century decline,[35] but those are not the causes. The unnatural effect of humans on the natural community in Texas has been catastrophic and continues.

So what is the ecological perspective of rural Texas? The background is the wide, lush panorama of virgin prairies. It moves forward through episodes of human assault with fire, axe, and gun to ever newer and more irresistible tools of destruction such as plow, bulldozer, and dragline, across two centuries of killing and destruction, of confiscation of resources from the surface of ever-widening stripped tracts and from ever deeper in the ground itself. So-called soil and water conservation programs along the way have mostly been no more than an application of ever more sophisticated technologies to milk the biosphere ever drier, or else palliatives keeping sick communities alive a little longer in a sort of intensive care. Paradoxically, rural development programs have mostly proved to be schemes to make the countryside less rural.

Modern settlers first appear in this perspective as little specks running around setting fires, blazing away with their guns, and axing a few trees — most irritating little specks to be sure, but hardly all-threatening. Then they bring in their animals, their plows, and their mechanical harvesters and start destroying the natural prairie. A little of that would not have been so bad, here and there, but the situation begins to look ecologically dangerous when almost the whole countryside becomes monoculture fields and the specks multiply until the action is like that of leaf-cutter ants stripping a tree and hauling it off in a million pieces to their nests. The rapaciousness of these leaf-cutter humans seems to know no bounds. They still act as if the prairies and their resources are infinite, even though from our ecological vantage point it is clear they are not.

Closer to us the scene is still changing. Some of these humans now seem bent on covering the prairies with the concrete of highways, airfields, and power plants, while others seem equally frantic to strip-mine or to quarry the surface away. The foreground of the picture becomes a sick scene. Here the cities grow together to form metroplexes

---

35. W. A. Price and G. Gunter, "Certain Recent Geological and Biological Changes in South Texas, with Consideration of Probable Causes," *Transactions Texas Academy of Science* 26 (1943): 146–47.

and metastasize until it is hard to get out of sight of a town by day or find a rural sky unlit by suburbs at night.

If we survey the scene from the beginning, the projection to the end is clear. Rural Texas is receding. It might vanish and the journey be over. But there is yet another possibility suggested by the total scene.

Here and there throughout the whole panorama are mighty storms and droughts, which remind us that the natural Texas environment will probably not remain quiet and die peacefully. Yet who takes this into account? The children of pioneers who shot every buffalo, trapped every beaver, grazed every blade of grass, and filled up every glade they could, devise ever more efficient means of taking it all—every bit of biomass, every drop of water—as surely as they are the last dregs of oil. They have come to depend on the full take. They extend themselves on the premise that they can always meet their needs. But Texas has had the diabolical habit of suddenly turning off the water, of coming up with extremes that wipe out herds or wreck facilities with great winds, shutting off all production. Frightful losses have resulted from these instabilities. Any valid projection would therefore have to include even more terrible reenactments of such losses as more and more people build more and more carelessly on everything, from the very islands where others were drowned to the Llano Estacado, where they perished of starvation and thirst. The end of rural Texas may not be peaceful.

We need not, however, follow the trends seen from this viewpoint. We are dominant, and could still start off on a new tack. We could yet limit ourselves and let the prairies recover. We could still restrain ourselves and become a cooperating part of the living community. We could, as Isaac Asimov suggested in an essay for *Time* in 1977, "return to the days before 1800, to the days before the fossil fuels powered a vast machine industry and technology." But the hour for rural Texas is late! As Asimov concluded in "A World without Fuel," "if we had only started 50 years ago, it would have been easy."

To his eternal credit, a man known to us only as "Gid," of Long Point, Texas, set out for all, in the 1861 edition of the *Texas Almanac,* the kind of choices that have to be made if our writings on it do not become the epitaphs of rural Texas:

> Now, that all the world "and the rest of mankind," are coming to Texas, it behooves those who intend to remain here, to look around them and see what portion of nature's wide-spread bounties can be saved from the destructive tramp of immigra-

Windmill in South Texas.
Photograph courtesy La Retama Public Library,
Corpus Christi.

tion. First, as most essential, I would point the attention of the investigating portions of our community to the analyzation of preservation of the best species of our great variety of superior indigenous meadow grasses; for it requires not the spirit of divination to see that the increasing number of farms, and with them cows, sheep, and other stock, aided by the insinuating action of the destructive plow, will soon put an end to our heretofore boundless fields of luscious pasturage. No country on earth could compare with this, as a stock-raising region, previous to the devastating tract of the incursive plow. It is plain, that our wide-spreading prairie pastures will soon be gone; when we shall be forced to resort to the grass-growing system, or our rich milk and butter and fat cattle will be gone too. . . . Some of our more thoughtful farmers, men whose minds and souls are not wholly engrossed with the all-absorbing "cotton, cotton, first bale of cotton," . . . are already beginning to speak of the waning grass . . . before the prairies shall all be plowed up.[36]

36. Gid [pseud.], "Native or Indigenous Texas Grasses," *Texas Almanac for 1861*, p. 139.

Walt Whitman maintained that the greatness of a land depended on its names, and J. Frank Dobie, who displayed more than amateur interst in the subject, noted that "the map is covered with names that tell stories, reveal character, betray sentiments, call up events, express facts." Names mark the first conquest of a wilderness — the signposts of the trailblazers. Place names can, and often do, reveal much about the values and aspirations of those who confer the names. If one considers the date at which certain Texas settlements were founded and named, one glimpses how naming the land changed with time and locale, how the westering dream varied among ethnic groups, and how the transition from a rural to an urban frame of mind can be documented in Texas town names.

3
From Eden to Uncertain: Observations on People and Place Names in Texas
Al Lowman

Among the feelings that have moved men powerfully, none has been more universal than love of the earth. Consciously or unconsciously, silently or in defiant proclamations, men have always identified themselves with their native soil. With their own countryside, with their home rock, they have associated the forces of their lives. Young men, not always in vain, have died for this ideal of the land; poets have sung it and old men have celebrated it in story. It has made some men narrow, but it has made others heroic. Famed or nameless, each of us is moved by this feeling for the place of his growth. Every man deserves a native heath.[1]

So wrote Harry Ransom in 1939. And how people choose to identify this place of their growth may tell us something of the outlook, the values held by those who claim it as their own.

The study of place names may be useful beyond the mere knowledge of how or why a particular landscape feature or habitat received its designation. Fred Tarpley, Texas' foremost onomatologist, points out that "from the origins of map names, linguists determine sources of names and foreign language influence; historians trace migrations and the impact of events upon names; folklorists discover local customs and whims in choosing names; scientists find boundaries of plant and animal life, minerals, and terrain reflected in place names. For everyone, the stories behind local place names provide fascination in the mystery and diversity of their sources."[2] Tarpley may have more confidence in the reve-

---

1. Harry H. Ransom, "A Man Deserves a Heath," in *Texian Stomping Grounds* (Austin: Texas Folk-Lore Society, 1941), p. vii.
2. Fred Tarpley, *Place Names of Northeast Texas* (Commerce: East Texas State University, 1969), p. ix.

latory qualities of onomatology than I do, for reasons that will soon emerge.

One might generalize and say that place names given by native Americans were usually derived from physical attributes of the surroundings, that place names conferred by the Spanish conquerers were often associated with their religious heritage, whereas the army of Anglo-American settlers in Texas frequently chose to honor themselves, their places of origin, or places of biblical significance.

However dangerous such generalities may be, place names can, and sometimes do, give insight into the aspirations and values of those who confer the names—names that reflect beauty, ugliness, hope, despair, altruism, vanity, success, failure, and the whole gamut of human response. The sources of place names are widely divergent. They stem from geology, flora and fauna, climate, religion and mythology, memories of other places, occupations, anecdotes and events, company and brand names, arbitrary assignment by postal authorities, and pure whimsy. But most Texas place names tend to memorialize individuals.

Indian Names

Indians, the original inhabitants of what is now Texas, were mostly driven away in the nineteenth century, but in isolated instances their place names bear testimony to their one-time occupancy—names like Texas itself, which allegedly stems from a Hasinai Indian greeting. Two of the state's metropolitan areas bear the names of tribes that once lived in those vicinities—Waco and Wichita Falls. The falls, by the way, are as long-vanished as the Indians. Tribal history is further recalled in such communities as Aransas Pass, Caddo, Cherokee, Comanche, Keechi, Kickapoo, Lipan, Nacogdoches, Seminole, and Tehuacana.

Aransas Pass takes its name from Aransas Bay, which in turn was named for a tribe or portion of a tribe that the Spanish designated the Aransuas. Cherokee in San Saba County derives its name from Cherokee Creek, so designated in 1854 by a surveyor in the Fisher-Miller land grant. The surveyor may have been inspired by the creek's proximity to the site of Gen. Edward Burleson's Christmas Day battle with the Indians fifteen years earlier, or he may have named it in honor of Polly Ann Rogers, a pure-blooded Cherokee, who was the wife of an area settler. Those who founded the town of Comanche on Indian Creek needed little imagination to produce such a designation. It was 1856, and tribesmen were all about them—adding gusto and uncertainty to an otherwise drab existence.

Keechi, in Leon County, was settled before 1860 on a site formerly occupied by members of the Kichai tribe. Allegedly the name means "peaceful." The Nacogdoches Indians were a Caddoan tribe, one of the nine Hasinai confederates. Pawnee in Bee County was so named because settlers found arrowheads in nearby Sulphur Creek that they believed to have been made by Pawnee Indians. Wild Indians had long been subjugated when Seminole was established on the Southern Plains in 1905, but the town was named for the Seminole Wells discovered by Seminole scouts who guided U.S. Army troops over the area thirty years earlier. Tehuacana, in northeastern Limestone County, was named for the Tawakoni Indians, who roamed the area between the Brazos and Trinity rivers in the 1840s. Oddly, the tribal name became anglicized while the place name remained Hispanic. Most often Spanish explorers were the first Europeans to leave a written record of their encounters with the natives, with the result that place names of Indian origin were first recorded and then remained in the Spanish language. Examples abound.

Anahuac, a cauldron of the Texas Revolution, purportedly derives from an Aztec word meaning "plain near the water." First given this name in 1849, the town was earlier known as Perry's Point and later as Chambersea. Henry Perry was an original settler and Thomas Jefferson Chambers was the area's largest landowner. Cibolo, in western Guadalupe County, takes its name from a meandering creek that originates in Kendall County and forms the northern and eastern boundary of Bexar County before entering the San Antonio River above Floresville. Cibolo, according to the *Handbook of Texas,* is both an Indian and Spanish word meaning buffalo.

There are other place names of Indian origin that reveal the significance of the buffalo in their culture. Tribesmen referred to a certain South Texas stream as Hide Creek (in their native tongue, of course). Early explorers called it Cuero Creek, a Spanish word with the same meaning. It is so designated on maps as early as 1745. The hides were buffalo hides. Anglo-Americans established the town of Cuero along its banks in 1846. Waxahachie, beginning about 1851, is named for Waxahachie Creek and is said to derive from an Indian word meaning "place where buffalo gather to drink." Others think, however, that a more accurate translation might be "buffalo dung," rather than "buffalo creek."

Folk etymology concerning the naming of Quitaque in the North Texas ranching country is surely more interesting than a faithful hewing to historical fact. Wild horses once had ranged here. Two nearby buttes reminded some earthy soul of manure piles, or *quitaque* in Indian tongue. One begins to wonder about these ubiquitous linguists who seem to wait in the wings with a ready explanation for such terms. Rarely are we told from which of many Indian dialects the word derives.

At Helotes, northwest of San Antonio, one finds a settlement said to have been populated originally by Mexicans who had intermarried with Apache Indians. Their principal crop was corn, and the word *helotes* is supposedly an Indian expression, borrowed by the Spanish, meaning "green roasting ear."

Not all so-called Indian names were applied by Spaniards certainly. Anglo-Americans occasionally applied Indian words, or what they thought were Indian words, to newly formed settlements. Eagle Lake, established as late as 1908 in southeastern Colorado County, takes its name from a natural body of water that received its designation years earlier. The name supposedly originates from a Karankawa Indian legend about a young girl (historians in tennis shoes have proclaimed her an honest-to-God princess, although it is difficult to imagine the destitute Karankawas understanding the concept, much less honoring the practice) who set two suitors in competition for her hand by having them cross the lake, climb a tree, and return with an eaglet. Fortuitously for legend's sake, competition was narrowed when one of the suitors drowned in the lake.

Eola was established in Concho County about 1900. It is said to derive from an Indian word meaning "good return from the blowing wind." Thirty years later Eola was at the southern limit of the dust bowl. Despite its founding as late as 1883, no one really knows how Falfurrias got its name. Those who are inclined to the romantic viewpoint tell of a Lipan chieftain seeking a new hunting ground. On sighting the flat, featureless terrain shimmering under a hot, noonday sun, he exclaimed: "Falfurrias," which in his language was supposed to mean "land of heart's desire." Perhaps.

Kemah, facing Galveston Bay, was known as Evergreen until 1910, when a post office was established. The name was changed to Kemah, an Indian term meaning "facing the wind." The origins of Kiomatia in Red River County may be traced to about 1819. The village name was appropriated from Oklahoma's Kiomatia River, which joins the Red River from the northwest at a point opposite the present town site. The Indian name means "clear water."

Tahoka Lake is a spring-fed body of water that furnished refreshment to Indians, soldiers, buffalo hunters, cattle herds with their drovers, and a diverse assortment of passers-through. The name purportedly means "deep" or "clear water" in one of the Indian tongues. When a settlement began growing some five miles to the southwest, the name of the lake was used also for the town. On the other hand, Teneha, deep in East Texas, is an Indian word meaning "muddy water." Established in 1885, it was named by the Hicks family for the old Tenehaw district, later Shelby County. Tioga, in the fertile blackland of Grayson County, is said to be an Indian word meaning "fair and beautiful." Gene Autry is the most famous person ever to hail from Tioga, Texas. At the height of his career he offered to buy the town site, provided the name was changed to Autry Springs. The offer was declined.

On several occasions Anglo-American settlers in Texas named their communities after certain noted Indian personalities. Katemcy, established about 1880 in McCulloch County, is the Anglo tribute to, and spelling of, Ketumse, a Peneteka Comanche with whom John O. Meusebach was believed to have negotiated a treaty some three decades earlier. Quanah, the seat of Hardeman County, began to shape up in the mid-1880s. It was named for Quanah Parker, chief of the Quahadi Comanches. Parker's father was Peta Nacona, for whom a town in Montague County is named. His mother, Cynthia Ann Parker, had been a member of the clan for which Parker County was named. Santa Anna in Coleman County was named for the mountain peaks just north of the settlement. The area was once the home of another Peneteka chief whose Hispanic name was Santa Anna. The peaks bearing his name began appearing on maps in the 1820s.

Generally speaking, then, place names honoring tribes and noted members seem to have been conferred largely by late-arriving Anglo-American settlers, as if to honor staunch friend or stubborn foe. Names that are alleged to be of Indian origin reflect the Indian impulse to describe physical characteristics. One suspects that something may have been lost in translation from Indian to Spanish to English.

Hispanic Names

Religion seems to have strongly influenced early Spanish explorers in their choice of place names. It was a pious custom of the Spaniards to name locations in honor of the saint on whose feast day the discovery occurred. To Alonzo Álvarez de Piñeda goes credit for having first charted the Gulf Coast of Texas as he sailed its rim in 1519. The bay that Piñeda entered on the feast day of Corpus Christi accordingly was named Corpus Christi Bay. The first written mention of Corpus Christi Bay is contained in a 1766 report submitted by Col. Diego Parrilla, who toured the area in a vain search for errant Englishmen. Historian Dan Kilgore of Corpus Christi notes that, en route to the bay, Parrilla had stopped at the settlement at Petronila, established earlier by Blas María de la Garza Falcón. Kilgore then surmises that the name for Corpus Christi Bay had been preserved by either Falcón or one of his employees.[3]

By 1840 Henry L. Kinney had established a trading post on the shores of Corpus Christi Bay. The United States' war with Mexico gave the embryo settlement a major boost. It became the seat of Nueces County in 1846, and, needing something more appropriate than Kinney's Trading Post for a postmark, Kinney decided to call it Corpus Christi, for the bay. The El Paso County town of Ysleta, the oldest permanent settlement in Texas, is a contraction of the phrase Corpus Christi de Ysleta.

In June, 1691, Domingo de Terán was en route to the site of a future metropolis: "On the 13th our royal standard and camp proceeded in the same easterly direction. We traveled five leagues over fine country — broad plains, the most beautiful in New Spain. We camped on the banks of a stream adorned by a great stand of trees. . . . I named it San Antonio de Padua because we reached it on his day."[4] Later, mission San Antonio de Valero and the presidio of San Antonio de Béxar were established in this vicinity. In 1731 the arrival of fifteen families of Canary Islanders formed the nucleus of the villa of San Fernando de Béxar from which the modern city of San Antonio has developed. The town of Anthony in El Paso County, although anglicized and established at a later date, is also named in honor of Saint Anthony, a thirteenth-century prelate and member of the Franciscan order.

The village of Navidad is located in a bend of the Navidad River in western Jackson County. The name is a Spanish word meaning "nativity" and refers to the birth of Jesus. Trinity, Texas, was named for another East Texas river which, in turn, had been called La Santísima Trinidad by the explorer Alonso de León in 1689. It was his homage to the Holy Trinity. In 1756 the Spanish established a mission and presidio on the lower reaches of the Trinity River. Years later the site was called Atascosita. In 1831 Francisco Madero, land commissioner for Texas, redesignated it Villa de la Santísima Trinidad de la Libertad (Town of the Most Holy Trinity of Liberty), a name that was quickly anglicized and shortened to Liberty. The first Republic of Texas post office was established there in December, 1836.

---

3. D. E. Kilgore, *Nueces County, Texas, 1750–1800: A Bicentennial Memoir* (Corpus Christi: Friends of the Corpus Christi Museum, 1975), pp. 5–6.

4. Mattie Austin Hatcher, "The Expedition of Don Domingo Terán de los Rios into Texas," in *Preliminary Studies of the Texas Catholic Historical Society*, vol. II (1933), p. 14.

Another of Alonso de León's accomplishments was the discovery and naming of a San Marcos River by members of his fourth expedition in 1689. The event occurred on the feast day of Saint Mark. The name originally was applied to the first sizable river east of the Guadalupe and may have referred to the Lavaca. But later explorers, notably Espinosa and Olivares in 1709 and Domingo Ramón in 1716, reinforced the claim of the present San Marcos River to the name.

San Saba in Central Texas takes its name from the San Saba River. An explorer named Don Juan Antonio Bustillo y Cevallos crossed it on December 5, 1732. He named it El Río San Sabá de las Nueces, honoring Saint Sabbas, whose special day it was. Saint Sabbas was abbot of the monastery near Jerusalem that now bears his name. The town of San Saba was first settled about 1854.

Santa Maria in western Cameron County is in an area first settled in the 1750s by José de Escandón's colonists. The community took its name from a chapel built there in 1824 by the Oblate Fathers, who sought to honor the Virgin Mary. San Elizario in El Paso County derived its name from the Presidio de San Elizario, which had been moved there in 1780 from the valley of San Elizario some fifty miles to the southeast. Possibly the valley was named by a friar, or someone familiar with the saints' calendar, who came to the valley on Saint Elzear's Day. Elzear was a French nobleman who achieved fame, and subsequent canonization, for his war against Henry VII in the invasion of Naples. San Ygnacio in Zapata County was founded about 1790 by Jesús Treviño, who named it for the patron saint of his native Guerrero. Like Elzear, Saint Ignatius was a member of the nobility who served his country as a soldier. Wounded while fighting the French, he turned to religion during his recuperation. About 1537 he went to Rome to organize the Society of Jesus, or Jesuits.

The town of Del Rio originally was called San Felipe del Río because it was reached on Saint Philip's day by a priest who established a mission there in 1808. Years later, when a post office was requested, there was already a San Felipe existing in Austin County and postal officials refused the longer name. Thus the name of the Val Verde County town was shortened to Del Rio. San Felipe de Austin was the capital of Stephen F. Austin's colony. The name was decreed in 1823 by Gov. Luciano Flores, who sought to honor the patron saint of Don Felipe de la Garza, commandant general of the eastern interior provinces of Mexico. At the same time he honored Stephen F. Austin, who was a lieutenant colonel in local charge of all military and civil affairs.

San Augustine, deep in East Texas, purports to be the first town in the state to have been laid out with a public square in the American tradition. The town derived its name from the act of the provincial legislature that created the municipality of San Augustine, a jurisdiction which at the time embraced all or part of six present counties. The legislators, meeting at Monclova, seem to have been influenced by clerics who wished to honor the memory of Saint Augustine, a fifth-century bishop whose base of operation was at Hippo in North Africa. The clergy at Monclova might have been more adept in their town naming than they realized, however. Saint Augustine was noted for his independence and his militance toward adversaries, characteristics for which the inhabitants of East Texas have long been noted.

San Augustine was commemorated in more than one Texas community. Laredo, on the middle Texas border with Mexico, dates from the arrival of settlers in 1755. The name Villa de San Augustine de Laredo had been affixed by the time a mission was established there in 1762. There is also speculation that José de Escandón suggested the name in honor of another Laredo in Santander, Spain. The Spanish town was on the seacoast; the Texas town was not. But both were hot and dusty.

Victoria, near the mid–Gulf Coast, was founded in 1824 by *empresario* Martín de León, who first named the town Nuestra Señora de Guadalupe de Jesús Victoria. Geronimo in northern Guadalupe County was named for Geronimo Creek. The creek, in turn, had that name at least by 1846. Possibly it was named by the Mexicans in honor of Saint Jerome, a fourth-century priest, doctor, and scholar who translated the Old Testament from Hebrew and the New Testament from Greek into Latin. Most assuredly the community was *not* named for the Warm Springs Apache leader who terrorized New Mexico, Arizona, and Sonora in the 1880s, this, despite a claim to the contrary in a recent directory of Texas place names.[5]

San Isidro, a farming community in northeastern Starr County, bears the name of the farmers' patron saint. Saint Isidore was a plowman who lived near Madrid, Spain, from about 1070 to 1130. He was said to be so devout that an angel plowed his fields while he was at prayer.

San Benito and San Juan, both in the lower Rio Grande Valley of Texas, were named by Hispanics in honor of lesser mortals. Ben Hicks and John Closner both were owners of town sites, and both were highly regarded by their Hispanic friends and neighbors.

Ben Ficklin was a stop on the Butterfield Overland Mail Route as

---

5. Fred Tarpley, *1001 Texas Place Names* (Austin: University of Texas Press, 1980), p. 92.

well as the first seat of Tom Green County, beginning in 1875. Seven short years later a disastrous flood wiped it from the map. The seat was moved to the nearby village of Saint Angela, which had begun life as a trading post for the soldiers of Fort Concho. The trader, Bart DeWitt, named his establishment for his wife's sister, a nun in a San Antonio convent. For a time the settlement was known as San Angela, but ultimately it became San Angelo when the Post Office Department objected to the masculine "San" coupled with the feminine "Angela." By 1882, when it became the county seat, it was already known as San Angelo.

When John McMullen and James McGloin established an Irish colony between the San Antonio and Nueces rivers, they named their capital San Patricio del Hibernia, for the Irish patron saint. The first settlers came in 1829 and within a year the town was well under way. It prospered for a few decades, then declined when the county seat was moved to Sinton in 1893. In 1834 other Irish empresarios, James Power and James Hewetson, established a town on the site of Nuestra Señora del Refugio, a mission which by that time was defunct. The town, of course, became simply Refugio.

The first Polish colony in America was established south of San Antonio at Christmas in 1854. These Roman Catholic immigrants honored the Virgin Mary by calling their settlement Panna Maria. Four years later another small group of Polish arrivals moved to a location nearer San Antonio, where one John Demmer had put down roots in 1852. Other Silesian immigrants swelled the ranks until, by 1868, the community had an impressive stone church and a name, Saint Hedwig — in honor of the duchess and patron saint of Silesia. As late as 1910 German Catholics settling in eastern Potter County named their community Saint Francis, for the twelfth-century founder of the Franciscan order.

In 1923 a discovery well was brought in on University of Texas lands in West Texas. The well was named in honor of Saint Rita, a fifteenth-century Italian mystic and patron saint of the impossible. Employees of the Texon Oil and Land Company and other companies associated with the development of the Reagan County field soon had a community that was named Santa Rita for the well. The railroad that served the region wanted the name changed, however, to Rita Santa in order to avoid confusion with a similarly named station in New Mexico.

Although the Spaniards were inclined to apply place names in honor of their saints, they did have it within their capacity to honor ordinary and extraordinary mortals. Medina, west of San Antonio, was named for the river that Alonso de León discovered and named for a widely respected Spanish scholar and engineer, Pedro Medina. In Comanche County the town of DeLeon was established in 1881 and named for the river on whose bank it stood. The river, in turn, had been named for the late Alonso by members of the Aguayo expedition in 1721. Bandera was named for nearby Bandera Pass, which, in turn, likely received its name from a military commander sent to this area to quell Indian depredations. Apaches were making life miserable for settlers until General Bandera fought a decisive battle against the Indians. The showdown occurred in the pass about 1720. When the town of Bandera was settled beginning in 1853, it took its name from the nearby pass.

A name that derives from similar circumstances is Uvalde, seat of Uvalde County, named for the Cañon de Ugalde, where in 1790 Capt. Juan de Ugalde had routed a Comanche war band. Although Reading W. Black and Nathan Stratton called their town Encino (Oak) when it was laid out in 1858, the name was changed to Uvalde after it became the county seat. Concepcion in Duval County and Mirando City in Webb County are examples of settlements that took their names from the land grant on which they were founded — Concepcion for the Santa Cruz de Concepción grant and Mirando City for that of Nicolás Mirando.

In many instances Anglo-Americans in Texas simply perpetuated or carried forward place names that were originated by Hispanics, but in other instances Anglos originated the name in honor of a Hispanic person. The name of Galveston Bay (and the city that emerged on its shore) resulted from a coastal survey ordered by Bernardo de Gálvez, Spanish governor of Louisiana from 1777 to 1783. The city itself was not properly founded until 1838, by Michael B. Menard, a French Canadian.

In 1839 settlers at Walnut Springs changed the name of their community to Seguin in honor of Juan N. Seguin, an ardent Texas patriot and hero of San Jacinto. Subsequently he was unjustly suspected of collaboration with the Mexicans and was forced into exile, but memory of his contribution was kept alive by the prosperity of the town that bore his name. Settlers in the Angelina County town of Zavalla sought to honor the first vice-president of the Texas Republic, although they added an extra "l" to the name.

Zapata on the lower Rio Grande border was first settled about 1770 by former residents of Revilla, Mexico. They called their community Carrizo. Zapata County was created by the Texas legislature in 1858 and named for Col. Antonio Zapata, a wealthy merchant and landowner, whose support for an independent Republic of the Rio Grande led to his execution by Mexican centralists in 1840. Carrizo itself was later renamed Zapata. In that same county is the town of Bustamente, named for Anastasio Bustamente, a former Mexican president.

Mexia in Limestone County was named for Enrique Antonio Guillermo Mexía. Vidaurri in Refugio County was named for the original grantee of the land on which the town stood, José Jesús Vidaurri, who was commissioner for the Power and Hewetson colony of Irish immigrants. Manchaca in southern Travis County was named for Menchaca Spring, which was the campsite of Gen. José Antonio Menchaca, an authentic Texas patriot who commanded a contingent that afforded protection to area settlers. Floresville bears the name of Don Francisco Flores de Abryo, who established a ranch headquarters northwest of the present town before 1832. When the San Antonio and Aransas Pass Railroad came through in 1885, the Flores descendants gave a town site that was designated Floresville.

Placido Benavides was the son-in-law of empresario Martín de León and a participant in the Texas Revolution. He also had the rare distinction of having two Texas towns named in his honor. The old Benavides homestead in Victoria County became the site of Placedo Junction when the Missouri Pacific and Texas and New Orleans railroads formed a crossing about 1910. The town of Benavides, in eastern Duval County, was founded on another of his grants.

Catarina in Dimmit County was named for a nearby ranch whose name in turn preserved the memory of a Mexican woman who had been killed there by Indians. Candelaria was called Gallina until the name was changed to honor a Presidio County beauty. Mercedes in the lower Rio Grande Valley was laid out in 1905 and named in honor of Mexico's first lady. The ulterior motive behind this gesture was to influence President Porfirio Díaz to curb Mexican bandit raids into the area. The effort was as useless as it was blatant.

On several occasions Anglo-Americans applied Hispanic names to their settlements, then botched the spelling. Weesatche was first called Middleton because it was halfway between Goliad and Clinton. Clinton later was eclipsed by Cuero, which prospered directly across the Guadalupe River from it. Middleton was renamed Westach, then Wesatche, and finally Weesatche in recognition of the huisache tree that grows abundantly in the area. After three tries they still didn't get it right.

Whon, in Coleman County, is another case of a phonetically (mis)-spelled Hispanic name. The name honors a Mexican ranch hand who worked for the postmistress's husband in 1903. Presumably the spelling looked acceptable to postal officials in Washington.

Buda, in eastern Hays County, is supposedly a corruption of *viuda,* the Spanish word for "widow." Originally the community was called Dupree, a further corruption of Do Pray. It seems that a pioneer citizen petitioned International and Great Northern Railway officials, "Do, pray, give us a railroad." A sizable number of the population liked the name, but Do Pray was a bit prosaic for local taste, so it was frenchified, and Dupree was the result. Within a short time, 1889 to be exact, residents requested a name change to Buda. Three Mexican widows— *viudas*—operated a hotel that was a focus of community life. Somehow the name Buda is said to have emerged from this fact. If the explanation is not entirely convincing, then the same must be said of numerous other Texas place names.

Juno, in Val Verde County, is said to have been thus named because the owner of a cantina offered a menu consisting solely of frijoles and beer. Nonetheless he continued to greet his largely Mexican clientele by asking, "What'll you have?" Their good-natured reply—in border English—was "Juno," i.e., "you know." Today Juno maintains an aura of uniqueness because residents operate a one-room school, one of the last of its kind, that educates four students. It exists because it would be too costly to transport the pupils forty-three miles to the nearest "city" school at Ozona. They would have to travel two hours a day along winding state highway 163, which is sometimes impassable when it rains.[6]

Spanish-speaking explorers and settlers were not limited in their place name choices to saints and others less saintly. They, like the Indians, could and did confer names on the basis of physical appearance. El Paso del Norte, the Pass of the North, was the name given by sixteenth-century conquistadores to a site on the Rio Grande where the great river makes a sharp bend to the southeast for eventual union with the Gulf of Mexico. Cabeza de Vaca crossed the river in the vicinity of the pass near the end of his long odyssey between 1528 and 1536. An expedition led by Fray Agustín Rodríguez and an old soldier nicknamed Chambuscado may have been the first to designate the vicinity as El Paso del Norte, in 1581. In 1873 the area that had included Hart's Mill, Franklin, Magoffinsville, and Concordia was incorporated as El Paso.

Settlers at Ragtown in the Texas Panhandle decided that their growing community needed a more appropriate designation, so they changed

6. *Dallas Morning News,* November 30, 1980.

the name to Amarillo—a name suggested by the presence of a stream known as Arroyo Amarillo by Mexican sheepherders. The phrase means "yellow creek," and was given because of the soil color along its banks.

When Europeans first cast eyes upon West Texas, they saw lots of open, flat land and reflected this fact in their choice of certain place names. *Llano* is Spanish for "plains." Early explorers from south of the Rio Grande encountered a Central Texas stream which they called the Llano, although the river rises and runs its entire course in the Texas Hill Country. In the mid-1850s the town of Llano evolved along its course. Plano, although named by Anglo-American settlers, received its designation because of its location on a plain, as did Pampa (another Spanish term meaning virtually the same thing), Plains (obviously), Vega, Lamesa ("the table"), and (again, the obvious) Levelland. Not so obviously, the town of Broadway in Lamar County was said to have been named in 1885 because of its location on an open prairie. In 1904 Danish settlers in Wharton County called their new community Danevang, meaning "flat country where Danes live."

There are many instances of places being named, in Spanish, for flora and fauna. Lampasas is a corrupt spelling of *lampazos* ("water lilies"). The town, in Central Texas, is actually named for the river. Possibly it was named by members of the Aguayo expedition in 1721 for the Mexican city of Lampazos de Naranjo, according to Fred Massengill, who did pioneering work on the origins of Texas place names.[7] Water lilies, however, do not appear to have been characteristic of the stream. Salado Creek supposedly refers to the saline qualities of its water, but it is a freshwater stream. There is speculation that the names of the Lampasas and the Salado were somehow transposed in history. The town of Salado, also in Central Texas, is named for the creek.

Los Fresnos, "the ash trees," was named because of its location on Rancho los Fresnos, which had been established as early as 1770 in what is now Cameron County. Not far away, in Hidalgo County, is Los Ebanos, "the ebonies," site of one of the last hand-drawn ferries across the Rio Grande. And a few miles to the northwest, in Starr County, is El Sauz—"the weeping willow." At the time of its naming Palito Blanco in Jim Wells County was shaded by numerous hackberry trees. On the South Plains the town of Tulia is named for Tule Canyon— Spanish for "bullrush" canyon.

Matagorda is the name given a bay, a peninsula, a community, and

---

7. Fred I. Massengill, *How Texas Towns Were Named* (Terrell, Tex.: privately printed, 1936), p. 5.

a county, all of which are on the mid-Gulf Coast of Texas. The name is a Spanish reference to the dense canebrakes that grew on the peninsula. Encinal in southwestern La Salle County and Encino in southern Brooks County were both named by Mexican pioneers for live oak trees that grow in the region.

The name Loco for a Childress County community does not, in this instance, describe a state of mind, exactly. About 1930 residents, mostly Anglos, were required to submit a new name for consideration by postal authorities. The name Loco, Spanish for "crazy," was suggested by the abundance of locoweed in the area. The name described the weed's effect when eaten by livestock.

A number of Texas communities have borne Hispanic names for animal life found in the region. Port Lavaca was established about 1841 as successor to Linnville, which never recovered from its sacking by Comanche raiders the previous year. Port Lavaca clung to life and prospered because of its status as a shipping point, especially for cattle and cattle by-products such as hide, tallow, and bones. The name Lavaca, or "the cow," was first applied by Spanish explorers to the river and bay beside which the town sits. The "cows" to which the Spanish referred were not Texas Longhorns, but buffalo cows. On the other hand, Bovina on the Texas–New Mexico border began as a line camp on the XIT Ranch and later became a switch on the Pecos and Northern Texas Railroad. At that point it was called Bull Town. Later, when a post office was applied for, the name Bovina was substituted.

Grulla, on the Rio Grande in Starr County, is an early Mexican settlement so-called because cranes, *grullas,* were a common sight on the lake near the town site. Viboras was the name given another Starr County ranching community by Don Manuel Guerra about 1890. The word is Spanish for "rattlesnake," and from the outset there appear to have been more reptiles than people within the city limits. *Lagarto* in Spanish means "alligator." Lagarto in southern Live Oak County was established about 1858 by Mexican settlers who noted the presence of these reptiles in the nearby Nueces River. No civic booster in his right mind would have chosen such a designation, but the village declined anyway when it was by-passed by the railroad around 1913.

On occasion place names in Spanish have commemorated events. For example Banquete—"banquet," in English—recalls a feast held on the site in 1832 when soldiers and settlers gathered to celebrate the opening of a road linking San Patricio and Matamoros, Mexico. El Campo in Wharton County was originally called Prairie Switch when it was established on a siding of the Texas and New Orleans Railway. Area ranches used the location as a campsite during roundups, and in 1890 the name El Campo, "the camp," was given.

The communities of Alvarado in Johnson County and Saltillo in eastern Hopkins County were both settled about 1850, and Cadiz in Bee County perhaps two decades later. All were named by Anglo-Americans. Alvarado's name was suggested by A. H. Onstott because he had participated in the capture of Alvarado, Mexico, during the war of 1846-48. The Mexican town, in turn, was said to have been named for a Spanish explorer with Cortéz. Saltillo, Texas, was named for Saltillo, Mexico, because one John Arthur simply liked its sound. Cadiz was first known as Lapara until a store owner named V. C. Howard changed the name in 1897 to honor his old hometown — Cadiz, Ohio.

A few Spanish-language place names hint at values other than religion, sense of self, or memories of other days and other places. Dinero in southern Live Oak County once was called Barlow's Ferry, but the name was changed in 1872 because the place was rumored to be the site of Gen. Antonio López de Santa Anna's buried gold. In 1895 Anglo-American promoters wanting to attract settlers to the barren landscape of what is now Schleicher County opted to call their town site Eldorado, after that mythical realm of indescribable riches. Those who agreed to come there were given free lots. One wonders why such a golden promise would require such a mundane lure. Settlers along the Rio Grande in Presidio County were only slightly less optimistic than those at Eldorado. They called their town Porvenir — meaning "things to come," although its future does not seem particularly bright.

Anglo-American Names

If the Indians awarded place names on the basis of physical appearance, and if Hispanic peoples were inclined to name places for saints and lesser mortals, then what approach did Anglo-American settlers adopt? They were drawn, of course, by land, which they found in abundance and variety.

One individual in search of a new beginning was David Crockett. On his way to immortality in the war for Texas independence, Crockett camped near what is now the Fannin County town of Honey Grove. He and his party found honey in virtually every tree. He referred to the campground as "the honey grove." These words subsequently were carved on one of the trees by W. B. Allen, who traversed the scene not long after. Crockett wrote a letter to his children in Tennessee.

> I must say as to what I have seen of Texas it is the garden spot of the world. . . .
>
> I expect in all probability to settle on the Border or Chactaw Br[anch] of Red River that I have no doubt is the richest country in the world. Good land and plenty of timber and the best springs and wild mill streams, good range, clear water and every appearance of good health and game aplenty. It is the pass where the buffalo passes from north to south and back twice a year, and bees and honey plenty. I have a great hope of getting the agency to settle that country.
>
> I have but little doubt of being elected a member to form a constitution for this province. I am rejoiced at my fate. I had rather be in my present situation than to be elected to a seat in Congress for life.[8]

Had not these early arrivals been possessed of unbounded optimism, there would have been no significant immigration. Disillusionment came later. More than one Texas village was called New Hope. In time a band of Wood County settlers chose for their community the name Little Hope. However different this West may have been in myth or reality, the pioneers carried with them as part of their cultural baggage a sentimental attachment to the teachings, the values, and the place names of their youth. These attachments often were revealed when new names appeared on early Texas maps.

Like the Indians before them, Anglo-Americans frequently called it as they saw it, as indicated in such names as Cedar Grove, China (berry) Grove, Elm Grove, Locust Grove, Oak Grove, Pine Grove, Walnut Grove, Pleasant Grove, and Shady Grove. Cactus in Webb County, Mesquite in Dallas County, and Notrees in Ector County are further examples, as are such inviting names as Apple Springs, Cherry Springs, Grapevine, Pearland, Pecan Gap, Plum, and Fruitland. Then, of course, there is Sweetwater and Sour Lake and Crystal City. At Crystal City a local historian described what happened the day artesian water was struck in the newly formed village, opening the way for it to become a rich agricultural center. "A great dome of water lifted of its own force and gushed to a crystal mound above a six-inch casing. Six glorious feet it rose, paused, turned, then rolled outward into a translucent umbrella and fell as liquid opal into the basin below. Old men sipped

---

8. James B. Shackford, *David Crockett: The Man and the Legend* (Durham: University of North Carolina Press, 1956), pp. 214–15.

it like wine and talked in short sentences as they stood in little clumps and let their quick, green dreams flash through. Beyond the clearing was empire; here was the essence!" In that burst of poetry, Crystal City got its name.

Not only did early settlers name their dominions for natural features of the landscape, they also reflected the variety of animal life in such towns as Antelope, White Deer, Quail, and Turkey in North and West Texas. The inception of these names seems straightforward enough.

Sometimes community designations had roots in actions taken by settlers themselves with regard to the land. In southern Hays County the old post road between San Antonio and Austin winds along the Balcones Escarpment. Settlement of this locale began in 1851. The first houses were strung out along a six-mile expanse of road between York's Creek to the southwest and Purgatory Creek to the northeast. It seemed perfectly logical then (and now) to call the place Stringtown. Far more obscure is the name derivation for Slide, southwest of Lubbock. Slide originated when a resurvey in 1903 caused two hundred sections of land to be located two miles farther west than first believed. After the new survey was completed, the settlers affected had to "slide over."

Like the earliest Spaniards, the earliest Anglo-American arrivals in Texas displayed their religious heritage in choosing place names. This seems to have been far more characteristic of pre–Civil War settlements than those that followed the war. One need only to flip through Fred Tarpley's monograph on *Place Names of Northeast Texas* to see the frequency with which pre–Civil War communities received names that were of biblical origin.[9] True enough that these communities may have consisted of nothing more than a church, a store, a blacksmith shop, or a saloon. Most were doomed from the outset and have long since disappeared from the highway map. Still, one may encounter a fugitive road marker that heralds such places as Antioch, Bethany, Bethel, Bethlehem, Canaan, Corinth, Ebenezer, Edom, Enon, Galilee, Gethsemene, Hebron, Jericho, Macedonia, Mount Carmel, Mount Moriah, Mount Pisgah, Mount Tabor, Mount Zion, Nazareth, New Jerusalem, Nimrod, Nineveh, Palestine, Providence, Sardis, Shiloh, Smyrna, and others.

In Grayson County there is a town called Bells, which originally was known as Gospel Ridge because of its many churches. The coming of the Texas and Pacific Railroad in 1873 provided the impetus for a name change to Bells since each church steeple had one or more of them.

9. Tarpley, *Place Names of Northeast Texas,* passim.

To the west of Bells, in Montague County, is Saint Jo. The town was named, not for Saint Joseph, but for Joe Howell, one of the town founders. As a member of the original survey crew in 1870, he had refreshed himself on a hot afternoon with a swig of unaccustomed whiskey. It made him ill. His partner, I. H. Boggess, remarked that "ole Joe" was so saintly that they would just call the town Saint Jo.

The relationship between God and man and land in West Texas is explored in chapter ten of A. C. Greene's classic book, *A Personal Country*. "West Texas is like the Biblical lands, a hot, dry desert country with low, blue hills along its horizons which are nothing but hot rocks when you reach them. Perhaps it is this kinship with the land of the Bible which causes it to hold to the fundamentalist religions, to cling to dry, feverish beliefs which demand more of a man than he is capable of offering even God; beliefs which promise him nothing on earth but sweat, frustration, and retribution for error."[10]

Despite the strong religious orientation among West Texans, one does not find quite so many biblical place names in this land of post–Civil War settlement. Nimrod in Eastland County was called Curtis until a post office was applied for in 1885. At that time the name was changed to avoid duplication with another community named Curtis. Jericho in Donley County recalls the biblical city whose walls tumbled down. Nazareth in the Texas Panhandle began in 1902 when a Roman Catholic priest brought fifteen settlers to the area. Much of the present-day religious influence in West Texas emanates from a single city that was established in 1881 by the Texas and Pacific Railroad and area cattlemen and that was named for a Kansas cowtown. Abilene is home for three denominational universities—one each representing the Baptist, Church of Christ, and Methodist faiths.

A number of early Texas settlers thought they had found heaven on earth, or at least pretended they had. Paradise in southwest Wise County is a case in point. The name is said to have been inspired by the flower-blanketed prairie that greeted the first arrivals there in 1873. Some forty years earlier Capt. Edward Smith described a portion of northeast Texas to a Louisiana audience in such glowing terms that a listener declared, "You have found Elysian Fields." The name stuck. In Navarro County an early arrival greeted the scene before him with the delighted cry, "Eureka!" And that name also stuck. Utopia, on the other hand, was discovered in Uvalde County about 1852 and was first called Wares-

---

10. A. C. Greene, *A Personal Country* (New York: Alfred A. Knopf, 1969), pp. 127–28.

ville. In 1886 settlers there finally decided that the location and climate placed them in Utopia.

Meanwhile a Lamar County storekeeper wrote postal authorities that he wanted to call his community Richland because of its fertile soil. His description was so ecstatic that an official replied, "Only Glory would do your town justice." And Glory it became. In 1887 Sublime, a Lavaca County community, sprung up in the wake of the San Antonio and Aransas Pass Railroad. Other examples are no less beguiling.

Eden in Concho County, for example. Named for the Garden of Eden, right? Wrong. It was named for Fred Eden, a local rancher and store owner. And then there is Garden City, surrounded by sagebrush and space in the trans-Pecos country. The town name proclaims a defiant optimism. Possibly, however, one need go no further for an explanation than to know that a Mr. Gardner operated the first store and was the first postmaster.

Another fine-sounding place name is Peerless in Hopkins County. Settlement began in the 1850s, and the community was subsequently and variously known as Gay's Mill, Hilldale, Fairyland (because, ahem, their young ladies attended dances looking like fairies), and Peerless. Why Peerless? In the early 1900s a family named Cotton planted a potato crop of the variety known as Peerless. Unusually heavy rains kept the crop from being harvested and potatoes rotted in the field, creating an unholy stench over the entire area. Peerless, indeed.

At places other than Peerless names were carefully calculated to reflect a sense of irony. Zephyr in Brown County was so named when a howling blue norther overtook a party of surveyors who laid out the original grants. This choice of a name was reinforced in 1903 when a tornado virtually demolished the town. Duster in Comanche County and Earth in Lamb County were resident reactions to the effect of high wind on loose soil. Duster was named in the 1880s by citizens who met at the local store to decide on a name. One man picked up a piece of paper that was covered with dust and, after shaking it off, set down his choice of a name. His friends agreed that the selection was an appropriate one. In Lamb County postal authorities had rejected two previous submissions for a name and demanded a third. The year was 1925, and the dust bowl was a-building. The postmaster looked out the window, saw much of the earth blowing by, and decided that Earth would be as suitable a name as any.

When Anglo-American settlers relocated in the West, they often preserved memories of earlier hometowns in their new ones. Little imagination is required to figure out the origin of settlers at Iowa Park in Wichita County or Tennessee Colony in Anderson County. Albany, Texas, for example, was named by former residents of Albany, Georgia. Athens, Texas, was named for Athens in either Alabama, Georgia, or Greece—possibly for all three. Atlanta, Georgia, was remembered in Atlanta, Texas. Buckeye in Matagorda County was designated by two former Ohioans. Columbus, seat of Colorado County, was named for the capital of the Buckeye State.

Anglo-Americans in Texas were not the only nationality to recall the Old World in place names given to the New. The Germans did not think of the unpleasant conditions that compelled their departure from the homeland when they gave their communities such names as New Braunfels, New Ulm, Oldenburg, and Weimar. Prince Frederick of Prussia was a member of the colonization society known as the Mainzer Adelsverein. He was regarded by German settlers in Texas as their friend. In 1846 John O. Meusebach named the town of Friedrichsburg in his honor. The Post Office Department anglicized the name in 1894. Nada in Colorado County was named by Czech settlers for the city of Nadja in the old country. They also named a town in Fayette County for Praha, the Czechoslovakian capital. A colony of Norwegians in Bosque County called their community Norse.

Other Texas place names were awarded for no other reason than that someone liked the sound. Bogata in Red River County was so designated in 1881 because someone thought Bogotá, Colombia, was such an altogether exotic place. But J. E. Horner's handwriting on the post office application was hard to read and was misconstrued as Bogata. Bogata it became, and residents pronounced it with the accent on the second syllable.

In naming the Ellis County town of Italy, Gabriel J. Penn recalled a trip he once had made to the Mediterranean. The village of Karnack in northeast Harrison County was so named, according to Fred Tarpley, because some erudite soul discovered that the distance between this settlement and Caddo Lake was the same as that between ancient Karnack in Egypt and the Nile River. Lexington in Lee County honors a Massachusetts town that figured prominently in the American Revolution.

Marathon, in the Big Bend area, was once the shipping point for the quicksilver mines at Terlingua. It was laid out and named in 1889 by Capt. Albion E. Shepherd, an employee of the Southern Pacific Railroad. Captain Shepherd, apparently well traveled, chose to call his town Marathon because he thought its surroundings were quite similar to those at Marathon in Greece.

From Eden to Uncertain

Perhaps as hard a sell as any was the name given by its promoters to the town of Riviera in 1907. Located on the Gulf Coast below Corpus Christi, this Kleberg County venture never quite captured popular fancy as did its namesake along the northern shores of the Mediterranean.

The same kind of temperament that would name a hometown for an exotic foreign metropolis might just as easily resort to literature or mythology for inspiration. Again there are numerous examples, with Shakespeare and Sir Walter Scott leading the pack in the realm of literature. Iago in Wharton County and Stratford in Sherman County, both dating from the early 1900s, reflect a Shakespearean influence. Stratford was named by an Englishman, Walter Colton, who thought the town's position on Coldwater Creek legitimized a comparison with Stratford-on-Avon. Sir Walter Scott is remembered in such towns as Ivanhoe and Waverley. Ivanhoe in Fannin County was Hawkins Prairie until the Post Office Department demanded a change to avoid confusion with Hawkins, Texas. Capt. Joe Dupree, C.S.A., was a Walter Scott fan and suggested the new name. Perhaps Mark Twain was not far from the mark when he blamed the Civil War on the South's overexposure to romantic novels like Scott's.

Other English authors are celebrated in names chosen for such towns as Bronte and Tennyson. The German author Ludwig Boerne also has a town named in his honor. Marfa in Presidio County was named by the wife of a railroad engineer for the heroine of a Russian novel she happened to be reading when her husband wanted a name for his new water stop, around which a town would later grow.

In the realm of mythology one may scan the Texas map and find Avalon, that mythical island near Paradise to which King Arthur repaired to recover from his battle wounds. Near the opposite end of the spectrum is Pandora, whose box loosed a host of troubles on the world. Hers was the name that some Wilson County settlers gave their community.

In some instances place names were related to events that had occurred on the site, or that in some way had affected the lives of those who dwelled there. Cat Spring, Flour Bluff, Impact, Independence, New Deal, and Slide are examples. Soon after moving to Austin's colony, Robert Kleberg killed a large wildcat as it came to a watering hole not far from his house on the prairie. Flour Bluff, near Corpus Christi, derived its name in the 1840s because Mexican smugglers, under pursuit, were compelled to abandon barrels of flour on a small elevation overlooking the beach. Impact came into existence as a tiny "wet" enclave huddled against the bone-dry bosom of Abilene. Abilene residents who desired alcoholic beverages found their needs met with a short drive to Impact, after Impact came into existence for the purpose of legitimizing such sales. Few town names were ever more appropriately chosen.

Independence dates from the signing of the Texas Declaration of Independence there in 1836. Known then as Coles Settlement, Independence was suggested by Dr. Asa Hoxey, who earlier was responsible for the naming of Washington a few miles to the east. New Deal, north of Lubbock, commemorates a landmark event in American political history. In some minds the term *welfare,* like New Deal, evokes an era of political history. Indeed there is a community called Welfare on the map of Kendall County. Travelers on Interstate 10 note its existence between Boerne and Comfort in the Texas Hill Country. The first inhabitants were Germans who came about 1846. Some suggest that the fertile bottomlands gave assurance that settlers would "fare well." The *Handbook of Texas* proposes that the name might spring from the German word *Wohlfahrt,* which means "pleasant trip."[11] Whatever the definitive answer, one may be certain that the name has no contemporary political connotations.

Other Texas place names—and these are of Anglo origin—seem downright frivolous. These range from Alpha (southeast of Richardson in Dallas County) to Omega (in Gregg County), from Fairy (in Hamilton County) to Gay Hill (in Washington County), and from Telephone to Telegraph. Fairy and Gay Hill were named for real people, however: Fairy for Miss Fairy Fort and Gay Hill for Thomas Gay and W. C. Hill. At Telephone in Fannin County Pete Hindman owned a general store that was the first business in town. He wanted a post office. After suggesting several names to authorities, all of which were rejected, he finally settled on Telephone because the one in his store was the only one in the area. This episode occurred in the late 1880s. Telegraph in Kimble County was so called because a work crew that was stringing a telegraph line across the country found ideal timber for poles growing nearby—timber which they proceeded to cut. As final examples of frivolity one might cite Bebe, in Gonzales County, named for a brand of baking powder; Wamba, in Bowie County, named for a then-popular coffee brand; and Trickham, originally called Trick 'Em until postal authorities decreed otherwise. Trickham, in Coleman County, was the hangout of some notorious pranksters whose outrageous behavior was widely heralded.

11. Eldon S. Branda, *The Handbook of Texas. A Supplement* (Austin: Texas State Historical Association, 1976), p. 1095.

On the other hand one can find instances where place names reflect some fairly substantial values on the part of those responsible. Commerce is a medium-sized town and Industry is a small one. The first name was conceived by a civic booster and the second simply described the life-style of the Germans who settled there. Actually, Industry more properly belongs in a league with such places as Energy in Comanche County and Pep, established in 1924 by German Catholics on the High Plains. Grit was a name applied to a Mason County community around 1901, and Pluck was established at an earlier date in Polk County. Forward (Lamar County), Rising Star (Eastland County), Progress (Bailey County), and Prosper (Collin County) all convey a similar spirit on the part of those who selected the names. Security in Montgomery County was promoted by the Security Land Company at the turn of the twentieth century. Comfort in Kendall County is so named because, according to one legend, a band of German immigrants camped there amid comfortable surroundings in 1854.

Somewhat more pessimistic were those who invested their future at Eulogy in Bosque County and at Uncertain in Harrison County. There are three stories as to how Uncertain got its name. Some say it was because a Texas attorney general threatened to contest citizens' incorporation efforts on grounds that it was a subterfuge to legalize liquor sales. As a result, the community was left uncertain of its legal status. Others say that ingress and egress in the area were rendered uncertain every time it rained because of the muddy roads leading in and out of the place. A third possibility is that the name originated in steamboat days, when ships had difficulty mooring at a place that came to be known as Uncertain Landing.

Fair Play, Harmony Hill, and Unity are East Texas settlements found in Panola, Rusk, and Lamar counties. The first settler at Fair Play was Judge John Allison, who owned a general store, boardinghouse, and blacksmith shop. The site is said to have been named by a traveler who was impressed by the rates and treatment he received at Allison's boardinghouse. The name Fair Play was continued when the post office was established in 1846. Harmony Hill was first known as Nip and Tuck. In the 1850s it was a prosperous community that profited from its proximity to Trammel's Trace, the Grand Bluff Road, and the Old Wire Road. Harmony Hill declined when railroads began bypassing it in the 1870s. Unity appeared on the map in 1905 when settlers at Dixie decided belatedly upon a name change.

Friendswood and Welcome appear, at least superficially, to say something of the attitude displayed by residents toward outsiders. Friendswood in Brazoria County was a Quaker settlement established in a wooded area of northern Brazoria County in 1895. Welcome, a German community in Austin County, was named by one J. F. Schmidt, who named the locale because of its inviting climate and terrain.

Loyal Valley in Mason County and Old Glory in Stonewall County were names conferred by their German inhabitants to affirm their devotion to the American Union. Those at Loyal Valley had supported the federal government during the Civil War. Old Glory was called New Brandenburg at its founding in 1903. In 1917, at the height of America's involvement in World War I, residents petitioned to have the name changed to Old Glory.

But above all else Texans named their settlements in honor of their heroes, their leaders, and most often for themselves. Among the Texas heroes who are commemorated in its place names are Austin, Bonham, Bowie, Crockett, Houston, and Milam. Among the state's leaders who have been honored are the Baron de Bastrop, Gov. Peter Hansborough Bell (Belton), Gail Borden (Gail is the seat of Borden County), Gen. Edward Burleson, President David G. Burnet, Henri Castro, George W. Childress, Gov. Andrew Jackson Hamilton, Gov. James Pinckney Henderson, Gov. Richard Hubbard, Gov. John Ireland, President Anson Jones (Anson is the seat of Jones County), Sen. Thomas J. Rusk, Gov. James Throckmorton, and Gov. George T. Wood (Woodville).

Heroes of the American nation were not neglected in the choice of place names either. Adm. Stephen Decatur and Gen. Robert E. Lee are only two examples. American presidents have been honored: Washington, Jefferson, Madison, Jackson(ville), Tyler, Cleveland, Roosevelt (Theodore), and Taft. Dallas was named for the county in which it was established, and the county was named for George Mifflin Dallas, who was vice-president during the Polk administration. Both Polk and Dallas were ardent supporters of Texas' annexation to the Union. Legend says that John Neely Bryan had preferred to name the county for Polk, but since there was already a Polk County, he pushed instead to honor Vice-President Dallas. Marshall in East Texas was named for U.S. Chief Justice John Marshall.

One of the enduring but erroneous Texas legends is that Judge Roy Bean named his seat of justice for Lillie Langtry, the celebrated English actress. Actually, it had been named prior to Bean's arrival for a civil engineer who directed a crew of Chinese laborers as they laid track for the Texas and New Orleans Railroad in 1881. Bean did, however, name his saloon "The Jersey Lily" for the legendary beauty and did not dis-

Coupland, Texas.
Photograph by Glen E. Lich.

courage her from believing that the town itself had been named in her honor.

The largest single category of Texas place names honors those who might otherwise have little cause to be remembered. A few managed to attach their full name to these places: Ben Bolt, Burkburnett, Calallen, Edcouch, George West, Maryneal, Samnorwood, and Tom Bean are examples. Sometimes, when frustrated by the threat of duplication, they resorted to reverse spellings: Notla, Reklaw, Remlig, Sacul, Setag, and Tinrag.

The propensity of early settlers to name places for themselves could be discussed at great length. It may, however, be illustrated by a single story involving a one-time New York and San Francisco barber named Daniel E. Hungerford, an Italian nobleman named Count Joseph Telfener, and the Texas cattleman named Shanghai Pierce. Hungerford had been a Mexican War foot soldier who had marched with the U.S. Army along the Texas Gulf Coast. The coastal grasslands impressed him greatly. Years later his daughter Louise met and married J. W. Mackay in a Nevada mining camp. Mackay was on the verge of becoming a bonanza king. When Mackay's ship came in, his father-in-law climbed on board. Hungerford now began calling himself "Colonel" Hungerford. Soon Hungerford and his other unmarried daughter, Edna, joined the Mackays for a trip to Italy. The trip proved fortuitous for Edna, who met and married a bona fide Italian count, Joseph Telfener. The marriage produced several children, one of them a daughter named Inez. Telfener had important connections. He had been a successful builder of South American railroads.

When his new father-in-law began describing the coastal plains as he had remembered them during his Mexican War service, Count Telfener had an idea. With Mackay's money he would build a Texas railroad utilizing Italian immigrant labor. In time Hungerford, Telfener, and Mackay toured the coast, then requested a charter for the New York, Texas, and Mexican Railway Company. Victoria became corporate headquarters. Soon twelve hundred Italian laborers were busy laying track. Area residents referred to the enterprise as the "Macaroni Line." The matter of town naming soon arose. "My family must live in perpetuity," declared Count Telfener. Accordingly his stations were named Telferner (*sic*), Inez, Edna, Louise, Mackay, and Hungerford.

Shanghai Pierce, through whose pastures the tracks extended, was miffed. He composed a stern letter to railroad officials. "The road runs over my land, and town naming must not be done to the exclusion of *my* perpetuity." He insisted that one station be named "Pierce" and

Sign, Brewster County.
Photograph courtesy Ellen Quillan Collection,
University of Texas Institute of Texan Cultures.

another "Shanghai." As an afterthought he demanded that a third be named "Borden" for his cherished nephew.

Pierce's Station was built all right, but old Shang had to pay for the lumber that the railroad hauled in free of charge. One day Pierce and his foreman sat watching a painter adding final touches to the new depot. At one end of the building the painter placed in large letters the words PIERCE STATION. Suddenly Shang came to life. "Hold on there, by God, Sir. Put the apostrophe S on it. I own it, don't I? I paid for it." Immediately the sign was changed to read PIERCE'S STATION. Shang was satisfied.

A few residents of Luling, Texas, have cherished a myth that the town was named for a certain Chinese laundryman—Lu Ling, of course. Fable dies hard when truth lacks flair. Charles B. Luling was a wealthy German refugee who helped finance Colonel T. W. Peirce's construction of the Galveston, Harrisburg and San Antonio Railway. Peirce honored Luling's contribution by naming the embryo rail stop for him.

The impulse to award names in one's own honor occasionally provoked rebellion. In West Texas an Irishman named Murphy owned the only convenient waterhole available to the Southern Pacific Railroad when it extended its tracks through Brewster County in 1882. He magnanimously agreed to allow the railroad use of the water if they would name the stop Murphyville. The water stop grew into a community. Residents grew weary of having to write out such a lengthy name on their correspondence. The matter came up for discussion at the general store. Walter Garnett picked up a post office directory and, while scanning it, spotted Alpine, Alabama. He and his friends at the store liked the name, thought it appropriate to their mountainous region, and circulated a petition for a name change, which followed in 1888.

Rebellion against names that are perceived as being inappropriate revives from time to time. In 1980 a significant number of residents in Clute, Texas, were dissatisfied with the name. Efforts to effect a change were defeated in 1970. But in the next ten years the population of this Brazoria County town substantially increased. Once again there was sentiment to come up with something more appealing, more enticing, than the present name, which honors a pioneer settler. The chairman of the town's charter review commission said, "We have received word that businesses won't move to Clute because of the name. We felt that Brazoswood would be more appropriate." Bright admitted he could not pinpoint the objection. "I guess the name Clute is abrasive to the ears," he concluded.[12]

12. *Austin American-Statesman,* December 19, 1980.

Controversy over place names is not new in Texas. Many communities have faced more than one name change. On the whole, however, Texas place names have stabilized in the twentieth century. In a backward glance one discerns that religion played an important role in the derivation of the earliest names. In the spiritual realm the native Americans placed heavy stress on the earth and its physical features. Their place names gave a similar emphasis. The first European arrivals in what is now Texas had strong religious motivation. To be a successful (i.e., surviving) conquistador called on all a man had of courage, stamina, and faith. Devout Roman Catholics that they were, it was to be expected that the landscape would be dotted with names traceable to the calendar of their saints.

Immigration from northern Europe to Texas mounted steadily after 1820. Those who came before the Civil War appear somewhat more prone to have lifted names from the Holy Scriptures. This trend declined somewhat after the war. Like the native Americans, Europeans could and did confer place names based on physical appearances, including the flora and fauna. Unlike the native Americans they also awarded place names in honor of their heroes, themselves, and the places of their youth. These things were dear to them above all else. Other values which they held—and which they reflected in place names—paled beside these. The assertion of self in this context has remained unwavering from the outset.

Doubtless there were many among them who, in the initial flush of optimism, hoped that their posterity would one day be enshrined in the name of a great metropolis. That rarely happened. Most of the settlements never survived the embryonic stage. Others achieved only modest success. It was never so much a case of communities outgrowing their names; most simply never grew into them.

Texas economic development can be interpreted in relation to the change in the state from a rural to an urban society. A significant shift in the patterns of rural Texas came from the movement of cattle raising from the western to the eastern part of the state when irrigated agriculture became increasingly important in West Texas. As business, especially oil, became more vital to the Texas economy, the evolution toward an industrial, urban society changed many aspects of Texas culture. These economic changes have brought environmental problems and created a growing concern for conservation and other environmental issues.

4
Cotton, Cattle, and Crude: The Texas Economy, 1865–1980
J. B. Smallwood, Jr.

Since the end of the Civil War, Texas economic conditions have undergone a radical transformation. In 1865 self-sufficient farms still dominated Texas life, but within less than a decade the transition to commercial agriculture became increasingly evident. Correspondingly, the range and cattle industry was transformed during the same period from that of the open-range cowboy to the large fenced ranches, which continue to dominate. In 1901 the discovery of oil at Spindletop produced a radical shift of Texas economic growth away from agriculture and provided the basis for the urban industrialization that has dominated the Texas economy since World War II.

Prior to the Civil War self-contained agriculture characterized the Texas economy, but after the war "Texans found themselves swept into a maelstrom of economic change caused by conflicting counter-currents of self-sufficiency and dependent commercialization." By 1900 this revolution had placed cotton in the premier economic position, moved cattle raising largely to the West, and provided the basis for industrial development in the state. Texas agriculture was well on its way to specialization in crops best suited to the climate and soil of each particular region. At the turn of the century, wheat, rice, sugarcane, and other crops shared commercial status with cotton and cattle.[1]

The Civil War took a greater toll from agricultural production than from the incipient industry, which had been stimulated to some extent by war needs. Both investment and profits per industrial shop had also suffered a loss, yet by 1870 manufacturing had increased substantially in both value and production. Financial institutions, adequate for the self-contained nature of much of the Texas economy in the 1870s, could not sustain a commercial economy. By 1870 Texans, especially the farm-

---

1. John S. Spratt, *The Road to Spindletop: Economic Changes in Texas, 1875–1901* (Dallas: Southern Methodist University Press, 1955), pp. 3, 37, 43, 48.

Monroe Henderson, rancher.
Photograph by June Van Cleef.

ers, simply had less on which to base their recovery. Those landowners who had preserved their property throughout the conflict often found themselves bankrupt and without an available labor force. In general, aggregate Texas farm value had declined by almost half. Problems of labor and capital eventually led to the institution of sharecropping and tenancy. In the struggle to recover from the effects of the war, the Texas farmer was increasingly attracted to the commercial production of cotton.[2]

After the Civil War cotton emerged as the chief agricultural product of the Texas economy and remained so well into the twentieth century, although grains, especially corn, were grown in almost all counties for local use. Ideally suited to the Texas climate and soil, cotton promoted the specialization and commercialization of Texas agriculture. Because cotton was more valuable per unit, depleted the soil less than many other crops, and was more resistant to severe weather conditions, Texas farmers favored its cultivation. As the railroad moved westward, lowering transportation costs, so did cotton cultivation. The commercialization of cotton production stimulated the development of other industries such as the manufacture of cottonseed products, ginning mills, and the construction of railroad equipment to serve the cotton farmer's needs. Texans also attempted to establish cotton textile mills before 1900, but most failed. In 1900 cotton remained central to the Texas economy and, along with the industries it stimulated, accounted for approximately 50 percent of all industrial investment.[3]

Throughout the last half of the nineteenth century agricultural prices experienced a general and at times drastic decline that always exceeded the decline in nonfarm prices. Although aggregate farm production in Texas increased substantially, offsetting some of the price decline, the great increase in the number of farms often meant that individual families failed to benefit from such production increases. Between 1860 and 1880 the number of Texas farms increased from almost 43,000 to almost 175,000, yet the size of the farms had decreased more than 27 percent; by 1880 tenants or sharecroppers made up more than one-third of all Texas farmers. In the struggle to recover from their plight the farmers increased their debt, which attracted them even more strongly

---

2. Rupert N. Richardson, Ernest Wallace, and Adrian N. Anderson, *Texas, the Lone Star State,* 3rd ed. (Englewood Cliffs, N.J.: Prentice-Hall, 1970), p. 221; Spratt, *Road to Spindletop,* pp. 9–11.

3. Spratt, *Road to Spindletop,* pp. 60, 70, 74, 82.

Simon Cotulla Ranch, Dimmit County.
Photograph courtesy William L. Cotulla,
University of Texas Institute of Texan Cultures.

to cotton culture. Becoming more commercial, Texans faced the paradoxical situation of producing more for lower prices.[4]

The problems of Texas farmers, like farmers in states farther east, were aggravated by several developments during the 1870s that ushered in a period of agricultural unrest. Basic to the farmers' plight was "the emergence of a commercial economy characterized by falling prices, tight credit," and often inequitable freight rates. Specifically, the panic of 1873 and the ensuing depression plunged farmers deeper into commercial economics with which they had little experience and of which they had little understanding. The resumption of specie payment in 1876 further aggravated the situation of Texas farmers, many of whom were tenants and sharecroppers or recent immigrants who depended heavily on credit. These conditions encouraged many of them to seek relief through membership in either the Grange or the Greenbacker party, or both. Generally unaggressive at first, the Grange became a more active political pressure group during the 1880s. Although Texas farmers never recognized the trend toward commercialization and mechanization of agriculture as basic to their situation, through the Grange they did attempt unsuccessfully to organize cooperatives for buying and selling. After initial success in attracting support, both organizations began to decline by the mid-1880s, yet they had kept the issues alive for future groups to pursue. The Grange also left a permanent legacy on Texas politics through its influence on the Constitution of 1876, drafted at the height of Grange support in the state. Most of the provisions limiting the taxing and spending powers of the government, as well as those restricting railroad and corporate activities, reflected Grange policy.[5]

The railroad represented a vital element in the development and commercialization of the Texas economy after the Civil War. With very few miles of navigable rivers and a limited number of good natural harbors, Texas experienced little growth until the 1870s. High rates for transportation restricted the cotton, cattle, and lumbering industries before the war. Prior to 1875 no railroads served the area west of Dallas, Austin, or Corpus Christi, yet by 1885 railroads extended into all areas of the state. At first, Texans eagerly embraced railroad construction and

---

4. Ibid., pp. 41, 74, 82, 279; Richardson, *Texas*, p. 221; Alwyn Barr, *Reconstruction to Reform: Texas Politics, 1876–1906* (Austin: University of Texas Press, 1971), p. 11.

5. Spratt, *Road to Spindletop*, pp. 13, 152, 162–163; Richardson, *Texas*, pp. 224, 233; Barr, *Reconstruction*, p. 38.

encouraged it, especially through a liberal land-grant policy established in 1876. Throughout the nineteenth century, trackage was extended until in 1904 Texas ranked first among the states in railroad mileage. The railroad helped to revolutionize Texas economic development by providing low-cost transportation that made commercial agriculture and business growth possible in many areas of the state. Although rates were often discriminatory, transportation costs actually declined between 1875 and 1900.[6] However, uncritical enthusiasm for the railroad companies did not survive the 1870s, as many Texans, especially farmers, began to demand regulation of their practices.

Farmers' distress continued throughout the 1880s, aggravated by a complex of factors. The transition from subsistence to commercial agriculture remained psychologically difficult for farmers, yet resistance to commercialization meant forgoing the advantages of civilized life available only through cash. Throughout the 1880s and 1890s Texas farmers sought various ways of solving their problems, but "the simple and evident answer of larger farms, more farm machinery, and fewer farmers appears never to have been seriously considered."[7] Their small farms and failure to adopt technology can partly explain the farmers' poverty. In the thirty years before 1900 the average improved acreage per farm in Texas increased from 48.5 to 55.6, while the value of farm equipment was less than eighty-five dollars per farm. To acquire larger farms, especially as land scarcity drove prices up, and to purchase more farm equipment, farmers had to increase their borrowing, yet national and state banking laws restricted it. Even when money was available, interest rates were high.[8]

Growing discontent among Texas farmers led to the formation of the Farmers' Alliance, which proposed both economic and political solutions to the farmers' plight. Controversy over Alliance involvement in political activities deeply split the membership between 1885 and 1887, bringing the organization to the brink of destruction. At the statewide meeting in Waco in 1886, C. W. Macune repaired the division by promoting expansion of the Alliance into a national organization and suggesting the establishment of a Farmers' Alliance Exchange of Texas, in which farmers would own all stock. Support for a farmers' exchange, which would concentrate on marketing cotton rather than discourage

---

6. Spratt, *Road to Spindletop*, pp. 25, 29–30; Richardson, *Texas*, p. 273; Barr, *Reconstruction*, p. 111.
7. Spratt, *Road to Spindletop*, p. 119.
8. Ibid, pp. 111–19; Barr, *Reconstruction*, p. 95.

its cultivation, as the Grange had, reflected a more realistic view of the farmers' economic circumstances. Established in Dallas in 1887, the Farmers' Alliance Exchange developed a systematic credit operation, yet, as with the Texas Co-operative Association, poor management that resulted "from the effort to operate with too little capital and overextension of credit"[9] doomed the experiment to failure.[10]

Allied with the farmers' protest in the 1880s was the emerging labor movement in Texas, which paralleled the industrial development of the state. Like the farmers, laborers saw little change in their conditions by 1887, but in 1888 Texas farmer and labor groups meeting at Waco called for abolition of national banks, government ownership of transportation and communications, a national usury law, opposition to alien landownership as well as land grants to corporations, coinage of silver, payment of national debt, a graduated income tax, and changes in the state's political structure and social service. By 1890 the Texas legislature was responding to some of the farmers' demands, and the state had become a center of independent political action. Although most farmers did not desert the Democratic party in the 1880s, their continuing discontent provided the basis for the statewide Populist movement in the 1890s. After 1890, when the Alliance had attempted but failed to dominate the Democratic party, many Texas farmers turned to the independent Populist effort as the best means for achieving their goals. Although Populist support came from various groups, at least two-thirds of the members were former Democrats. Populism appealed to those groups who felt abandoned by the traditional parties. Drawing support largely from the poorer areas of west central and East Texas as well as the "less-favored portions of generally more prosperous counties in Central and North Texas," Populist membership was largely Anglo and evangelical.[11] In addition, southwest Texas sheep ranchers joined the movement after Cleveland's administration reduced the tariff on wool. The Populist program, with the exception of the subtreasury plan which they were the first to promote, reflected the platform of earlier farm movements.[12]

An issue of continuing importance to farm groups after 1870 was railroad regulation. Because of the railroads' operating abuses—rebates, drawbacks, high short-haul fares, and rate discrimination—as well as

9. Spratt, *Road to Spindletop*, p. 202.
10. Ibid., pp. 187–89, 194–97; Barr, *Reconstruction*, pp. 93–94.
11. Barr, *Reconstruction*, p. 150.
12. Spratt, *Road to Spindletop*, pp. 206, 239–40; Richardson, *Texas*, p. 298; Barr, *Reconstruction*, pp. 103–109, 143, 145, 150–51.

their poor service, farmers were growing hostile toward railroad owners. The Constitution of 1876, influenced by the Grange, provided a basis for regulatory legislation, but effective implementation and enforcement of such regulation was not forthcoming. After the legislature in 1889 approved an amendment permitting creation of a commission to implement and enforce the laws, James S. Hogg supported its ratification in his campaign for governor the next year. Voters, despite opposition from the Populists, endorsed the amendment and elected Hogg governor (1891–95), and the Texas Railroad Commission was established in 1891.[13]

The panic of 1893 worsened the plight of the farmers, helping to bring Populist support in Texas to its peak in 1894. In that year the Populist candidate for governor, Thomas L. Nugent, made significant gains in support from the drought-ridden farmers of West Texas and even from blacks. Although in 1896 the Populist candidate for governor won 44 percent of the votes, Texas remained under Democratic control.[14]

Although the Populists never controlled Texas politics, they raised questions that Progressive leaders subsequently dealt with somewhat more successfully. Former Texas Populist leaders also helped organize and develop the Farmers' Union, which became an important national pressure group in the twentieth century. By 1900, as relative prosperity returned to the farming community, most Texas Populists drifted back into the Democratic party.[15] Essentially, Governor Hogg understood better than the Populists did that "control of the state government rested primarily on the economic and ethnic diversity of Texas . . . the very reform and views which brought [the Populists] a huge following repelled an even larger block of voters. . . . Culture and tradition rivaled economics as influences on Texas voting patterns."[16]

An industry long associated romantically as well as economically with Texas was cattle raising. Spawned originally from Spanish cattle that arrived with the early priests and settlers, cattle herds by 1830 had been augmented with English and French stock. Cattle raising in the eastern part of the state differed greatly from that elsewhere in Texas. In East

---

13. Spratt, *Road to Spindletop,* pp. 23, 25, 28, 214; Richardson, *Texas,* pp. 294, 297; Barr, *Reconstruction,* pp. 112–19.
14. Richardson, *Texas,* pp. 294, 297–99; Barr, *Reconstruction,* pp. 119–21, 142, 157–71.
15. Richardson, *Texas,* p. 299; Barr, *Reconstruction,* pp. 172–75.
16. Barr, *Reconstruction,* p. 174.

Texas it "began as a part of the system of self-contained agriculture."[17] In the west it originated as a commercial enterprise. While the eastern areas experienced a substantial increase in cattle between 1870 and 1900, the increase in the West was enormous during the same period, especially in the Panhandle. Prior to 1880 limited water supply, few available markets, and the presence of the buffalo and the Indian restricted development of the cattle industry in West Texas. As these problems gradually disappeared after 1880, an era of cattle drives and boom conditions ensued. A short but exciting period in the cattle industry followed, characterized by the open range and cattle drives to the railroad in Kansas.[18]

Although other agricultural prices declined, between 1880 and 1885 cattle prices boomed as capitalization for cattle companies exceeded that of railroads. Although informal agreements provided for dividing the range according to its capacity to support cattle, many areas were overstocked, bringing devastation during dry years. By 1890 "the crowded ranges, the westward advance of farmers and railroads, the introduction of barbed wire, and the utilization of drilled wells and windmills for obtaining water economically [had] transformed the open range into a country of big pastures."[19] Fencing, prevalent throughout Texas by 1885, met resistance initially, especially because the large land companies controlled by eastern or foreign capital erected the first fences. Fencing, however, made possible better control over grazing lands as well as the initiation of stock improvement. Farmers too began to challenge the cattlemen for possession of the land, which at first led to violence. But as land prices increased ranchers sold part of their land to farmers, resulting in peace if not amity between the two groups.[20]

Once the boom of the 1880s had passed, cattlemen experienced much the same conditions as the farmers; cattle prices declined to approximate those of other agricultural products. Cattlemen also shared the farmers' problems of poor "rainfall, shortage of money and credit, [and] high interest rates," as well as discriminatory freight charges.[21] In an attempt to deal with many of these problems, a group of Texas ranchers in 1877 organized the Stock Raisers' Association of North West Texas. Cattlemen in other areas founded similar organizations, which even-

17. Spratt, *Road to Spindletop*, p. 110.
18. Ibid., pp. 85, 91; Richardson, *Texas*, pp. 257, 260; Barr, *Reconstruction*, p. 12.
19. Richardson, *Texas*, p. 262.
20. Spratt, *Road to Spindletop*, pp. 15–18, 89, 93, 95–102, 120–26; Richardson, *Texas*, pp. 260, 262–65.
21. Spratt, *Road to Spindletop*, p. 147.

tually led to the formation of the Texas Cattle Raisers' Association in 1893. Between 1880 and 1890 the number of cattle in Texas peaked at about 10 million head, after which a slow but steady decline began. Despite the romantic association of cattle raising with Texas' past, the products of the range never exceeded the value of cotton or corn crops during the late nineteenth century.

Conflict between cattlemen and farmers for control of West Texas, especially the Panhandle, became particularly intense during the governorship of John Ireland (1883–87). Ranchers and railroads fenced not only their property but areas they did not own, including school lands on which ranchers failed to make lease payments. The actions also prevented many farmers from having access to water, resulting in a fence-cutting war. In 1884 the legislature attempted to control the situation by making fence cutting a felony, at the same time prohibiting fencing of unowned land, public or private. The controversy continued, however, as an issue in the gubernatorial election of 1886, and led Gov. Lawrence S. Ross (1887–91) to replace the State Land Board with a land commissioner and to make other changes in the state's land policy.[22]

In 1895, after having disposed of more than 91 percent of the public lands, Texas began an era of revision in its land policy. By 1898 Texas had granted 32 million acres of land for railroad development and had reserved 50 million for public schools and colleges. The following year the state abandoned its homestead policy after the courts ruled that the state no longer had public lands to distribute. In 1900 the legislature placed all unsurveyed and unappropriated lands in the Permanent School Fund, which in 1939 also acquired all lakes, bays, islands, and submerged lands off the Texas coast. In 1905 the state legislature adopted a more orderly procedure for selling land. By the last quarter of the twentieth century the Texas public domain consisted of 22.5 million acres, much of it submerged lands off the coast and lands held by public institutions, especially the University of Texas, which were valuable or potentially so as oil property.[23]

Although oil production was not of major economic significance in Texas during the late nineteenth century, activities in that period laid much of the groundwork for the state's oil boom during the twentieth century. Local production of oil in the Nacogdoches area, discovered

22. Spratt, *Road to Spindletop*, pp. 85–86, 103–108, 121, 147–48; Richardson, *Texas*, pp. 267–68, 276–78, 279; Barr, *Reconstruction*, pp. 12, 81–82.

23. Richardson, *Texas*, pp. 276–77; Barr, *Reconstruction*, p. 84; *Texas Almanac, 1980–81* (Dallas, Tex.: Dallas Morning News, 1980), p. 617.

while drilling for water and used for lubrication or medicine, dated back to the 1850s. By 1880 other fields had been developed in Brown and Shackelford counties, but the commercial production of oil began at Corsicana. In 1897 J. S. Cullinan of Pittsburgh, Pennsylvania, organized the field, which produced 836,000 barrels per year by 1900. Cullinan combined with the Cotton Belt Railroad in 1898 to develop an oil-burning locomotive, which greatly expanded the use of petroleum. Cullinan also inaugurated modern oil refining in Texas with completion of his Corsicana facility in 1901. In an attempt to prevent the waste associated with development of the Corsicana field, in 1899 the state legislature passed a law governing drilling and other oil field practices. The success at Corsicana encouraged deliberate attempts to find oil. By 1890 the association of oil deposits with salt domes had attracted considerable attention. An 1892 attempt to locate oil in the Spindletop salt dome failed, but a second try in 1901 proved successful, ushering in a new era in Texas economic development. On January 10, 1901, A. F. Lucas, an Austrian immigrant and mining engineer supported by Mellon money from Pittsburgh, brought in a well that gained nationwide attention. Yielding unheard-of production by a single well in the United States, Spindletop attracted tremendous investment to the area. In 1901 Texas chartered 491 oil companies authorized to issue $239,639,999 in stock. Although in 1900 the Texas economy remained largely based on farming, ranching, and processing of raw materials, after Spindletop the state began to evolve the characteristics of a complex industrial society.[24]

In the first two decades of the twentieth century Texas responded as did many other predominantly agricultural states of the South and Midwest "to meet the challenge of growing commercialization in agriculture, industrialization, and urbanization, as well as individual specialization and interdependence in the state and national economy and society." The impulse for reform, which had declined noticeably with the defeat of Populism, combined with the emerging commercialization to usher in an era of business-oriented progressivism. Between 1880 and 1900 manufacturing establishments had grown from 2,998 to 12,289, and the Spindletop discovery presaged an economic revolution in the state, yet progressive reform enjoyed a revival between 1900 and 1920. Composition of the state legislature reflected the economic changes occurring in Texas. Prior to 1890 farmers made up 50 percent of the legislature, but by the mid-1890s attorneys and businessmen accounted

24. Spratt, *Road to Spindletop*, pp. 271-72, 274-79.

for two-thirds of the membership. Politicians such as E. M. House and Joseph W. Bailey, though supportive of some reform measures, reflected the "new industrial and business interests, especially oil companies."[25] This business progressivism was reflected in the good roads movements of the 1920s, a boon both to business development and the commercialization of agriculture.[26]

During the first decade of the new century Texas lawmakers substantially revised the state's tax laws, which brought a somewhat more equitable distribution of the tax burden. Prior to 1900 property taxes had constituted the main source of tax revenue. In addition to taxing intangible corporate assets, the Texas legislature increased franchise taxes, passed a full rendition in 1907, and established a tax board in 1909. Despite these changes, property still bore the major burden of taxation until the coming of the oil industry and the automobile shifted the burden to natural resources and their products along with special sales taxes. Throughout the late nineteenth century the legislature made various provisions for collection of school taxes; between 1908 and 1919 the government substantially raised the ad valorem taxes for school districts while applying the laws more uniformly throughout the state.[27]

By 1900 general agricultural prosperity had returned to Texas and remained for two decades. Although individual farmers may not have benefited, the overall value of the state's agricultural production steadily increased between 1880 and 1920, maintaining a fairly stable condition even during the 1920s. Between 1880 and 1930 the value of the average farm increased from one thousand to seven thousand dollars, representing largely new farms and the increase in value per acre on existing ones. While from 1910 to 1920 the harvested cropland in Texas increased by more than 30 percent, much of the increase represented marginal land productive only under ideal conditions.[28]

The trend toward commercialization in agriculture accelerated during the twentieth century, but as one scholar observed, even though commercial agriculture prevailed as the main industry in Texas by 1900, the "doom of agricultural leadership in Texas was sealed at Spindletop."[29] Several factors encouraged commercialization. Among these, tenancy not only promoted the trend but was itself accelerated by the

25. Barr, *Reconstruction,* pp. 218–20, 228–34, 240, 249.
26. Richardson, *Texas,* p. 320.
27. Spratt, *Road to Spindletop,* pp. 134–35; Richardson, *Texas,* pp., 301, 305–306, 310, 403; Barr, *Reconstruction,* p. 234.
28. Richardson, *Texas,* pp. 280, 287, 316, 383–84.
29. Spratt, *Road to Spindletop,* p. 285.

very commercialization it fostered. In 1900 tenants operated 50 percent of Texas farms. Tenants who needed money to pay their rent and sharecroppers, encouraged by landowners, both turned to the production of commercial crops. The tremendous increase in farm mortgages also stimulated commercialization. By 1910 Texas farmers were more able to handle their mortgages, largely by turning to commercial production to meet the payment on their debts. Another factor of major importance in promoting commercialization of Texas agriculture after 1900 was irrigated farming, which at the turn of the century was confined to about ten counties, mostly in South Texas.[30]

Among the commercial crops, cotton not only prevailed but became increasingly important, until by 1910 cotton culture occupied one-half of the cultivated acreage in Texas. Despite critics who condemned the specialization in cotton and who blamed farming's ills on cotton culture, the Texas farmer persisted in planting cotton for many reasons. In the analysis of one scholar, "cotton almost always returned more income per acre than other crops suited to his land, labor, and machinery resources. Cotton was the most dependable of the southern crops; . . . it did not exhaust the soil as quickly as many other crops. And the machinery for marketing cotton was more advanced than other commodities.[31] Lured by the development of the rich water resources that lay in the Ogallala Aquifer beneath the Panhandle, cotton culture shifted perceptibly from East to West Texas began during the 1920s. More adaptable to mechanization, irrigated cotton accelerated the commercialization of Texas agriculture. Although in 1918 West Texas produced only 50,588 bales of cotton, in 1926 the soil of that area yielded 1,130,713 bales. Commercial development of the citrus industry in the lower Rio Grande Valley also began in the 1920s.[32]

As in the late nineteenth century, some Texas farmers turned to farm organizations for solutions to their problems. The Farmers' Union had achieved a membership of eighty thousand in Texas and other states by 1905. The organization attempted to regulate both cotton acreage and prices, but the panic of 1907 had already undermined the system of Union stores. The panic of 1914 ended a later attempt to establish a clearinghouse for buying and selling. Although the Farmers' Union declined rapidly after World War I, it reemerged as the "most militant

---

30. Ibid, pp. 55–59; Richardson, *Texas*, p. 313.
31. Richardson, *Texas*, pp. 279–80.
32. Seth Shepard McKay and Odie B. Faulk, *Texas after Spindletop* (Austin: Steck-Vaughn, 1965), pp. 93–98.

farmers' organization" after World War II. The union exercised some influence in state politics and did have some effect in achieving higher prices for farmers' products while moderating the prices farmers paid for their purchases.[33]

As the Farmers' Union declined during the 1920s, Texas farmers turned to membership in two other organizations: the Farm-Labor Union and the Farm Bureau Federation. Established in 1920 at Bonham as a "dirt farmer" organization, the Farm-Labor Union spread rapidly throughout Texas, but by 1925 bad management, the failure to establish a successful marketing system, and rising prices had destroyed it. The more successful Farm Bureau Federation, which came to Texas in 1920, faltered until 1936, when the Texas group associated with the American Farm Bureau Federation. With a membership of 100,000 by 1960, the federation represented basically a conservative group that promoted agricultural education and research, animal health laws, and better farm roads.

Already weak by the middle of the 1920s, agricultural prices plummeted after the crash of 1929. In that year the federal government established a $500 million revolving fund under the supervision of the Federal Farm Board. Although two of Texas' leading commodities, cotton and wheat, proved costliest to support, prices continued to decline, until in 1932 cotton sold for five cents a pound. Because President Franklin Roosevelt placed a high priority on revival of agricultural prosperity, much New Deal legislation affected Texas farmers. Especially important were parity payments, various soil conservation programs, better credit facilities for farmers, aid to very poor farmers, and the 1934 Cotton Control (Bankhead) Act that forced farmers into an allotment system.[34]

The Spindletop discovery fostered wild speculation and chaotic conditions in southeastern Texas, a situation reminiscent of that in western Pennsylvania after the discovery of oil there. Between 1900 and 1901 Texas oil production increased from 836,000 to 4,393,658 barrels. The discovery of abundant petroleum reserves at Sour Lake in 1902 only depressed oil prices further. Although developments were already under way that would make possible substitution of oil for coal for many uses, perfection of such processes lagged behind oil production. By 1905, outside capital had helped expand Texas production to over 28 million barrels, after which production declined for several years. State officials

33. Richardson, *Texas*, p. 381.
34. Ibid., pp. 329, 381–83, 384–86; McKay and Faulk, *Texas after Spindletop*, pp. 127–28.

recognized the need for some regulation of the petroleum industry as early as 1903. A constitutional amendment in 1917 provided for greater state control, and in the same year the Pipeline Act created the pipeline division of the Railroad Commission. In addition to supervising pipeline rates and practices, the commission monitored waste and poor drilling practices.[35]

By 1928 oil and the industries it spawned dominated the state's economy, as Texas led the nation in crude oil production. Overproduction by the mid-1920s caused the Railroad Commission to attempt voluntary production quotas. The opening of fantastic new fields in East Texas during the 1930s brought disaster to Texas oil producers as the price dropped to eight cents per barrel. With the support of the courts, the Railroad Commission met protest and resistance to its authority as it attempted to cope, often inconsistently, with the mounting problem of overproduction. In 1931 Gov. Ross Sterling (1931–33) declared martial law to enforce production limits, an act declared illegal by the courts in February, 1932. Under these critical conditions the state legislature voted the Railroad Commission power to establish allowables, and the federal government aided with the "hot oil" clause of the National Industrial Recovery Act of 1933. Using a policy of proration, Texas developed a more rational and effective policy for controlling oil production by the late 1930s. In 1935 Texas joined five other states in a compact to prevent waste and to encourage maximum recovery of oil. Although the signatories denied any intent to fix prices, the agreement tended to restrict production to demand.[36]

The search for petroleum often led to the discovery of natural gas, which assumed some commercial importance during the early twentieth century. Extensive fields of natural gas opened in the Panhandle during the late 1920s. In 1935 the legislature attempted to reduce wastage in manufacture of products from gas, and in 1946 the Railroad Commission prohibited flaring of gas. Chemicals represented another industry closely associated with petroleum production. Begun in Freeport in 1912, the industry prospered even during the Great Depression, providing chemicals not only for the oil and gas companies but also for synthetic textiles, paper, and other manufacturing processes.

Although depletion of forests caused a decline in lumbering after

---

35. Richardson, *Texas*, pp. 281, 393–94; McKay and Faulk, *Texas after Spindletop*, pp. 6–8.
36. Richardson, *Texas*, pp. 281–83, 345, 383, 394–95; McKay and Faulk, *Texas after Spindletop*, pp. 100–104, 126–27; *Texas Almanac*, p. 410.

1907, the industry remained significant throughout the twentieth century, with Orange and Beaumont important sawmill centers. The development of a technique for making sulfate paper from yellow pine in 1911 increased the demand for Texas lumber. By 1939, although cutting of timber exceeded a billion board feet, production of trees exceeded depletion. Cotton-associated industries, such as the production of cottonseed oil and cake for cattle feed, remained important after 1900, although attempts to establish cotton mills prior to 1930 were never very successful. With the establishment of two modern plants at Fort Worth in 1901, meatpacking emerged as a major industry in the state.[37]

Despite a generally exploitive attitude toward natural resources, some Texans shared with progressives throughout the country a concern for the depletion of the nation's resources. The abundance of cheap land undermined most early attempts to encourage good farming methods designed to preserve soil fertility, but inauguration of demonstration work in 1910 spread throughout the state in subsequent decades. Establishment of the Texas Forest Service in 1913 focused attention on Texas' declining timber resources. With acquisition of the first state forests in 1924, Texas began to provide demonstration and research facilities in forest culture.[38]

Water resources, always a major factor in the settlement of Texas, received official consideration with the establishment of the office of a state reclamation engineer in 1909. Initially, water programs such as flood control, water supply, irrigation, and industrial uses were dealt with separately by local communities, but by the 1920 the developing idea of approaching a watershed as a unit had begun to influence the state's program for managing its water resources. In 1929 the legislature established the Brazos River Conservation and Reclamation District, granting to it powers greater than any other such agency. Reflecting the increasing urbanization of the state, in 1932 Texas law granted cities first priority above all other uses for water. Gov. Pat Neff (1921-24) encouraged conservation of the state's natural resources. With the establishment of a nonsalaried state park board in 1923, Neff also moved toward the establishment of a state park system, which proved difficult since by that time Texas had little public land. The state had to solicit donations to provide land for recreational use. As was true in other

---

37. Richardson, *Texas*, 280-81, 283, 342, 343, 345, 395; Barr, *Reconstruction*, p. 218; McKay and Faulk, *Texas after Spindletop*, pp. 100-101.
38. Richardson, *Texas*, pp. 388-89.

states, the New Deal stimulated and supported conservation programs in Texas, especially soil and forestry conservation. Much of the soil conservation effort focused on the fragile ecology of West Texas, where the land was easily damaged by overgrazing and poor farming techniques. In 1935 the federal government, on invitation of the state legislature, began purchasing forest lands in Texas. During the 1930s Gov. James V. Allred (1935–39) urged the establishment of a planning board to develop comprehensive plans for conservation and use of natural resources. In response, the legislature authorized the Texas Planning Board for a four-year period.[39]

During the twentieth century the continued development of a variety of transportation systems stimulated economic growth in Texas. Railroad construction continued rapidly from the end of the Civil War until 1913, after which there was minimal activity until 1925. Mileage grew gradually until trackage peaked in 1932 at 17,078 miles. After that date, a steady decline began and continued, until in 1980 the state had only 13,000 miles of railroad. With the growth of bus and air travel during the 1960s, most railroads discontinued passenger service. Although rail freight tonnage generally increased, trucking became a major competitor in that area. By 1978 truck and bus service in Texas represented an investment of nearly $5 billion. Because two-thirds of Texas' communities depended exclusively on truck transportation, it was even more important in Texas than other states.[40]

The state's natural harbors are generally shallow and poor, which is why shipping presented problems from early days. A leading cotton and grain shipping port, Galveston, located on an island at the entrance to Trinity Bay, remained the state's major port until well into the twentieth century, despite improvements made at other ports. Interest in a ship channel to Houston began before 1900. Opening of the channel in 1916 diverted much of the shipping, especially of petrochemicals, to Houston and other ports along Trinity Bay, and Houston has remained the leader among the state's thirteen Gulf ports.[41]

Responding to the development of the automobile, Texans initiated a highway system when in 1907 the state permitted counties to issue bonds for road construction. By 1925 the state extended its control over the nascent highway system and in 1932 assumed full responsibility for construction and maintenance. Because of the vast distances within the

39. Ibid., pp. 320, 332–33, 387–88, 390–91.
40. Ibid., pp. 349–50; *Texas Almanac*, pp. 453, 471.
41. Richardson, *Texas*, pp. 353–54; *Texas Almanac*, pp. 453, 459–60.

state as well as perhaps the frontier independence that prevails among the people, Texans placed a high priority on automobile use. By 1950 the state could boast one of the better highway systems in the nation. Second only to California in motor vehicle registration in 1980, Texas led the nation in total road and street mileage. Stimulated by World War I, air transportation developed rapidly in Texas; Houston formally dedicated the first airport in 1928. By 1980 Texas airports had gained major significance in national air transportation.[42]

In many ways World War II marked a significant milestone in the development of the Texas economy. Although the basis for industrial growth had been laid during the first four decades of the century, soon after the war began, "the rate of industrial activity was the highest ever known and the total income surpassed all previous records."[43] Much postwar industrial development focused on the South and on Texas in particular. Population shifts had made Texas the third most populous state by 1978, and personal incomes rose faster than the national average, although a significant portion of the Texas population remained below the federal poverty level. Wage scales lower than those in other parts of the country partially explained both the spectacular industrial development of the state after 1950 as well as the relative poverty of many Texas workers. The socioeconomic conditions of ethnic minorities and illegal aliens contrasted particularly with the emerging California-style affluence of many Texans.[44]

Despite petroleum's dominance of the state's economy by 1955, more Texans relied on cotton than on oil for their livelihood. Texas agriculture followed trends similar to those in most other agricultural areas of the country, as agribusiness gradually replaced the small, traditional farm. The trend toward larger and fewer farms was noticeable as early as the 1930s. Since World War II, Texas farms "have become fewer, larger, specialized, more expensive to own and operate, but far more productive."[45] By 1960, although the number of farms had declined by almost 50 percent, the size of the units had doubled. During the 1970s, Texas ranked third in the nation in total farm and ranch marketing.

Indicative of the changes in Texas agriculture was the decline between 1940 and 1978 in the number of farms, from 418,000 to 200,000,

42. Richardson, *Texas*, pp. 350–52, 356–57; *Texas Almanac*, pp. 453, 459.
43. Richardson, *Texas*, p. 358.
44. Barr, *Reconstruction*, p. 250; *Texas Almanac*, pp. 192, 420; George Brown Tindall, *The Emergence of the New South, 1913–1945* (Baton Rouge: Louisiana State University Press, 1967), pp. 695–703.
45. *Texas Almanac*, p. 557.

with a corresponding increase in average farm assets from $6,196 to $214,748. Whereas in 1940 one out of three Texans lived on farms, only one in eighteen did in 1966. The decline in tenantry from 301,600 in 1930 to 37,800 in 1964 helped significantly to reduce one negative factor in Texas agriculture. Several factors contributed to the remarkable changes in Texas agriculture after World War II, most important among which were continued federal price supports, greater mechanization, and the use of better scientific knowledge and management. The increased use of machinery and chemicals, however, brought labor problems and increasing protest from environmentalists. After World War II, irrigation revolutionized agriculture in the High Plains, an area that by 1978 accounted for 65 percent of all the irrigated land in the state. Between 50 and 60 percent of the total value of Texas crop production in 1978 derived from irrigated lands. Because 80 percent of all irrigation waters came from wells, the increasing cost of fuel and a serious decline of water levels in the Ogallala Aquifer underlying the Panhandle region posed critical problems for the future prosperity of West Texas agriculture as well as its industrial growth.[46]

Traditionally a major crop in the state, cotton continued to dominate agriculture in Texas. Leading the nation in cotton production in 1978 with 3,828,000 bales, Texas shipped as its main agricultural export $652 million worth of the white fiber. Significant changes occurred in cotton production after World War II. Attracted by irrigation waters for the rich soils of the Panhandle, the center of cotton culture shifted from the eastern part of the state to West Texas. Machine harvesting, which began in 1947, solved one of the major production problems, and by 1971 Texas cotton farmers no longer used hand labor for that purpose. The processing of cottonseed oil remained an important auxiliary activity associated with cotton production. Grain crops also continued to figure significantly in Texas agriculture. Sorghum displaced rice as the second most valuable grain crop, and wheat stood third in cash value. Corn ranked third in value but was used as livestock feed and so was not generally sold. The production of fruits and nuts became increasingly important to certain areas of the state. With grapefruit most significant, fruit from the Rio Grande Valley ranked Texas third in the production of citrus, while pecans, grown throughout the wetter parts of the state, made Texas second in production of that crop. In 1977 Texas ranked third among the states in harvested acreage, production, and value of fresh market vegetables. A considerable amount of Texas agri-

46. Richardson, *Texas*, pp. 386–87; *Texas Almanac*, pp. 557, 560–61.

cultural land has been devoted to forage crops, either native grasses, introduced forage, or machine-harvested hay and silage.[47]

Ranching continued to be important to the Texas economy in the years after World War II; livestock and their products accounted for approximately one-half of agricultural cash receipts. Despite a slow decline beginning in 1974 in the number of beef cattle, sheep, and lambs, which has reduced wool production, Texas still led the nation in production of all cattle. Several factors brought significant changes to the livestock industry during the twentieth century. Poor market conditions between 1920 and 1927 resulted in a shift of ranching from the western part of the state into the Edwards Plateau, the trans-Pecos area, and the southern coastal plain. As ranching developed in the broken and semiarid areas of Central Texas, goat and sheep production increased, until by the late 1970s, Texas ranchers clipped almost one-half of the world's mohair. More recently, livestock production has moved into the moister eastern part of the state. Dairying, despite a steady decline in the number of cows, remained an important economic activity in the eastern part of the state. Also important in the agricultural economy of Texas were horses and poultry. In spite of the continued importance of agriculture to the Texas economy, its decline in relation to the emergence of industrialization and urbanization has shifted political and economic power toward the cities in the post–World War II era.[48]

A part of the "Sunbelt phenomenon" during the 1970s, Texas experienced rapid economic growth. Among the factors that stimulated such growth were the absence of either personal or corporate income taxes and minimal state regulation of business activities. In addition, only 13 percent of Texas labor was unionized by the late 1970s. In the 1980s not all conditions are favorable for the continued prosperity of the Texas economy. Lack of sufficient local capital has made it necessary to obtain investment money from sources outside the state for further growth. As the production and value of crude oil has begun to decline, continued dominance of Texas business and industrial development by petroleum production has meant potential problems for the economy in the future. Diversification into the production of computers, transportation equipment, and communication products as well as the electronic and aerospace industries represents a move toward a more balanced industrial economy, but these developments remain insufficient

---

47. *Texas Almanac*, pp. 557, 561–62, 565–70.
48. Ibid., pp. 557–58, 574–79; Richardson, *Texas*, pp. 267, 342, 387; McKay and Faulk, *Texas after Spindletop*, p. 97.

to compensate for the inevitable decline in the importance of petroleum production.[49]

Throughout the post–World War II era, petroleum and associated industries have profoundly affected the lives of Texans. With the discovery of new fields in the 1940s and 1950s, Texas crude production reached a billion barrels by 1951, and by 1966 Texas provided one-third of the nation's oil and 9 percent of the world's. Despite a yearly decline in Texas oil production since 1976, of the $19.6 billion of raw material produced in the state in 1978, mineral fuels accounted for $18.4 billion, of which $9.7 billion represented oil production. After a decline in the output of natural gas during the depression, war demands stimulated production, which continued to increase until 1966, when Texas produced over 7 trillion cubic feet of gas. Despite a decline in production from 1977 to 1978, Texas still provided one-third of the nation's natural gas. Auxiliary products distilled from natural gas have also been important in the state's economy. By 1976 Texas ranked among the top ten states both in the value of its manufactured products and value added. Much of the $77.1 billions of goods shipped as well as the $27.6 billions of value added was associated with the petrochemical industry. The chemical industry, which has grown rapidly in the years since World War II, provided more than 50 percent of the total value added by all mineral-related manufacturing. Petrochemical activities have concentrated along the Gulf Coast near Houston and Beaumont, as have refining industries. By 1967 Texas ranked second among the states in value added by chemical manufacturing.[50]

In 1978 mining and mineral-derived manufacturing employed approximately 382,000 workers, or 7 percent of all jobs in Texas. With the development of the energy crisis during the late 1970s, the future for the mining of Texas coal, almost all of which was lignite used for mine-mouth steam electric production, brightened greatly. Despite renewed interest, several problems confront Texas coal mining. Estimates indicated that 12.2 billion short tons of lignite lay near the surface, of which 6.7 billion short tons could be recovered profitably with existing technology. Another 100 billion tons rests in deposits from five hun-

---

49. *Texas Almanac,* pp. 404, 424; for an interesting presentation of the "Sunbelt phenomenon," see Kirkpatrick Sale, *Power Shift: The Rise of the Southern Rim and Its Challenge to the Eastern Establishment* (New York: Random House, 1975); for a typical example of investment promotion in Texas see the pamphlet, *A Special Kiplinger Report: Texas* (Washington, D.C.: The Kiplinger Washington Editors, 1980).

50. *Texas Almanac,* pp. 404, 406, 410–11; Richardson, *Texas,* pp. 343, 345–46.

dred to five thousand feet below the surface. Texas coal exists generally in thin seams, requiring costly removal of overburden. Demands by environmentalists for reclamation of stripped land under the environmental protection laws add another dimension to the problem of coal removal. Other groups have protested the polluting effect of increased use of coal for generating electric power. Texas remains the nation's leading sulfur producer (indeed, it is among the world leaders), an industry valued at more than a million dollars by the 1960s.[51]

Metallic minerals mined in the state constitute only 1 percent of the nation's total output. Important among these are iron ore, magnesium, of which Texas is a major producer, and uranium. Iron ore, mined largely in the eastern portion of the state, supplied the mills of the Lone Star Steel Company in Morris County. Consistently mined in Texas for more than seventy years, silver has been produced only in moderate amounts. Other products mined in the state include gypsum, of considerable importance; helium and salt (Texas has been a leading producer of both); and sand and gravel, important in the construction industry. Several other industries, both old and new ones, have contributed to Texas business growth in the post-1945 era. Steel production in East Texas, copper smelting in the El Paso area, magnesium processing at Freeport, and aluminum processing at various places have added to the state's economic prosperity. By the 1960s food processing employed seventy-five thousand workers. Textile manufacturing grew after World War II, until the 1960s forty-six hundred workers operated eighteen plants. Stimulated by war, the aircraft industry has developed a continuing economic importance for the Fort Worth–Dallas area.[52]

Texas forest resources continue to contribute both economically and recreationally to the well-being of Texans. After 1930 a reversal occurred in the depletion of Texas forests as a consequence of both public and private efforts to reduce fires, increase tree planting, and encourage natural regrowth. The 1950 Cooperative Forest Management Act encouraged better private management of forests, resulting by 1966 in tree farms that covered almost 4 million acres. By 1977 regrowth in East Texas exceeded harvesting by 34 percent, yet as lands devoted to rights-of-way, water impoundment, real estate development, and park and wilderness areas have reduced forested areas, demand promised to outstrip production unless remaining lands were more fully developed. Of the harvested timber, four-fifths of which was pine, the pulp and

51. Richardson, *Texas*, p. 345; *Texas Almanac*, pp. 404, 416, 418–19.
52. Richardson, *Texas*, pp. 342–45; *Texas Almanac*, pp. 404, 417–19.

Texas Hardiness.
Photograph by June Van Cleef.

paper industry constituted the chief use, with construction lumber second in importance. Production of railroad ties constituted the main use of hardwoods, while plywood production increased in importance. By 1977 the estimated market value of Texas timber approached $4 billion. In the same year timber from Texas tree farms sold for "an estimated value of $216 million."[53] Outdoor recreation, watershed management, and livestock production as well as wildlife preservation represent other benefits Texans derived from their forests. The four national forests and two national grasslands in the state practiced timber management, which permitted cutting of one-third of the estimated 200 million board feet of lumber they contain.[54]

As Texas became increasingly industrialized and urbanized, an adequate supply of usable water emerged as critical to the economic prosperity of the state. Demands for water from agriculture, industry, and cities grew tremendously after World War II. A series of droughts during the 1950s spurred interest in a more systematic development of the state's water resources. Beginning with the creation of the Lower Colorado River Authority in 1935 through attempts in the 1960s and 1970s to promote the Trinity River barge canal and the Texas Water Plan, Texans have searched for various ways to meet the water needs of a rapidly urbanizing society.[55]

The 1980s pose both opportunities and problems for Texans. The leveling-off of oil production suggests that Texans develop a more diverse industrial economy less dependent on petroleum, yet international crises in oil-rich regions of the world have temporarily stimulated secondary recovery efforts in vast oil fields of the state. Depletion of irrigation waters on the High Plains foreshadows radical readjustments in agricultural patterns in that area, which has contributed substantially to the state's agricultural productivity. An adequate supply of usable water remains a problem, an issue that demands intelligent and thoughtful planning for a state half of whose area lies beyond the twenty-inch

53. *Texas Almanac*, p. 569.
54. Richardson, *Texas*, pp. 388–89; *Texas Almanac*, pp. 103–105; 107, 569–70.
55. For a discussion of the development of the Lower Colorado River Authority, see Comer Clay, "The Lower Colorado River Authority," in *Public Administration and Policy Formation: Studies in Oil, Gas, Banking, River Development, and Corporate Investigations*, ed. Emmette S. Redford (Austin: University of Texas Press, 1956), pp. 189–237; for a discussion of the controversy surrounding the Trinity barge canal project and the Texas Water Plan, see papers by J. B. Smallwood, Jr., "Texas Water Politics: Opposition to the Trinity Barge Canal" and "Texas Water Politics: Opposition to the Texas Water Plan," both in possession of the author.

rainfall line. In its economic development Texas faces a challenge in the last quarter of the twentieth century. The programs and policies provided by its business, agricultural, political, and intellectual leaders could easily determine whether future generations of Texans continue to enjoy the state's developing prosperity or whether they face a declining quality of life as their environment and opportunities slowly deteriorate around them.

The rural landscape, the farmhouse, and the hearth warm our memories of a traditional past, but that past was not as mellow as we might like to remember. The vernacular dwelling — jacal, adobe, dugout, log cabin, or Fachwerk — *is a record of the stark realities of that bygone world. Remembering the link between homes and values is vital to understanding the changing styles and quality of the houses of Texas farmers and ranchers from 1870 to 1970.*

5
Whatever Happened to the Little Frame House on the Prairie?
Clarence C. Schultz

Today's urban dweller often envisions yesterday's rural environment by conjuring up an image of a small white frame box house with a long rambling porch across the front and possibly down one side. A chimney made of local stone protrudes skyward from one end of the sharply pitched, rusting tin roof. In the background are several weathered plank barns, a stock pen, and a small watering tank endlessly replenished by the slowly spinning blades of a windmill.

This landscape, like many other mental constructs, is a myth blended from hard truth and romantic imagination. For the rural home of Texas both yesterday and today, like that of the nation, is not a monomorphic cultural entity. Rather, it reflects the diverse geography and climate of the area, the pluralism of the settlers, the scientific and technological revolutions of the twentieth century, and the social-historical vicissitudes of the past hundred years.

The rural households of Texas in the nineteenth century were in part adaptations to the multiple natural geographic regions of the state. With time and pioneer ingenuity and cultural traditions, these households took new forms. The Coastal Plains, extending from the eastern boundaries of the state to the Balcones Escarpment in the heart of the Lone Star State, looked to settlers like a giant topographical chameleon changing in hue and form as they moved across it from east to west or north to south. A pioneer crossing into the northeastern part of the state found the dense "Piney Woods" standing in readiness for his axe and hand to carve a wooden home for his family. If he pressed on westward, the sentinel pines gave way to the legions of post oak, and still far-

---

Clarence C. Schultz acknowledges with gratitude the action of the Department of Sociology-Anthropology of Southwest Texas State University in granting him time to research and write this essay on rural housing in Texas.

A dugout cabin.
Photograph courtesy
University of Texas Institute of Texan Cultures,
from the Erwin E. Smith Collection of
Range-Life Photographs in the Library of Congress,
with permission from Mrs. L. M. Pettis, Bonham, Texas.

ther to the west, the rich blacklands beckoned him to fulfill his agrarian destiny. To the south of the pine belt, the enterprising migrant found the coastal prairies with their rich cover of grasses and, still farther south, the brush country of the Rio Grande Plain with its prickly pear, cactus, and mesquite, challenging the armies of settlers like some barbed fortification. North of the Rio Grande Plain and west of the Coastal Plains, the immigrant entered the Edwards Plateau and the Hill Country. Here the settler found an abundance of stone to be quarried and fashioned into durable abodes for a possession of generations.

Those who ventured north from the Hill Country or west from the blacklands (passing through the East and West Cross Timbers) emerged upon the rolling prairies of the North Central Plains, navigating their prairie schooners through the treeless sea of grass in search of new homes. For those among western pilgrims who dared to homestead this area, the earth became the dwelling place not only of the dead but also of the living. Homes were created by using the only natural resource in abundance, the soil, to fashion dugouts and sod houses. In the late nineteenth century the railroads penetrated this region and provided a means for importing timber, changing the whole character of the settlement of the plains. The coming of the railroads also linked East Texas with the farthest reaches of West Texas, the Llano Estacado ("Staked Plains") with the mountainous trans-Pecos region. With this linkage from east to west, the regions of the state became interdependent; as a consequence, the impact of local topography on the household was lessened, and the influence on housing by the cultural traditions of the major ethnic groups represented among the rural settlers of Texas became tempered.

Mexican, German, and Anglo-American populations were the major ethnic groups among Texas immigrants in the nineteenth century. The Mexican and German populations were often either immigrants or descendants of immigrants; the Anglo-Americans were predominantly migrants or children of journeyers from other southern states. This southern dispersion was from both the upper South (Arkansas, Kentucky, Missouri, Tennessee) and the lower or Gulf South (Alabama, Georgia, Louisiana, Mississippi). In general, the upper southerners tended to settle in the central and north central counties, the Gulf southerners in the eastern counties, the Germans in a narrow line of counties extending northwest from Calhoun County on the Gulf to Mason County in west central Texas (plus a branch from this line running northeast from Guadalupe County to Washington County), and the Mexicans in the counties roughly south of a line drawn east to west through San Antonio.[1] Each group contributed significantly to the architectural styles of rural Texas—the Anglos with the log house and its plank successor, the Germans with their native stone abode emerging from the *Fachwerk*, and the Mexicans with the *jacal* and adobe huts.

These distinctive architectural styles, found in rural Texas throughout the last half of the nineteenth century, should be thought of as composing the "folk architecture" of Texas. Construction did not follow some formal design or represent the mind's eye of some distant and fashionable architect, but rather reflected housing traditions of each ethnic group. The origins of these styles, like the ancestry of most of their practitioners, remain for the most part obscured or unrecorded. Each builder, while following the outlines of his folk tradition, altered the structure to meet the exigencies of the environment. The resulting dwelling became simultaneously an affirmation and an adaptation of the cultural heritage of the individual settler.[2]

The folk housing of the Mexican Americans took two forms: the adobe house, principally in far West Texas, and the *jacal* in South Texas. The adobe structure represented an adaptation to the range of temperatures of the western section of the state and a response to the available building resources. Typically, this one-room house built of sun-dried brick was not larger than fifteen by twenty feet and was located on a hillside to reduce potential weakening of the structure by collection of rainwater around the bottoms of the walls sitting directly on the ground. Sometimes the characteristic flat roofs were equipped with water spouts to direct any rainfall on top of the house away from the dried-clay walls, but more often the poor families who lived in these houses could not afford such a convenience and simply left matters to fate. Until milled lumber became available, mesquite was cut and used for the lintels of the doors and windows, while a combination of felled cottonwood and mesquite provided support for the bricks used for the roof. Increasingly in the late nineteenth and early twentieth century, a gabled roof replaced the flat roof and, when income would permit, the walls

---

1. Terry G. Jordan, "The Imprint of the Upper and Lower South on Mid-nineteenth-century Texas," *Annals of the Association of American Geographers* 57 (Dec., 1967): 670–72.
2. Terry G. Jordan, *Texas Log Buildings: A Folk Architecture* (Austin: University of Texas Press, 1978), pp. 3–4; Amos Rapoport, *House Form and Culture* (Englewood Cliffs, N.J.: Prentice-Hall, 1969), pp. 47–49.

Mexican *jacal* of the Rodriguez family
near San Benito, Texas.
Photograph courtesy University of Texas
Institute of Texan Cultures and
Mrs. Clara Zepeda, San Benito, Texas.

were stuccoed. Both of these features were as much prestigious ornamentation as functionally motivated modifications.[3]

South of San Antonio, Mexican ranchers fashioned for themselves a home the style of which would influence the design of the contemporary rambling ranch house, so often idealized today as a hallmark of Texas living. One room wide and two to three rooms long, these dwellings had walls constructed of caliche or sandstone blocks finished with plaster and whitewash, a porch spanning the front, and sometimes a shingled roof. Beamed ceilings and a fireplace completed what many persons now regard as the epitome of the early cattleman's residence, but this was not the characteristic abode of people in this area in the nineteenth century.[4]

In South Texas the distinctive folk dwelling was the *jacal*. The typical family occupying one of these "shacks" or "huts" faced a daily existence in a dirt-floored one-room rectangular space from 160 to 200 square feet in size. The walls might be made of any material—wooden branches, adobe, gravel and stones—to be found, and plastered inside and out with a mixture of mud and lime. The finished wall was whitewashed both for appearance and to make the plaster less susceptible to the deterioration from rainstorms. Some combination of wooden poles, leaves, grass, and animal skins was used to construct a thatched roof, which was sharply pitched to allow quick drainage. The furnishings of these homes were often as impoverished as was their construction—a wooden stool or two, perhaps a table, and beds made of mesquite or pallets of sheepskins (fur side for the cold nights and leather side for the warm ones).[5] Although the *jacal* was not an uncommon form of housing among some Mexican Americans in South Texas into the twentieth century, it was also a badge of poverty reluctantly worn by its inhabitants. Therefore, as the opportunities increased around the turn of the century to occupy small wooden homes, the *jacal* began its welcomed decline as the housing of the common people.

---

3. Joe Graham, "Folk Housing in South and West Texas," *Proceedings: An Exploration of a Common Legacy—A Conference on Border Architecture* (Austin: Texas Historical Commission, 1978), pp. 44–45.

4. Willard B. Robinson, "Colonial Ranch Architecture in the Spanish-American Tradition," *Southwestern Historical Quarterly* 83 (Oct., 1979): 131–33, 148–49; Workers of the Writers' Program of the Works Progress Administration in the State of Texas, *Texas: A Guide to the Lone Star State* (New York: Hastings House, 1940), pp. 152–53.

5. Graham, "Folk Housing," p. 40; Robinson, "Colonial Ranch Architecture," p. 131.

Little Frame House on the Prairie

In time, the wooden house became a substitute folk housing for the Mexican Americans of South Texas. Starting as a one-room dwelling of not more than 180 square feet, the entire structure—walls, floor, roof—was made of wood. Rectangular, it also resembled the *jacal* in having a pitched roof, but differed from its folk predecessor by having a porch across the front and rooms added in the back as the family grew. Commonly, a kitchen was the first room built immediately behind the original room. This was followed by a bedroom, to which later another bedroom would probably be attached. As the rooms were added, the original roof was extended backward at less and less of an angle, thereby lowering the ceilings of the back rooms. Although it is highly likely that the shape of this wooden home was an adaptation of the *jacal*, the use of board and batten most likely reflected diffusion of a trait of Anglo folk housing.[6]

The frame house of rural East Texas, the prototype of the typical Texas home of the small farmer in the late nineteenth and early twentieth centuries, evolved from the log house brought to Texas as part of the cultural tradition of the Anglo-American migrants from the South. The use of log houses peaked in Texas in the period from the 1850s to the 1880s. It has been estimated that more than half of the rural homes in the state in the 1870s were constructed of logs. Thereafter, the percentage began to drop sharply, spurred on by the increasing availability of milled lumber for houses and the negative social status associated with occupying a log home. Nevertheless, during the Great Depression of the 1930s some rural residents, especially in East Texas, turned once again to log construction for their homes.[7]

Back in the heyday of log cabins, structures built with round logs were usually thought of as temporary dwellings, whereas houses made of hewn logs were intended as more permanent residences. The size

---

6. Graham, "Folk Housing," pp. 41–42.
7. Drury Blakeley Alexander, *Texas Homes of the Nineteenth Century* (Austin: University of Texas Press, 1966), pp. 13–14. Swedo-Finn and German colonists along the Atlantic seaboard are usually given credit for introducing the log dwelling into America. Scotch-Irish and English colonists nearby apparently borrowed the idea and carried it westward. Terry G. Jordan, "Some Comments on Log Construction in Texas," *The Architecture of the Texas Frontier: A Series of Papers Delivered at the 1972 Winedale Workshop* (Austin: The Texas State Historical Survey Committee and the University of Texas at Austin Winedale Inn Properties, 1972), pp. 60–61 (mimeographed). C. A. Weslager, *The Log Cabin in America: From Pioneer Days to the Present* (New Brunswick, N.J.: Rutgers University Press, 1969), pp. 38–41; Jordan, *Texas Log Buildings*, pp. 5–9, 27–29; Hugh Anthony Crosby, "Architecture of Texana, 1831–1883" (Master's thesis, University of Texas at Austin, 1975), p. 17.

A log cabin at Deep Creek Crossing.
Photograph courtesy University of Texas
Institute of Texan Cultures
and Dr. M. W. Sharp, Castroville, Texas.

of a room, called a "pen," in a house or cabin was dictated by the length of available tree trunks. Thus in East Texas, with its tall pines, each wall of a single room might average sixteen to twenty feet, whereas farther to the west, where only shorter trees grew, the walls might each be only ten feet long. The hewn logs, cut flat on all four sides, were notched on each end to make them fit and hold together as they were stacked to form the walls.[8] Of course, the hand-cut logs did not stack perfectly, and the cracks between logs had to be closed with some type of filler, a process called "chinking." Clay mixed with grass or broomweed was a common type of filler; another was a combination of limestone and sand; all else lacking, mud was used. The end walls of the log house were gabled, and the resulting pitched roof commonly was covered with wooden shingles referred to as "shakes." If the shakes could not be fastened, preferably by nails, to the horizontal roof timbers called "purlins," then they were kept in place by putting rocks or poles on top of them. Sometimes the roof was covered with boards rather than shakes. Floors were either dirt or puncheon (made of split logs). Door and window frames were formed from split logs or sawed boards put into place after the walls had been erected. Window openings were closed by wooden shutters. The construction was completed with the building of a fireplace and chimney at one end of the house. Chimneys might be made of stone where such was available, but chimneys of sticks and mud were quite common in East Texas. Not surprisingly in those cases, chimney fires frequently occurred, and often the only way to stop these was to knock down the chimney—leaving a chilled family on a cold day.[9]

As the young pioneer's family grew, the single-pen log house was frequently expanded into a double-pen dwelling, commonly called the "dog-run" or "dog-trot" house.[10] The second pen was built seven

---

8. Jordan, *Texas Log Buildings*, pp. 12, 105–107; Jordan, "Some Comments," p. 68. A scholarly debate, utilizing statistical as well as logical arguments, has developed concerning the diffusion of notch types to Texas. Milton B. Newton Jr., and Linda Pulliam-DiNapoli, "Log Houses as Public Occasions: A Historical Theory," *Annals of the Association of American Geographers* 67 (Sept., 1977): 360–83; Terry G. Jordan and Carl Parker III, "Southern Folk Housing: A Reply and Critique," *Annals of the Association of American Geographers* 68 (Sept., 1978): 448–50; M. B. Newton, Jr., and Linda Pulliam-DiNapoli, "Comment in Reply," *Annals of the Association of American Geographers* 68 (Sept., 1978): 450–52.

9. Seymour V. Connor, "Log Cabins in Texas," *Southwestern Historical Quarterly* 53 (Oct., 1949): 111–15; Weslager, *Log Cabin in America*, pp. 40–41; William Bennett Bizzell, *Rural Texas* (New York: Macmillan, 1924), p. 397.

10. It has been suggested that "dog-run" or "dog-trot" house is a name more

to fifteen feet away from and in line with a gabled end of the original pen, but the two pens were connected by a common roof that extended over the open space between them. The resulting breezeway served many functions for the family: a covered and cool place to sit, work, or visit during the hot summers or on rainy, humid days; a shady place to store all manner of things; a place, depending on the season, where an overnight guest might sleep; and a place where dogs could trot, sit, lie, or sleep any day. At the time the second pen was added, it also was customary to build a porch across the entire front of the house. Still later, the breezeway might be enclosed, creating a third room (often a parlor) or a central hall.[11] When milled lumber became increasingly available for construction, the log house came to symbolize backwoods poverty. Therefore, some owners of log houses eventually covered the outer walls with planks to create the illusion of the East Texas frame house.[12]

The basic plans of log and frame houses were quite similar, since the latter was essentially an outgrowth of the former.[13] The original

---

likely applied to these homes by later generations, and that the original builders referred to the structures by such labels as "two-pens-and-a-passage" or "hallway house." In any event, this style of folk architecture appears to have developed first in southern Tennessee. Fred Kniffen, "Folk Housing: Key to Diffusion," *Annals of the Association of American Geographers* 55 (Dec., 1965): 561.

11. T. R. Fehrenbach, *Lone Star: A History of Texas and the Texans* (New York: Macmillan, 1968), pp. 297-98; Charles Jeffries, "Early Texas Architecture: Its Dis.tinguishing Marks Were Indubitable Reflections of the Character of the Builders," *Bunker's Monthly*, June, 1928, pp. 906-908; Jordan, "Some Comments," pp. 69-70; Jordan, *Texas Log Buildings*, pp. 113-19; Ailene Stegner, "The Evolution of and the Development of the Houses of Early Texas," A Group of Themes on the Architecture and Culture of Early Texas by Students in Course A. 350 Taught by Professor Samuel E. Gideon (Austin: University of Texas at Austin, 1942), pp. 26-27 (mimeographed); Sarah E. Stripling, "Frontier Design for Living," A Group of Themes on the Architecture and Culture of Early Texas by Students in Course A. 350 Taught by Professor Samuel E. Gideon (Austin: University of Texas at Austin, 1942), p. 34.

12. Crosby, "Architecture of Texana," p. 18.

13. The general plans of both the "double-pen" log house and the East Texas frame house are thought to be descendants of the Greek Revival plan (equal number and size of rooms on opposite sides of a central hall), which was common in America from 1700 to 1870. Alexander, *Texas Homes*, p. 87; Elliott A. P. Evans, "The East Texas House," *Journal of the Society of Architectural Historians* 11 (Dec., 1952): 1. In addition, the significance of the central-hall plan common in English medieval houses as part of this evolution has been noted by Crosby, "Architecture of Texana," p. 184.

frame building known as a "double house" commonly consisted of two rooms of equal size located across the central hall from each other. Later, as additional living space was needed for the family, two shed type rooms, typically called "side rooms," were frequently added simultaneously to the back of the house. When still more space was needed, a small room, logically referred to as the "room-on-the-porch," might be created by closing in one end of the porch. Sometimes a second story consisting of two rooms was built directly over the original two rooms. Ell additions, rooms constructed at right angles to the existing building, were rarely made until late in the nineteenth century, perhaps because such appendages were more difficult to incorporate structurally with those rooms already standing.[14]

The skeleton of the early East Texas frame houses contained much lumber and used diagonal timbers to strengthen the corner posts of the rooms; but as milled lumber became more plentiful in the late nineteenth century, simpler types of framing—balloon, plank, and western—replaced the earlier braced frame construction. Also notable in the later types was the extensive use of nails rather than mortise and tenon to join the frame, which was commonly sided with clapboard.[15] Windows on either side of fireplaces located at each end of the house and also windows on either side of the door opening onto the porch were typical, especially after glass and sash could be fairly easily obtained.

The porch stretching across the front of the house provided the family with a place to escape the heat of the long Texas summers. Those which were an integral part of the frame house plan were typically either of the cut-out or shed variety. In the former, the roof of the house was pitched at an angle allowing it to cover the rooms and the porch without a break in the slope. In the case of the more common shed porch, the roof over the rooms was at a steeper angle than the roof over the porch. Typically, six rectangular pillars or posts supported the roof of the porch. Two-story houses sometimes had a second porch over the

14. Crosby, "Architecture of Texana," pp. 20–22; Evans, "East Texas House," pp. 2–3; Jeffries, "Early Texas Architecture," p. 906; John Edward Short, *Survey 69: East Texas—A Visual Biography* (n.p.: National Council for the Arts, 1969), p. 9. For an interesting discussion suggesting the possible influence of the I house design, diffused from the Middle Atlantic states, on the style of the two-story farmhouse found in Texas, see Kniffen, "Folk Housing," pp. 553–55.

15. Alexander, *Texas Homes,* p. 13; Crosby, "Architecture of Texana," pp. 21–24, 48–51.

first. In such cases, stairs to the second floor might be located inside the porch, allowing a second, perhaps related, family access to the upstairs without going through the lower floor of the house.[16]

The choice of color of paint to cover the outside of the East Texas frame house probably provided one of the most distinguishing traits of the stereotyped conception of the home of the small farmer in Texas. White appears to have been the exterior color chosen by most rural homeowners throughout much of the last half of the nineteenth and on into the twentieth century. At least two strong reasons existed for this choice. The high lead content of the white paint was believed to make it last longer than other colors, and white deflected the sun's heat more than darker colors, thereby providing greater protection for the weatherboarding.[17]

The site for the rural East Texas home, like the selection of paint and other aspects involved in building the frame house, was a functional choice circumscribed neither by governmental regulation nor by some architect's tract plan. Hence, a rural home frequently was built near the center of the owner's property and on a small hill, where it could take advantage of cooling breezes. Homeowners would construct a road to reach the house rather than locate the house in relation to the main road. Emphasis in rural home construction in nineteenth-century East Texas, as in other sections of the state, was on the practical, the natural, and the simple.[18]

Like the Anglos of East Texas, the German pioneers in the central section of the state resorted temporarily to log cabins. However, this type of dwelling was abandoned in a very short time and replaced by

---

16. Evans, "East Texas House," pp. 3-4; Clovis Heimsath, *Pioneer Texas Buildings: A Geometry Lesson* (Austin: University of Texas Press, 1968), pp. 30-33. Roofs broken by dormers were uncommon among rural East Texas houses, but could be found on houses in towns in the locale; Heimsath, *Pioneer Texas Buildings,* p. 68.

17. Crosby, "Architecture of Texana," pp. 190-91.

18. Jeffries, "Early Texas Architecture," pp. 914-15; David R. Williams, "An Indigenous Architecture: Some Texas Colonial Houses," *Southwest Review* 14 (Autumn, 1928): 63. See the paintings, no doubt idealized through memory, of "primitive" artists Velox Ward (*Sunday Afternoon*) and Clara McDonald Williamson (*A Day's Work Is Done*) for strong suggestions of the simplicity and family orientation of the rural homes of late-nineteenth-century Texas. *Catalogue* of the Collection, 1972 (Fort Worth: Amon Carter Museum of Western Art, 1973), pp. 174-75, 178-79. Also see the interesting examples of East Texas houses depicted in E. M. "Buck" Schiwetz, *The Schiwetz Legacy: An Artist's Tribute to Texas, 1910-1971,* selected under direction of John H. Lindsey and with notes by the artist and John Edward Weems (Austin: University of Texas Press, 1972), pp. 58, 63.

Fachwerk houses, a form of construction combining stone or mud bricks with a timber frame of posts and diagonal braces and frequently finished with a coat of plaster or whitewash. German immigrants subsequently discarded this adaptation of building methods practiced in their homeland as they discovered that local stone could be used for erecting homes without the elaborate timbering employed in the *Fachwerk* house. Stone remained the principal building material for the houses of the Germans from approximately 1860 to 1890, when construction of frame houses—sometimes of board-and-batten style—became the mode.[19]

The early stone houses of the Germans, whether of one or two stories, were typically only one room deep. A shed type room was usually located at the back of the main room. When additional rooms were added in a row behind the shed room, each might be provided with a gable roof, producing a sawtooth roof pattern rather than a straight roof line. Not infrequently, a spacious attic existed over the front room of the one-story house, and it was reached by outside stairs going to a door cut into one of the gables formed by the roof. The roof (like some other parts of the house—floors, windows, doors, joists, etc.) was often made of wood, although metal (tin) roofs appeared as early as the 1850s. Cedar, cypress, and oak, available in the area, were the woods commonly used. The necessary stone was quarried by these pioneers using centuries-old and tedious methods, and the essential mortar was produced in lime kilns made by the home builders.[20] Thus, through an assiduous blending of skills and natural resources, the German settlers developed in the last half of the nineteenth century a style of house that exemplifies successful, ecological adaptation.

Equally ingenious in meeting the challenge of the environment were the dugout and the sod house, which early became standard responses to the need for shelter on the open prairies of the frontier roughly west of the 100th meridian. Consisting of one room, the dugout was made

19. Alexander, *Texas Homes,* p. 16; Terry G. Jordan, *German Seed in Texas Soil: Immigrant Farmers in Nineteenth Century Texas* (Austin: University of Texas Press, 1966), pp. 166–67; Stegner, "Evolution and Development of Houses of Early Texas," pp. 24–26.

20. James Keys, "Stone Construction," *The Architecture of the Texas Frontier: A Series of Papers Delivered at the 1972 Winedale Workshop* (Austin: The Texas State Historical Survey Committee and the University of Texas at Austin Winedale Inn Properties, 1972), pp. 101–105; Stegner, "Evolution and Development of Houses of Early Texas," pp. 28–29. Stone ranch houses also were not uncommon on some parts of the western frontier of Texas in the 1870s. For the story of some of these and the families who occupied them, see Mary Whatley Clark, "Historical Stone Ranch Houses along the Clear Fork of the Brazos," *Cattleman* (Jan., 1947): 19–21.

The original stone house on the
Johanna Wilhelm Ranch, Menard County, Texas, ca. 1894.
Photograph courtesy University of Texas
Institute of Texan Cultures
and heirs of John F. Wilhelm, Menard, Texas.

by excavating a spot in a low hillside to a depth half of the intended height of the room. Then the remainder of the walls were made either by stacking squares of dried sod on top of each other around the edges of the dirt hole to the desired level of the ceiling or, if some timber was available, by using logs to complete the remainder of each wall. If boards or logs were not handy for the ceiling, one was created by using a series of poles topped with brush and then covered with sod and soil. Holes in the wall, curtained with corn sacks, served as substitutes for windows, and an earthen fireplace and chimney at the rear of the room provided facilities for cooking and heating. The sod house, composed of stacked squares or "bricks" of plowed prairie sod, was similar in construction to the upper half of the dugout but was built entirely aboveground and frequently had more than one room. Such primitive housing conditions—combined with the threat of Indians, opposition from cattlemen, scourges of grasshoppers and prairie dogs, and devastating drought—slowed the settlement of the western half of the state. Nevertheless, after 1880 the number of migrants to the area grew dramatically, and by the close of the century the frame house became as common in West Texas as elsewhere in the state. The catalyst of this social transformation of the area was the railroad—the Texas and Pacific, the Southern Pacific, the Sante Fe, and the Fort Worth and Denver.[21]

In the last quarter of the nineteenth century, the railroad map of Texas changed from a sparse structure serving Galveston and Houston to that of a complex communications system permeating the entire state. The rails became like cultural pipelines, bringing raw materials and ideas that began to obliterate the folk distinctions of the various regions within the state, paralleling a similar process occurring on the national level. Thus linked to the eastern United States, Texans discovered the asymmetrical and elaborate Victorian style of architecture. Some Victorian edifices did come to dot the landscape like wooden castles symbolizing the status and power of their owners; but small frame houses, built in the East Texas tradition and made possible by the importation of milled lumber via the railroads, became home for the typical rural

21. Roberta F. Biles, "The Frame House Era in Northwest Texas," *West Texas Historical Association Yearbook* 46 (1970): 167–68; William Curry Holden, *Alkali Trails or Social and Economic Movements of the Texas Frontier, 1846–1900* (Dallas: Southwest Press, 1930), pp. 228–32; Jordan, *Texas Log Buildings*, pp. 111–13; Carl Coke Rister, *The Southwestern Frontier, 1865–1881* (Cleveland: Arthur H. Clark, 1928), pp. 257–58; Workers of the Writers' Program of the Works Progress Administration in the State of Texas, *Texas*, p. 154; Holden, *Alkali Trails*, pp. 63–66.

The Paris Cox family's typical Anglo frame house, ca. 1890.
Photograph courtesy University of Texas
Institute of Texan Cultures
and the Museum of Texas Tech University.

Texan.[22] The image of the little frame house on the prairie for several decades hence would symbolize the panorama of rural Texas. But it also reflected the standardization of American life fostered by an emerging technology that ultimately would leave the decaying, empty small frame house in the field as an archeological reminder of the era of the small farmer.

Central to this technological transformation of Texas rural life was the railroad, connecting the state's farmlands and their produce to the northern and eastern markets of the nation. Other factors abetting the growth of commercial farming in Texas in the last two decades of the nineteenth century were the need for cash crops to offset the spiraling costs of buying land, the introduction of barbed wire to guard crops from cattle, and the consumer demand for cotton—which made it the number-one cash crop across the state. From 1870 to 1900 the number of farms in Texas increased from approximately 61,000 to more than 352,000, and the general solvency of this era is reflected in the fact that at the turn of the century more than three-quarters of the almost 172,000 existing farm homes were free of mortgage.[23]

In the early twentieth century the number of farms in Texas, as in the nation, continued to increase, reaching a total of 436,000 by 1920. But the number of tenants, rather than owners, operating farms in Texas also changed upward—from 37.6 percent in 1880 to 53.3 percent in 1920, compared respectively with 25.6 percent and 38.1 percent for the nation. The much larger percentage of tenant farmers in Texas in contrast to the national average in 1920 is largely explained by the focus of agricultural production in the state on one crop—cotton, a situation particularly adaptable to a tenancy system.[24]

---

22. John D. Hicks, George E. Mowry, and Robert E. Burke, *The American Nation: A History of the United States from 1865 to the Present*, 4th ed. (Boston: Houghton Mifflin, 1965), pp. 120–21; Short, *Survey 69*, p. 7; Alexander, *Texas Homes*, pp. 167–69; Biles, "The Frame House," pp. 168–73.

23. Richard Mathis, "The Process of Urbanization in Texas," in *Population Mobility: Focus on Texas*, ed. Harley L. Browning and Larry H. Long (Austin: Bureau of Business Research, University of Texas at Austin, 1968), pp. 125–26; Rupert N. Richardson, Ernest Wallace, and Adrian N. Anderson, *Texas: The Lone Star State*, 3rd ed. (Englewood Cliffs, N.J.: Prentice-Hall, 1970), pp. 279–80; *Texas Almanac and State Industrial Guide* (Dallas: A. H. Belo, 1925), p. 95; U.S. Department of Commerce, Bureau of the Census, *Historical Statistics of the United States, Colonial Times to 1970*, Bicentennial ed., pt. 1 (Washington, D.C.: Government Printing Office, 1975), p. 459; *Texas Almanac and State Industrial Guide* (Dallas: A. H. Belo, 1914), p. 200.

24. Karl E. Ashburn, "Economic and Social Aspects of Farm Tenancy in Texas,"

A sample, numbering almost one thousand and about equally divided between white farm owners and tenants in Texas, in the early 1920s revealed that the average house of the independent farmer had 5.6 rooms compared with 4.4 rooms for the home of the tenant farmer. The owner's family being smaller (4.6 persons) than the tenant's (4.9 persons), the latter lived under more cramped conditions. The average size of all farmhouses in the study was less than 950 square feet, but the dwellings were not judged to be overcrowded by then-current standards. Another study, conducted at about the same time, of Texas farm families in the blacklands region rather surprisingly found the average size of the owners' families to exceed slightly those of tenants. Nevertheless, this study found, as did the previous study, that owners' families were less cramped for room space. Moreover, although the typical home of each was wooden, the average owner's house had a value of more than twice that of the tenant's home, reflecting the generally lower quality construction and greater disrepair of the tenant's dwelling. Landlords tended to be indifferent about improvements, believing tenants did not care and would not appreciate them; tenants tended to be apathetic about seeking improvements, believing landlords did not want to do anything.[25]

By 1930 the number of farms in Texas had grown to 495,000 and those operated by tenants reached a high of 60.9 percent. Meanwhile, the living conditions of both owners and tenants did not change appreciably. In 1930 a study was made of farm women in five Central Texas counties. The sample was about evenly divided between wives of farm owners and those of farm tenants or laborers. All of the women in the sample were white and most had lived all of their lives in the same county in which they resided at the time of the survey. More than half used wood fires for cooking, and most of the remainder used coal oil. Almost all did their washing chores with "rub-boards," tubs, and boiling water heated in iron washpots, and about two-thirds of them completed this frequent cleaning ritual by pressing the dry clothes with flatirons. In fourth-fifths of the homes lighting was provided by

---

Southwestern Social Science Quarterly 15 (Mar., 1935): 299; Bizzell, *Rural Texas*, p. 387; T. J. Cauley, "Agricultural Land Tenure in Texas," *Southwestern Political and Social Science Quarterly* 11 (Sept., 1930): 135; Bureau of the Census, *Historical Statistics*, p. 459.

25. Ashburn, "Economic and Social Aspects," p. 304; Ellis Love Kirkpatrick, *The Farmer's Standard of Living* (New York: Century, 1929), pp. 130–33; U.S. Department of Agriculture, Office of Farm Management and Farm Economics, *Farm Ownership and Tenancy in the Black Prairie of Texas*, by Jesse T. Sanders, Bulletin No. 1068 (Washington, D.C.: Government Printing Office, 1922), pp. 50–53.

oil lamps. Not surprisingly, then, only a small number had radios, but about one-half had a home-delivered newspaper. As expected, a similar study of black women found them even more culturally deprived than the whites with respect to electrical and mechanical amenities.[26]

In Texas, as in other states, the federal government during the Great Depression sought to assist those farmers with low standards of living to cope with their hardships. Money was made available at low interest rates to buy or improve farmhouses. The government also experimented with farm resettlement programs such as the Ropesville Farms in Hockley County in northwest Texas. Here, individual farm families already in the area were moved into new but small frame houses, each located on approximately 120 acres. The typical house, a four-room box, was one version of a general house plan that government architects of the day thought would be ideal for the average farm family. The basic model was a five-room rectangle of about 950 square feet. Across the front of the house were three rooms, consisting of a bedroom to each side of a central living room. In the back part of the house were another bedroom and a kitchen–dining area combination. A bathroom was not part of the plan, although a small storage area could be converted to such in the future. A small screened-in porch was located in the rear of the house, and a front porch—the width of the living room—was built on the face of the house.[27] The little white frame house at this time was probably at its zenith as the symbol of the typical farmer, for forces were at work across the nation that would soon make the small farmer and his frame home anachronisms in the rural environment.

Contributing to the impending metamorphosis were government responses to the Great Depression: controls on crops through acreage allotments with an accompanying trend toward diversification in crops. These developments began to erode the cotton economy on which the still-prevalent tenant system largely depended for its existence. Moreover, in the 1930s Texas was on the precipice of a technological revolution

---

26. Ashburn, "Economic and Social Aspects," p. 299; Bureau of the Census, *Historical Statistics*, p. 459; Ruth Allen, *The Labor of Women in the Production of Cotton* (Austin: University of Texas, 1931), cited by Ralph W. Steen, *Twentieth Century Texas* (Austin: Steck, 1942), p. 53.

27. Paul V. Maris, "Farm Tenancy," *Farmers in a Changing World: The Yearbook of Agriculture, 1940* (Washington, D.C.: Government Printing Office, 1940), pp. 887–906; Richardson, *Texas* p. 386; Steen, *Twentieth Century Texas*, p. 52; Rupert B. Vance, Gordon W. Blackwell, and Howard G. McClain, *New Farm Homes for Old: A Study of Rural Housing in the South* (University, Ala.: University of Alabama Press, 1946), pp. 63–65.

in agriculture. Soon, propelled by these converging forces, tenant farmers and small owners would desert their frame houses in increasing numbers and move to nearby towns and cities, forming a new immigrant class seeking to accommodate itself to the new and different demands of urban life.[28]

The rural population of Texas exceeded the urban population for the last time with the tabulation of the 1940 census. At that point in the state's history, more than one-half of the farm homes (compared with two-thirds for the nation) were more than twenty years old, but 90 percent of the existing farm dwellings were occupied (similar to the rate for the nation as a whole). The vast majority of these homes were inhabited by single families—approximately two-fifths by owners and three-fifths by tenants. Houses of farm owners had an average of five or more rooms, but those of tenants were typically smaller and more crowded, as in earlier decades. Moreover, although a distinct minority of all farm dwellings possessed electricity and indoor plumbing, proportionately many more farm owners' homes enjoyed these conveniences than did those of tenants; and generally the homes of owners were less likely to be in need of major repairs than were those occupied by tenants. Although Texas in 1940 contrasted favorably with other states as to the average age of farm homes, the state did not fare as well in comparisons of the median size of farm homes and lack of overcrowding of rooms, the availability of facilities such as electricity and plumbing, and the general condition of the dwellings. This lower status of Texas farm homes doubtless reflected the much higher rate of tenant-occupied houses in the state in 1940 than in the entire nation.[29]

In the next twenty years, from 1940 to 1960, the farm population of Texas dropped drastically, and, with it, the general nature of farms

---

28. *Texas Almanac and State Industrial Guide* (Dallas: A. H. Belo, 1936), p. 228; *Texas Almanac and State Industrial Guide* (Dallas: A. H. Belo, 1945), p. 179; *Texas Almanac and State Industrial Guide* (Dallas: A. H. Belo, 1955), p. 252.

29. Vernon Davies, "Comparison of Farm Housing Factors Among the States," *Social Forces* 25 (March, 1947): 430–31; *Texas County Basic Data* (Philadelphia: Market Research Department, Farm Journal, Inc., 1948), pp. 1–2; U.S. Department of Commerce, Bureau of the Census, *Sixteenth Census of the United States, 1940: Housing*, vol. 3, *Characteristics by Monthly Rent or Value*, pt. 1, *United States Summary*, pp. 20–21; U.S. Department of Commerce, Bureau of the Census, *Sixteenth Census of the United States, 1940: Housing*, vol. 3, *Characteristics by Monthly Rent or Value*, pt. 3, *New Jersey-Wyoming*, pp. 615–16. For a related and insightful discussion of farm housing in the 1940s in an adjoining state, see Robert T. McMillan, "Farm Housing in Oklahoma," *Southwestern Social Science Quarterly* 26 (Dec., 1945): 228–38.

A white frame house pictured in
the *Yearbook of Agriculture, 1940*,
in connection with a discussion of farm tenancy.
The caption accompanying the photograph read,
"By appropriate steps, such houses as this can be built
to strengthen the foundations of our democracy."
Photograph courtesy U.S. Department of Agriculture.

and farming within the state was transformed. From the high point of 501,000, reached in 1935, the number of farms in Texas sharply declined to 227,000 by 1960, a reduction of almost one-half in a quarter of a century. The size of farms in the state increased by about two and one-quarter times, to an average of 631 acres each. The proportion of tenants versus owners residing on farms reversed, with two-thirds of all farms in 1960 being occupied by the owner. The trend toward consolidation of units, as in urban businesses, was marked by increasing mechanization, specialization, and commercialization, particularly after World War II. Farming was losing its focus as the way of life for a family and was becoming instead a business enterprise. In the process, the small, marginal farmers were being eliminated from economic competition in agriculture, as was true at the national level. Increasingly, everywhere, the vacant small frame houses that these farmers left behind were to be found mutely standing like decaying monuments.[30]

By 1960 the number (203,000) of occupied farm dwellings in Texas compared with the total (516,000) in 1940 had dropped by 60.6 percent. By contrast, the figure for the nation dropped 49.8 percent during the same period. In both instances, the greatest decline occurred in the number of units occupied by tenants or renters. The remaining inhabited farmhouses in the state, two-fifths of which had been built since 1940, were generally in good condition and larger than the typical farm home of two decades earlier. Three-fifths of the houses had from five to seven rooms, compared with only one-third with such accommodations in 1940. Indoor plumbing and bathrooms now existed in a majority of the homes. Washing machines, home freezers, telephones, and television sets were becoming commonplace, but clothes dryers and central air conditioning were still uncommon. The use of wood as fuel for cooking had almost disappeared, although about one-sixth of the homes were still using wood for heating.[31]

---

30. Glenn H. Beyer, *Housing and Society* (New York: Macmillan, 1965), p. 392; U.S. Department of Commerce, Bureau of the Census, *Eighteenth Census of the United States, 1960: Housing*, vol. 1, *State and Small Areas*, pt. 8, *Texas-Wyoming*, pp. 45-7; Bureau of the Census, *Historical Statistics*, pp. 458–61; Larry H. Long, "Patterns of Migration for Short Periods, 1930 to 1960," in *Population Mobility: Focus on Texas*, ed. Harley L. Browning and Larry H. Long (Austin: Bureau of Business Research, University of Texas at Austin, 1968), p. 49; *Texas Almanac* (1955), pp. 252–53; *Texas Almanac and State Industrial Guide* (Dallas: A. H. Belo, 1965), p. 389.

31. Bureau of the Census, *Sixteenth Census, 1940: Housing*, vol. 3, pt. 1, pp. 20–21; pt. 3, pp. 615–16; U.S. Department of Commerce, Bureau of the Census, *Eighteenth Census of the United States, 1960: Housing*, vol. 6, *Rural Housing*,

Perhaps most indicative of the changes that were occurring in farm housing were the types of new farm homes most frequently approved for mortgage loans by the Farmers Home Administration in the early 1960s—brick, three bedrooms, one or more bathrooms, and with built-in stoves, central heating, and other facilities common to new urban homes of the period. Thus, the operators of agribusiness were adopting urban styles in their daily living and in their housing. The small white frame house as the abode of many Texas rural inhabitants was passing into history, where it would become a symbol of a romanticized conception of an earlier, supposedly idyllic existence.[32]

In the 1960s trends in Texas agriculture and farm life apparent since World War II continued apace. By the end of the decade one-fifth of the state's population was still rural, but only 3.5 percent actually lived on farms and ranches. The number of farms dropped to 214,000 and the average size increased to 668 acres. The characteristics of rural housing also continued to change. More than four-fifths (690,958) of the occupied rural housing units in 1969 were nonfarm, the much smaller remainder (152,440) being truly farm dwellings. Two-fifths of the farmhouses had been built since 1950, and two-thirds of them had from five to seven rooms. In addition, all but one-tenth had complete bathrooms; one-half had air conditioning; more than three-fourths had washing machines; another one-third had clothes dryers; two-thirds had home freezers; and almost all had television sets. These improving living conditions reflected, among other things, the fact that three-fourths of all farm home residents in Texas were now also the owners of the houses. Parallel changes were also occurring at the national level.[33]

---

pp. 1–4; Bureau of the Census, *Eighteenth Census, 1960: Housing*, vol. 1, pt. 8, pp. 45:5–45:11.

32. Wilson Gee, *The Social Economics of Agriculture* (New York: Macmillan, 1954), pp. 416–17; Louis D. Malotky, "Better Housing in the Country," *A Place to Live: The Yearbook of Agriculture, 1963* (Washington, D.C.: Government Printing Office, 1963), p. 185. Recognition is due Paul H. Johnstone, Senior Agricultural Historian, Division of Farm Population and Rural Welfare, Bureau of Agricultural Economics, who in the late 1930s understood the changes occurring in American agriculture and foresaw the growing chasm between the myths and the realities of American farm life. Paul H. Johnstone, "Old Ideals versus New Ideals in Farm Life," *Farmers in a Changing World: The Yearbook of Agriculture, 1940* (Washington, D.C.: Government Printing Office, 1940), pp. 164–67.

33. U.S. Department of Commerce, Bureau of the Census, *1970 Census of Housing, Detailed Housing Characteristics: Texas* (Washington, D.C.: Government Printing Office, 1972), pp. 201–207; U.S. Department of Commerce, Bureau of the Census, *Census of Housing: 1970, Detailed Housing Characteristics, U.S. Sum-*

The rural landscape of Texas in 1970 was no longer principally the domain of the independent farmer, certainly not the small farmer so lauded yesterday in politics, literature, music, and art. Most of the remaining farm residents were owners whose homes emulated those of their peers of equal affluence residing in the city. Tradition as a determinant of their choices in architectural design was gone.[34]

For the future, attention to rural housing needs to be shifted from farm residents to the rural nonfarm population, both in the open country and small towns. Perhaps as much as one-quarter of the homes of this population in Texas are in need of major repairs or replacement, almost twice the proportion of urban homes in a similar condition.[35] Meeting these needs will require innovative as well as customary remedies that the state may take a lead in instigating. Among possible actions are enactment of a statewide building code for rural areas, support of research for experimental house designs and uses of building materials, development of a program of low-interest loans financed by tax-exempt bonds to stimulate repair or replacement of rural homes, improved educational programs and stronger licensing for individuals entering the building trades, and the creation of housing counselors to aid the rural poor in constructively adapting their life-styles to take advantage of any improved housing made available to them. Thus, one of the first goals of rural planners and residents of today should be to develop an acceptable housing accommodation to the changed rural environment of the present, just as the little frame house on the prairie and elsewhere represented an accommodation to a different rural environment of an earlier time.[36]

---

mary (Washington, D.C.: Government Printing Office, 1972), pp. 235, 281–83, 287–89; Bureau of the Census, *Historical Statistics,* pp. 459–61; *Texas Almanac and State Industrial Guide* (Dallas: A. H. Belo, 1975), p. 391.

34. Rapoport, *House Form and Culture,* pp. 6–7.

35. Department of Community Affairs, *Texas Housing Report: Results of Comprehensive Survey of Texas Housing Conditions and Occupant Attitudes* (Austin: Office of the Governor of Texas and Texas Department of Community Affairs, 1972), p. 18.

36. Texas Rural Development Commission, *Building Rural Texas: Final Report of the Texas Rural Commission* (Austin: State of Texas, 1973), pp. 65–69.

Women saved the frontier from backsliding. Men were often seen as the heroes for whom the West was a mythic idea, a personal rite of passage. Women, however, sustained the life cycle and maintained continuity and culture. They were the true preservers of the wisdom of the past, which they pieced and stitched into a new social fabric.

6
Women on the Land
Martha Mitten Allen

Popular images of rural women in Texas are colorful and varied. Rodeo queens and freshly scrubbed 4-H girls flash by in an imaginary parade, while Lady Bird Johnson, Anne Armstrong, and Janie Briscoe pose in rural settings and remind us of their links to the land. "Miss Ellie" Ewing, star of the television series "Dallas," shines brighter than bright, larger than Texas: the Texas Earth Mother who, although part of an immense oil empire, finds meaning in her beloved Southfork ranch. These popular images are attractive and appealing, but are they representative of rural women in Texas today? Who is the rural woman, and how has her life changed in the twentieth century?

A century ago, all of Texas was rural. Everyone lived on the land, or in small towns that were dependent upon the production of the adjacent land. The twentieth century brought dramatic changes to Texas as industrialization and urbanization became the wave of the future. Cities offered jobs, services, and salaries at the same time that mechanization, drought, and bad crops drove people from farms and ranches. Farm and ranch life came to be seen by many city folks as old-fashioned and out of the mainstream. In the last three or four decades, however, factors have intervened again to blur the differences between rural and urban people in Texas. During those decades the lives of women in rural areas have been radically altered. Yet, within this new framework, a remarkable diversity of life-styles still persists among the women on the land in Texas. Documenting these changes and the richness of the fabric of rural life presents quite a challenge.

Standard historical sources provide little information on rural women in Texas. Except for studies of such flamboyant subjects as the Austin colony, the Republic of Texas, and the cattle business, studies of rural life in Texas are practically nonexistent. Once the frontier phase was past, rural life quickly took a backseat, as an historical topic, to politics, business, and oil wells. Women were given a secondary role or none at all. Even when women wrote about phases of rural life in Texas, they often failed to tell about women's life-styles, concentrating instead on

Sixty Years' Attendance.
Photograph by June Van Cleef.

what was considered the central theme, men. Cordia Sloan Duke, with fifty years' ranching experience, wrote, with Joe B. Frantz, the story of life on the XIT ranch, but it contains little or nothing about what the XIT experience was like for women.[1]

The only rural women in Texas who have received much notice are those who have achieved national prominence for some other claim to fame, for example, the prototype "bad" western woman, Belle Starr, or the prototype "good" Southern lady, Lady Bird Johnson. Great numbers of rural women are largely unknown to us, except through scattered diaries and local historical collections, where they usually appear in the shadow of their men.

Not only are the sources on Texas rural women few and far between but the literature on rural women in general is sparse, and sheds little light on the situation in Texas. In rural studies, as in other areas of women's studies, the first focus has been on identifying some rural women and writing oral histories or short biographical studies of individuals.[2] These first-stage studies are important, but the critical integration and interpretation have yet to be done.

Even the rapidly expanding literature on sex roles pays comparatively little attention to rural women and their changing roles and status. This factor is further complicated by the pervasive and confusing use of a stereotypic view of rural women. Two authors who attempted to deal with the changing roles and status of rural women point out that "the stereotypic image used to describe all rural women as isolated farm wives who do little else but prepare meals, raise children, and help with the farm chores is misleading. 'Farm wife' is not synonymous with 'rural woman,' and the roles and responsibilities of women in rural areas today are much more complex and diversified than this image suggests."[3]

In order to secure some new material that would reflect on rural

---

1. *6,000 Miles of Fence: Life on the XIT Ranch of Texas* (Austin: University of Texas Press, 1961).

2. One of the most engaging of these is Sherry Thomas, *We Didn't Have Much, But We Sure Had Plenty: Stories of Rural Women* (Garden City, N.Y.: Doubleday, Anchor Press, 1981), an oral history collection about rural women from California to Maine, but including no Texans. Another valuable work on rural women is Joan M. Jensen, *With These Hands: Women Working on the Land* (Old Westbury, N.Y.: Feminist Press, 1981), a documentary collection. Only two Texas references are included in this extensive work.

3. Linda Bescher-Donnelly and Leslie Whitener Smith, "The Changing Roles and Status of Rural Women," in *The Family in Rural Society*, ed. Raymond T. Coward and William M. Smith, Jr. (Boulder, Colo.: Westview Press, 1981), p. 167.

women in all of Texas, and that would document change and offer some analysis of the causes of change, I sought the aid of county extension agents for home economics of the Texas Agricultural Extension Service. From previous experience in 4-H work in another state, I knew these agents to be concerned, aware, and observant, and to know the rural woman's situation and needs in a unique way.

I devised a simple, one-page questionnaire that asked each county agent to describe the typical situation for rural women in her county; changes for rural women in her county during her tenure; and the greatest changes for rural women in Texas in the twentieth century, along with the causes for these changes.[4]

As the responses poured in from all corners of the state, three conclusions became clear. Use of the term *rural* is problematical. A new rural woman has emerged in the last thirty to forty years. The diversity of experiences and life settings for rural women in Texas is great.

The problem with *rural* was partly that of definition and partly that of stereotypical connotations. What does *rural* mean? Does the rural-urban distinction have any meaning in modern-day Texas?

The once clearly drawn lines between rural and urban in Texas have become vague, if not indistinguishable. Two recent trends accent this confusion: the trend for farm families to move to town, and the back-to-the-country movement of suburbanites. Moving to town can be seen, on one hand, as an opportunity for broadened horizons and more social activity, or, on the other hand, as the measure of the decline of the family farm.[5] The movement of city folks to the country is seen with mixed emotions also. Tarrant County farm- and ranchland, for example, is rapidly becoming urban as the growth of the Dallas–Fort Worth Metroplex makes it "more profitable to subdivide land for housing and industry than it is to farm it."[6] One county agent from another area views with disgust the influx of city people who want an acre or two in the country: "My wish is that the city people would do us all a favor by staying in town. They are a different kind of people with different values. Their buying acreage and subdividing it into

---

4. The questionnaire was approved by the state agent, Judy Sanders, who provided the names and addresses. The responses to this survey, identified by name of respondent and county, provide the major source for the information and interpretation that follows. Subsequent references to data and quotations, unless otherwise identified, are from the questionnaires, which remain in the author's possession.
5. Thelma Kulik, Childress County; Mabel Walker, Brazos County.
6. Jalyn Burkett, Tarrant County.

small plots is killing decent country living . . . (and) turning our countryside into a rural slum."[7]

And what of the rural image? A woman from East Texas stated that she hates the term *rural* because of the former social connotations of being "backwoods" instead of "sophisticated."[8] "The old stigma of 'You can tell a country woman a mile off' is no more, because today there is no difference"[9] is a theme that was echoed by a number of county agents from all parts of Texas.

Once the respondents got past the problems with the category of "rural women," they began to sketch a picture of today's rural women that compares favorably with urban women. One response described the rural woman as being "as well-informed and progressive as other women."[10] Another described her as being "as at home in the city as an urban woman . . . informed on world affairs and . . . involved in [her] community."[11] Rural women were seen as progressive in ideas and willing to adopt new methods "a little faster than most, and many times ahead of people in town."[12]

From the responses to the survey, a composite portrait gradually emerged of a new rural woman in Texas, one who is neither "backwoods" nor "country," who retains the positive elements of country living—love of land, neighborliness, concern for family, pride in good work well done—while embracing the positive elements of city life—household conveniences and labor-saving devices; comfortable, attractive homes; fashionable dress; opportunities for education, jobs, and involvement. Putting the two influences together, she is "a more responsible woman, a person with a better self image," with pride in her roots and her life-style, and confidence in her ability to function as a modern woman, not just as a country woman.[13]

Time and again, both in the questionnaires and in my search for examples of rural women in my area of the state, I met energetic women who live on farms and ranches but who are also inseparably connected with the wider scene of contemporary life.

Joyce Rosenbusch, who was born and raised in the country near Georgetown, has raised her family on a farm. She remembers her child-

---

7. Patricia Hohensee, Concho County.
8. Name withheld by request.
9. Peggy Sullivan, Hill County.
10. Rita Diffie, Upton and Reagan counties.
11. Pat Bandy, Erath County.
12. Elinor Harvey, Gaines County.
13. Sullivan.

Above Vlasta Mekolik and her husband, full-time farmers, have raised five children, as well as cotton and maize, on their blackland farm.
Photograph by Terry Hagerty.

Top right Joyce Rosenbusch is proud that she has lived in the country all her life. She worked on the farm when her three children were small. Now she works full-time in town, and her husband, who works for the county, shares the work on the two-hundred-acre ranch with their son, who teaches "ag" and manages another ranch on the side.
Photograph by Terry Hagerty.

Bottom right Esther Weir and her husband built the rock house in which they have lived for thirty-five years on their thousand-acre ranch. She taught in public schools and college and sent her son to Harvard and daughter to the University of Texas, despite the ups and downs in the cattle market.
Photograph by Terry Hagerty.

hood spent "in the saddle all the time or atop the windmill." Yet she works in town every day and is equally at home in the alumni office of Southwestern University or working with livestock on the farm.[14]

Etta Rush Dees can make the transition from looking after her sheep and goats to presiding over a meeting of the American Association of University Women or Delta Kappa Gamma quicker than anyone else I know. No one calls her "country."

Esther Weir, a widow who runs a 1,000-acre cattle ranch near Georgetown, is a retired teacher and very active in the community. She and her children have invested in the restoration of several commercial buildings in Georgetown, and she is an advisor for the Sweet Adelines, a member of the Heritage Society, and a frequent consultant for all sorts of projects. She plays tennis every morning, and her hospitality at the ranch is legendary.

Four changes have played the largest role in the emergence of the new rural woman: improved transportation, especially automobiles, and farm-to-market roads; rural electrification and access to labor-saving technology; access to information sources: television, magazines, and education; and the effects of the women's movement. All four have exerted their greatest influence recently, bringing about changes in the post–World War II rural Texas scene that have been more revolutionary than the cumulative changes in rural life in Texas from the days of the Texas Revolution to the 1930s.

Better transportation helped women to overcome the challenge of rural isolation and to make the distance from town less consequential. Isolation was long a problem for the whole rural family, but it often had more serious implications for women. While men went to town to conduct business transactions and children went to school, many farm women in the "old days" were severely limited by the daily demands of housework, cut off from social contacts and cultural enrichment.[15] Better transportation was a key factor in broadening opportunities for rural women in Texas and providing a measure of independence; "whereas the family used to have only a pickup . . . when the wife got a car, she was able to go places on 'her own.'"[16]

Rural electrification "brought homemakers into the twentieth cen-

---

14. Joyce Rosenbusch, interview, Dec. 1, 1983, Georgetown, Tex.
15. David B. Danbom, *The Registered Revolution: Urban America and the Industrialization of Agriculture, 1900–1930* (Ames: Iowa State University Press, 1979), p. 10.
16. Georgia Langford, Home Demonstration Club member, Stephens County.

tury."[17] It freed women from drudgery and chores by making available to them electrical conveniences formerly available only in city homes, thereby helping remove the stigma of being "from the country." Earlier, inventions and improvements in farm machinery had helped reduce the men's toil, but women's work did not get much relief until the revolution brought by rural electrification. Household timesavers freed women to help on the farm, work in town, or get involved in volunteer work or other activities outside the home. From the days of chopping wood for the fire and carrying water to heat on the stove for laundry, to the days of electric stoves, indoor plumbing, and washing machines, women's work was transformed at last.

Technology affected farm life in ways far more extensive than revolutionizing housework. Many rural people who could not adapt to modern mechanization were forced out of farming and off of the land. "Modern farm machinery has made farming less of a 'family affair,'" and made management skills more important than manual skills.[18] Often the rural wife has a key role in the management of the farm operation as recordkeeper and bookkeeper. Bigger and better farm machinery cut down the number of workers needed in the field and hence cut down the work for women in feeding the hands. Mauna Loa Cleek remembers as a girl helping cook on a coal stove for a threshing crew of twenty men. She now lives on three and a half sections of farmland that is worked with the labor of two men.[19]

It is not just a coincidence that the time of expanding opportunity and improved life-style for rural people was also the time of a precipitous decline in the number of Texans on farms and ranches and in the number of farm units in Texas.[20] Agriculture is still important in Texas, but the farmer is rapidly becoming an endangered species. No wonder a new rural type has evolved — it is necessary for survival.

Modern technology gives rural people ready access to processed goods and encourages specialization in farm and ranch production, making the self-sustaining farm a thing of the past. Thus, many chores that were at one time routine have been eliminated entirely. As Georgia Langford, a Home Demonstration Club member from Stephens County,

17. Roxie Dinstel, Llano County.
18. Arleen Atkins, Palo Pinto County.
19. Mauna Loa Cleek, telephone interview by her daughter, Donna Cleek Connor, Dec. 17, 1983.
20. U.S. Bureau of the Census, *Historical Statistics of the U.S., Colonial Times to 1970*, Bicentennial edition, pt. 1 (Washington, D.C.: Government Printing Office, 1975).

reports, "Very few farmers milk cows anymore. They don't have chickens and butcher hogs. So they don't churn, make lard, make soap, pluck ducks for feather pillows. . . . Very few quilt. However, they do still have gardens and freeze produce. Some still can fruits and vegetables."

Not only do women have access to labor-saving technology but they also have instant access to information about how other people live and about current events. Television and magazines open new vistas for rural people. Rural women are better educated than they once were and have access to continuing education. One woman cited television as one of two factors causing the greatest changes in rural women: "Seeing women in other roles on TV has caused rural women to see their lives as less complicated than in other areas. They are not as satisfied with the simple life."[21]

The fourth factor cited as a major influence in recent years is the women's movement. Unlike the first three factors, which would probably be recognized as important by everyone, the extent of influence of this fourth factor is controversial. The controversy may, however, be a superficial reaction against "women's lib" rather than a deep disagreement with the issue of women's rights and opportunities. "Although most rural women declare they are against E.R.A. and say they are not 'women's libbers,' a more detailed conversation reveals agreement with and feeling for some of the basic premises of the women's movement. This has affected attitudes more than is at once obvious."[22]

The influence of the women's movement on rural women is seen by the county agents in three ways: in the opening of doors to employment for them, in their increased involvement in politics and business, and in their heightened self-awareness and self-confidence. "Women have gotten out of the home and become community and social oriented. They have their own goals even apart from their husbands. They enjoy financial independence through employment. . . . The woman now has a mind and a voice of her own—and she has gained self-respect and self-confidence. She is more important than a mere wash woman on Mondays."[23]

Not all of the news about the impact of the women's movement is quite so liberating. Equal participation does not always add up to equality. Carolyn Lehmann, from Blanco County, stated that "rural

---

21. Judy Beavers, Mills County.
22. Name withheld by request.
23. Jerri Ray, Kerr County.

women take an active part in their husband's business or occupation, but still do not make major decisions. Society continues to stereotype them and applauds submissiveness and non-aggression in women." One woman from West Texas, who asked not to be identified, wrote that instead of having a liberating influence, the women's movement had had the opposite effect. It caused farmers to reaffirm their "hold" on their wives, and she thought the wives liked it that way.[24]

The new rural woman in Texas may not march for "women's lib," but she clearly demonstrates the heightened consciousness and feeling of confidence and self-worth that is at the heart of the movement for women's rights. She has been influenced whether or not she knows it, or likes it.

Over the last forty years, then, the lives of rural women in Texas have been radically changed. Hellon Catlett of Bowie County in East Texas put together a chronological framework, adding a prediction for the 1980s: "Rural electrification and farm-to-market roads probably changed the lifestyle the greatest in the 1940s and 50s. In the 60s, the pill and fewer children; in the 70s acceptance of women working because it was necessary rather than because she wanted to. Prediction for 80: inflation and energy cost will influence lifestyle again."[25]

Despite all the agreement on factors causing changes for rural women in Texas, and despite the evidence that seems to support the existence of a new rural woman in Texas, several respondents to the survey, who asked not to be identified, remarked that it is difficult if not impossible to describe the typical rural woman, even in one county. Part of the vitality and richness of the rural scene in Texas is its variety; that variety is reflected in the diversity of life-styles and situations of rural women. The story of rural women in Texas would not be realistic without a sampling of this diversity.

Through the reports of the county extension agents we can tour Texas, from region to region and county to county, to see what life is like today for rural women. In East Texas, rural women live on small diversified farms ranging in average size from 10 acres or less in Morris County to 335 acres in Kaufman County. In Marion County 50 percent of rural families are of racial minorities. The average age of the typical rural woman there is fifty; she has four children, a tenth-grade education, and works outside the home. In the area around Franklin, Camp, and

---

24. Carolyn Lehmann, Blanco County; name withheld by request.
25. Hellon Catlett, Bowie County.

Titus counties, the typical rural woman is white, has two or three children, lives on a 100-acre farm or ranch, and, if she is in the twenty-to-forty age group, probably works away from home.

Velma Bowden lives on forty acres on the edge of Bettie, thirty miles from Longview. Although she is retired now and not as active as formerly, she has been very heavily involved in the community life of this small rural town in northeast Texas. She grew up in Bettie, went to school there, and married and raised her family there. She helped with elections, the farm census, worked as a clerk in the post office, and worked one year in a variety store. Her children have moved away to cities and she is now one of the few longtime residents left in Bettie. Her life has been centered in a rural village rather than on a farm. She remembers life in Bettie when there was no electricity or air conditioning or even screens on the windows. Electricity came to Bettie early, about 1917, as did the railroad, and both widened the horizon for the rural folks of the community.[26]

Along the Gulf Coast the picture shows even greater diversity. Orange County has a few large farms of about eight hundred acres, but more small farms with diverse "crops," including Christmas trees and crawfish. Ethnic groups represented are Caucasian, Louisiana French, black, and Vietnamese.

At the southern tip of Texas in Willacy County, the Raymondville area, we encounter a pattern that will be repeated in West Texas. Two types of rural women predominate there: white, middle-aged women of German background, wives of farmers, full-time homemakers with five to seven children and a high-school education; and Hispanic women, in their twenties to middle aged, wives of farm workers, full-time homemakers with large families and a ninth-grade education.

Rhoda Ellen Long, a great-grandmother, lives alone on a three-thousand-acre ranch in parts of Jim Hogg and Webb counties, close to Encinal. Five miles from her nearest neighbor, she is quite independent. She quilts, cans, gardens, and supervises the cattle operation. Each of six or seven pastures has its own herd of cows, windmill, and catching pen. She rides out in a pickup with a helper to look over the herds and select animals to sell. The hospital pasture is south of her house, and she keeps an eye on heifers due to calve. Her daughter says that people who grew up in that isolated area were about a generation behind people growing up in the Houston–Corpus Christi area. She remembers that it was 1942 when they finally got a telephone. The daugh-

---

26. Velma Bowden, telephone interview by Mary Briggs, Dec. 15, 1983.

ter very proudly tells how her mother, who was an orphan and never finished high school, married at seventeen, moved to Oilton, east of Laredo, and worked hard making a home for her family on forty acres outside of town while her husband worked in the oil fields. Today Mrs. Long, a widow, is a competent modern rancher, never happier than when on the ranch.[27]

Moving up into Central Texas, we encounter the transition from farming to ranching, with diverse examples of each. For many of these counties, Sunbelt publicity has brought a rapid influx of city people, subdivisions, and suburbs. In Comal County, northeast of San Antonio, the "city woman gone country" coexists with the ranch wife who is typically over fifty and German, has eight to twelve years of education, and is not employed outside the home. In a number of these counties — Mills, Burnet, Williamson, Comal — the trend is for the younger rural women (under fifty) to work outside the home whereas the older women do not. The average Central Texas farm or ranch ranges in size from fifty acres or less in Brazos County (Bryan) to 820 acres in Blanco County (Johnson City). The Central Texas area is split between farming and ranching; cotton, grain sorghum, and livestock are the most important products. The Milam County agent reported three types of rural women in her area. The first owns fifty-seven acres, leases forty more, runs seventy-five head of cattle. She is white, forty-two years old, has a high-school education, has six children, and works outside the home four days a week as a housekeeper. The second type is white, age forty-six, owns twenty-seven acres, raises a few cattle, has two children, and she and her husband both work away from home. The third type is black, in her mid-thirties, lives on thirty-five acres, raises a few cattle, has a high-school education, and works away from home.[28]

"Mama" Cox lives on five acres on the outskirts of Andice, a tiny rural community in Williamson County. She grew up in Central Texas and, although she did not attend college, three of her six children have graduated from Southwestern University and moved to urban areas to teach. Myrl works at a day care center in Georgetown during the day and in the evening often helps feed cattle or chase stray livestock back into the pasture.

In north central Texas the typical rural woman in Erath County, near Stephenville, lives on a dairy or peanut farm of 250 to 300 acres, has two children, and enjoys a higher income than most farm women,

---

27. Joanne Long Morse, interview, Dec. 18, 1983, Georgetown, Tex.
28. Vivian R. Pittman, Milam County.

without working away from home. In Wise County, northwest of Fort Worth, a similar picture can be seen, with dairying being the typical farm enterprise. The farms and ranches are large, 300 to 600 acres, and prosperous. The average rural woman in this area has a high-school education and a family of two or three children. There are few rural blacks or Mexican Americans in north central Texas.

Much of the rural land in north central Texas has been affected by Sunbelt growth and the spreading Dallas–Fort Worth Metroplex. In North Texas, four miles north of Sherman, lives Suzan Fincher, formerly a "city girl," who grew up in Tyler and married a man whose medical career took them to Galveston, California, Connecticut, South Carolina, and the District of Columbia but whose roots were in the farmland of North Texas. The family of four moved to Sherman more than ten years ago and bought their dream farm of 112 acres. They moved to the farm nine years ago and raised beef cattle and a big garden. Recently the highway department took about one-third of their land for a superhighway right through the middle of their farm. Since access was limited from one side to the other, they sold the other part and are now down to about 40 acres and six cows and a bull. They raise beef for their family and friends and put up lots of canned goods; many jars go to their church. Their orchard furnishes apricots, peaches, apples, and plums. Despite the looming freeway, Mrs. Fincher loves the farm and "would have real regrets if we had to leave."[29]

In the Panhandle, in Ochiltree County, the typical rural woman lives and works on a farm of several sections of land, producing wheat and milo, and probably does not work away from home. In the area from Amarillo to Lubbock the farms are large, approximately a thousand acres, much of it irrigated, and the women are either Anglo wives of farmers or Mexican American wives of farm laborers. In Hale and Castro counties the typical rural woman lives in town while the husband commutes to the farm. Few of these women work outside the home.

Mauna Loa Cleek lives three and a half miles from Panhandle, a town of about two thousand in Carson County. She and her husband, with help from a son who has moved back to the area, farm three and a quarter sections of land, about half of it in pasture and half in cultivated crops. They both grew up in the area, graduated from college, married, and settled down in Panhandle, where she was active in volunteer work and church activities and has taught school off and on while they raised two children and he worked the land. Eventually they

29. Suzan Fincher, telephone interview, Dec. 17, 1983.

built a house and moved out to the farm, where she worked around the house and cultivated a large garden and orchard. Asked if she ever worked in the fields, she commented that she cultivated some row crops once back in the 1950s, but then it did not rain and all those little plants she had worked so hard to cultivate just shriveled up and died, and she could not stand it. That was the last time she rode a tractor. Now she does housework, volunteer work, club work, and puts up enough vegetables and fruit from her garden and orchard to last her family till the next season.[30]

From Lubbock to Midland, the average farm or ranch ranges from about five hundred acres in Dawson County to about fifteen hundred acres in Yoakum County. In the northern part of this area, in Gaines, Terry, and Yoakum counties, the owners or part-owners are Anglo and many farm workers are Mexican American. In the southern part of this area, Dawson and Howard counties, a high percentage of rural women (Howard County—99 percent) are Anglo, have completed high school, have three children, and are not employed outside the home.

In West Texas, in Midland County, the typical rural woman is a rancher's wife, age thirty-five, who has three children and two years of college. The ranch is approximately fifty-seven hundred acres and runs cattle and goats. This woman has two homes, one on the ranch and one in town. She and the children stay in town during the week for school but spend weekends and summers on the ranch. Farther south in Crockett County the typical rural woman is a college graduate, about fifty years old, a rancher's wife living on about ten sections of land raising sheep and goats and receiving further income from gas and oil.

Thus a pattern can be outlined. In East Texas rural women of diverse ethnic backgrounds live on small farms relatively close to urban centers where many of them work. Farther west the ethnic diversity declines and the size of the farm or ranch increases dramatically. In far West Texas distance from town becomes great enough that many ranchers maintain two homes, one on the ranch and one in town. In East Texas rural women are generally wives of the owners or renters of farms, but in West and South Texas many rural women are the wives of farm or ranch hands.

In each area there are many other types of rural women. Patricia Hohensee of Concho County (east of San Angelo) lists the "untouched" farm wife, or traditional rural homemaker (often a widow); the typical

---

30. Mauna Loa Cleek, telephone interview by her daughter, Donna Cleek Connor, Dec. 17 and 21, 1983.

rural housewife who "works hand in hand with her husband, and is not removed from feeding stock, hauling cotton trailers, drenching sheep or going to town for tractor parts" (the majority fall into this category); the farm wife with a town job who works because of financial need or because she was a city girl who "couldn't tolerate total country living"; and city folk gone country who are rural only by location, not by nature. The survey of county extension agents shows that these four categories exist in many, if not all, counties in Texas.[31]

If one looks for the typical rural woman in Texas, one must look in diverse settings. She may be living on a ten-acre farm in East Texas or on ten sections of ranchland in West Texas. She may be within minutes of major shopping centers and have access to all modern conveniences, or she may live a hundred miles away from any large city, thus limiting shopping to mail order and television reception to one station. She may devote all of her energy to home, family, and farm, or she may work full time away from home. She may be Anglo, German, Mexican American, or black. She may be involved in cotton, grain, livestock, dairying, peanuts, oil production, or even crawfish farming. Wherever she is, whoever she is, the rural woman in Texas has experienced changes in her life-style that would have amazed her grandmother. These changes are the result of the impact of rural electrification, modern technology, improved transportation, mass media and education, and the women's movement. Out of the dynamic flux of the past forty years has emerged a new rural woman in Texas, one who cherishes country living but who also looks forward to the future with confidence, knowing that she is not the timid country cousin, but the equal in every way of her knowledgeable and competent city sister.

31. Patricia Hohensee, Concho County.

The seed for modern country-and-western music was planted in the South in the seventeenth and eighteenth centuries when Anglo-Scottish-Irish settlers began arriving with their music from the Old Sod. During the years of their westering the old songs met new sounds from churches and camp meetings, from blacks and Cajuns and Mexicans, and from Tin Pan Alley and vaudeville and minstrel shows. These styles and sounds fell upon pickers and singers who were living strongly and precariously and close to the frontier soil, and the result was the folk music of Texas and the South — songs to dance and play to and songs of careless love and stockade blues — the songs that were later to give their sound and spirit to the country-and-western music that grew out of it.

7
Texas Folk and Modern Country Music
Francis Edward Abernethy

In the early days of Texas most of the music was country, rural music because most of the people were living in the country, and the songs they sang and the music they made were parts of their rural heritage. Even the urban areas were rural in the sense that they were dominated by an agrarian economy. Their musical heritage was the folk music of the rural South that could trace its ancestry back to a similar environment in the Old World. Texas singers and players personalized the songs and changed the lyrics to fit their own times and places and situations. The settlers were conscious of themselves in this new and exciting area and adventure. Usually they viewed their lives with humor, but at times a sadness came in as they reflected on their isolation and the distance between themselves and the homes of their past. Still, most of their songs were optimistic. The settlers had lost out somewhere else and they did not come to Texas to lose again. As long as there was a frontier, there was a place of hope.

This early musical expression of themselves and what they did is not history. It is not documented, nor is it actual or factual, except in spirit. In some respects, however, it is more important than history because it reveals how the settlers saw events and felt about them at the time. History can provide statistics on the number of people who migrated during a particular period, but the folklore and the folk music of the time can tell how they really saw themselves in the midst of that great adventure.

This early folk music has traveled many years and many miles from then to now, and it underwent many changes during its lifetime. But the feeling of closeness to the soil and identity with the land and the strong emotion never died. The music mixed with many cultures and styles and borrowed from others and loaned of itself. As Texas became more urban, the country-folk style was diluted, but just as it lost some of its countriness, it gained from the new urban sounds that it encountered. The modern result of country music's evolution of a hundred years or more is a broad spectrum of musical style called country-and-western music. It is urban in spite of its rural roots because, farmers and ranchers included, we are all wired and televised into the urban scene. We are too close to our rural heritage, however, to give it up or forget it.

The people who were eventually to cover the mountains of Kentucky and Tennessee and Arkansas with their sounds and those who sang the old songs through the coastal states of the Deep South in their journey to Texas were a motley group of pilgrims and pioneers. Many were the offspring of the criminal, the indentured, and the dispossessed—the unwanted flushed out of England to the colonies. After they had served their time and indenture, they left the coastal land of the tidewater and the plantations of Virginia and the Carolinas and about 1769 started westward through the Cumberland Cap, then along the ridges and through the long valleys of the southern mountain states. About a generation later another migration began moving south toward Georgia, then west along the southern coastal states. Earlier migrations of Scotch-Irish and Germans moved southwest from southern Pennsylvania along the Blue Ridge Mountains. Generations of moving followed as families came to new ground, planted and plowed till the earth got poor, then moved west again, scattering their seed and their songs as they went.

A later wave of westward migration included more prosperous settlers who came to establish new plantations and businesses and to guarantee established social positions for their offspring, but these were not the main carriers of the music that we are talking about. Ours are the ones who stayed with the soil, the ones who became the crackers and the rednecks and the hillbillies, the ones who covered the rural South like seed ticks, filling all the pockets of the Smokies and the Southern Appalachians and the Ozarks, praying some nubbin-eared corn out of sand that could barely grow a pine tree, maybe lucking into enough creek-bottom loam to raise a money crop. Living about as close to the land as their aboriginal predecessors, they moved with very little baggage, a wagon and a mule maybe, a team if they were lucky, some pots and pans to cook in, enough covers to keep from freezing, and some seed corn. That was about all they owned and about all thay had room for.

What these early settlers *did* have room for was their folklore, that part of them that was as much a piece of their lives as their livers and their lights. They brought a mind full of cures that they could find by the side of the roads they traveled and an eye for the signs that they knew to plant their sweet potatoes by and castrate their pigs and cattle by and signs to tell how bad the winter was going to be. They brought their religions and their old faiths. They brought legends and tales from an old and other world. And they brought the customs and traditions that had always been a part of them and of the ways of life that would later bind them to the Texas soil.

But best of all, they brought to Texas great stores of songs that had been given to them before they had crossed the blue water, and they brought along some that they had gotten in the East before they made their journey to the West. And like the miracle of the wine at the wedding in Galilee, these songs were continually growing, and they were continually changing shape and sound as they were bred to new songs and pastured in new ground and hazed along by an ever-increasing number of new owners.[1]

There was usually an underlying optimism in the songs of the pioneers on their way to Texas. This spirit is seen in an invitation song that was sung by some early nester who was trying to get a woman to share with him the challenge of opening up new country. The title of the song is "Shoot the Buffalo" and it is a play-party song. It is also sometimes referred to as a "rise-you-up." A rise-you-up is a song to start off the dancing. It gets the women out of their chairs and onto the floor. This song was supposed to go one step further. It was supposed to get the ladies in a wagon and across the Sabine River into Texas. It is a folk song because there is no telling where the tune came from or how many tales it told before some poet made it fit the circumstances of the western migration.

Shoot the Buffalo
Rise you up, my partner dear,
And present to me your hand,
'Cause I know you want to marry
And I'd like to be the man.
And I'll take you out to Texas,
Where I know you want to go,
And we'll rally round the canebrake
And shoot the buffalo.

1. The following songs and the information concerning them are natural accumulations of a lifelong interest in all kinds of music. The material is not documented because for the most part the songs were learned informally and the information is the result of observation rather than research. All of the songs, with their music, can be found in F. E. Abernethy, *Singin' Texas* (Dallas: E-Heart Press, 1983).

Chorus
Shoot the buffalo,
We will shoot the buffalo,
We'll ramble through the canebrake
And shoot the buffalo.
Rise you up, my partner dear,
And present to me your hand,
And we'll take a little journey
To a fair and distant land.
Where the boys will scrap and rassle
And the girls will sit and sew,
And we'll rally round the canebrake
And shoot the buffalo.
(*Chorus*)
Well, the buffalo is dead;
We've done shot him in the head,
So let's all form a circle
And we'll have a dance instead.
And the hawk will chase the buzzard,
And the buzzard chase the crow,
And we'll rally round the canebrake
And shoot the buffalo.
(*Chorus*)

   I sometimes wonder when I hear "Shoot the Buffalo" why any woman would respond to that sort of invitation. It is easier to understand why the following song might have an appeal to some prospective settler. When the old-timers were looking for land to settle on, they looked for white oak trees because they knew that where the white oak grew, the land was rich and fertile. This old play-party song is a romantic description of what every settler was looking for.

Coffee Grows on White Oak Trees
Coffee grows on white oak trees,
Rivers flow with brandy-o,
Choose that girl to roam with you,
Sweet as sugar, like candy-o.
Chorus
Grab your partner and we'll all dance Josey,
Grab your partner and we'll all dance Josey,
Grab your partner and we'll all dance Josey,
Hello, Susie Brown.

Coffee grows in a white oak stump,
Rivers flow with sugar lumps,
Choose the girl that you love true,
Choose the girl to roam with you.
    (*Chorus*)

The other side of the picture is a song that was popular all the way up and down the frontier. In East Texas it is called "Texas Boys" and it is a "come-all-ye," one of those folk songs whose main purpose is to give advice.

Texas Boys
Come all you young ladies and listen to my noise,
And don't you go marrying those Texas boys,
'Cause if you do your life's gonna be
Johnny cake and venison and sassafras tea,
Johnny cake and venison and sassafras tea.

When they come a'courtin' I'll tell you what they wear,
An old tattered shirt all patched and bare,
An old straw hat more brim than crown,
And a pair of leather britches that they wear the winter round,
A pair of leather britches that they wear the winter round.

They'll take you out to some tall pine hill
And leave you to starve against your will;
They'll leave you alone out there in the sand,
And that is the way with a Tex-i-an,
That is the way with a Tex-i-an.

They'll take you to a house with hewed log walls,
And it ain't got no windows at all,
A pine-shake roof and a puncheon floor,[2]
And it's that way all Texas o'er,
It's that way all Texas o'er.

And when they come in the first thing you'll hear
Is "Madam, your old man's shot you a deer."
The very next thing when they sit down
Is "Madam, your johnny cake's too durn brown,
Madam, your johnny cake's too durn brown!"

---

2. A puncheon floor is made of split logs—hewed side up, rough side down.

> So, candy's candy any way you fix it;
> Brandy's brandy any way you mix it.
> When other good folks are asleep in bed
> The devil is a-workin in a Texan's head,
> The devil is a-workin in a Texan's head.

"Texas Boys" is a traveler, as are most folk songs. The tune and general idea can be found in songs from Kentucky, Kansas, and Nebraska, at least. Carl Sandburg has a "Kansas Boys" in his *American Songbag* that has nine verses describing in detail the dangers of marrying a frontiersman. The dangers, you will notice, aren't Indians, Mexicans, or wild animals. The dangers lie in the character of the man himself, the frontiersman who was his own breed of cat and who was moving into the open spaces of the Southwest in order to live without the social restraints of the more sophisticated society back East. Any woman who decided to tie her destiny to his shirttails did so at her own risk. But then, most of the women who made the trek west were cut from the same piece of cloth as the men. Some of them sang the following verse, or one like it, to the old fiddle tune "Shady Grove" or "Old Joe Clark" or "Cindy":

> If I had a needle and thread
> As fine as I could sew,
> I'd sew my skirt to his shirt tail
> And through the world we'd go.

The pioneers came in three waves. The first wave on the southwestern frontier was made up of the takers, the warriors and hunters looking for adventure, land, and a fresh start, and the cattlemen looking for free range. The next wave was mostly squatters looking for a piece of free land they could clear easily, wear out, and then leave to the persimmon sprouts. The land was pretty well tamed by the time the third wave arrived; the Indians had been pushed on and the bears and panthers hunted out. This group consisted of the settlers and the businessmen who came to put down roots and make new lives and new towns.

The first wave into West Texas had some of the most disreputable takers that ever raped the American frontier. These were the buffalo hunters, who came west to take advantage of the government bounty on buffalo and the high price of hides back East. After the Civil War the push of the western frontier was into the tall grass of the plains area west of the Cross Timbers. The cattlemen wanted the land, most of which was controlled by the Plains Comanche and Kiowa, who migrated with and lived off the great buffalo herds. The simple solution, for the settlers at least, was to kill off the buffalo and force the Indians onto the Oklahoma reservations. Between 1870 and 1880, 13 million buffalo were killed. Those buffalo hunters who did the job are now pictured as a mangy and lawless lot whose brief time in history was the cause of the destruction of a culture and of the noblest symbol of the Great Plains. A folk song that has come down from that time views it differently. Buffalo hunting to the maker of this song was a hard job necessary for survival, and going out on the buffalo range was like working for a summer in the oil fields. The song dealt with the hardships of the hunt, not the plight of the buffalo or the Indian. And this is the way they saw that time in their history.

The song those hunters left was called "The Buffalo Hunters." Like folk songs generally—and buffalo hunters in particular—it had been something else before it got to Texas. It began as an Old World love song entitled "Caledonia," then was taken into the fold of English sea chanteys, and later as "Canaday-I-O" described the hardships of logging in the far north. It might have drifted down to Texas with some lumberjack–turned–buffalo hunter. Whatever happened, somebody changed the song to fit the circumstances of the buffalo hunters in Jacksboro, Texas, in the spring of 1873 and came up with a classic.

The Buffalo Hunters

'Twas in the town of Jacksboro in the spring of seventy-three,
A man by the name of Crego came stepping up to me,
Saying, "How do you do, young fellow, and how would you like to go
And spend one summer pleasantly on the range of the buffalo?"

It's me being out of employment, to Crego I did say,
"This going out on the buffalo range depends upon the pay.
But if you pay good wages and transportation, too,
I think, sir, I will go with you to the range of the buffalo."

So now our outfit was complete, seven able-bodied men.
With navy six and needle gun our troubles did begin;
Our way it was a pleasant one, the route we had to go,
Until we crossed Pease River on the range of the buffalo.

It's now we've crossed Pease River, our troubles have begun.
The first damned tail I went to rip, Christ! how I cut my
    thumb!
While skinning the damned old stinkers our lives they
    had no show,
For the Indians waited to pick us off while skinning the
    buffalo.

He fed us on such sorry chuck I wished myself most dead,
And all we had to sleep on was a buffalo robe for a bed;
The fleas and graybacks worked on us, O boys, it was not slow;
There's no worse hell on this old earth than the range of the
    buffalo.

Our hearts were cased with buffalo hocks, our souls were cased
    with steel,
And the hardships of that summer would nearly make us reel.
While skinning the damned old stinkers our lives they had no
    show,
For the Indians waited to pick us off on the range of the
    buffalo.

The season being near over, old Crego he did say
The crowd had been extravagant, was in debt to him that day.
We coaxed him and we begged him and still it was no go—
So we left old Crego's bones to bleach on the range of the
    buffalo.

Oh, it's now we've crossed Pease River and homeward we are
    bound,
No more in that hell-fired country shall ever we be found;
Go home to our wives and sweethearts, tell others not to go,
For God's forsaken the buffalo range and the damned old
    buffalo.

After the buffalo and the Indians were cleared from the prairies the cattlemen moved in, and the ultimate Texas symbol, the cowboy, became a part of this nation's history and folklore. Most of those who were to trail the great herds from Texas to the northern railheads were flotsam from the recently defeated South who had no place to go but west. They found their places in the cow camps and lost some of their lonesomeness in company with other boys who were a long way from home and family. History records the size of the herds and tells about the events of the trail. The songs they sang tell about how they felt about it all.

Even in the midst of their time and work, cowboys felt that they were different. They felt the heroic stance of their lives in the midst of the loneliness of the prairie and the hardships of the trail. They laughed a lot about the trouble of wild cows and salty horses, and they also sang sadly of their separation from the homes that they had left behind and would probably never see again.

One of the sad songs they sang was "Bury Me Not on the Lone Prairie." The tune and the mood of the song were well established by the time it got to the prairies of the Southwest. Like most Texas folk songs —and some of the people—it was something else before it came to this part of the country, in this case a popular ballad called "The Ocean Burial." The words to "The Ocean Burial" were written in 1839 by Rev. Edwin Chapin and published in the *Southern Literary Messenger.* The story was a sailor's lament about being buried at sea and far from home. George N. Allen set the poem to music in 1850, and it became popular enough to become the vehicle for parody.

The situation for the sailor and cowboy was the same. They were dying far from home, and their last words were please not to be buried in the alien depths of the "deep, deep sea," or the foreign soil of "the lone prairie." Cowboys and sailors had much in common in their ways of life. Their sense of separation and aloneness was as strong as their sense of the uniqueness and romance of their lives. Both groups existed in a vigorous male-club society, and the setting for the action of their lives was lonesome and without relief.

Bury Me Not on the Lone Prairie
"Oh, bury me not on the lone prairie,"
These words came low and mournfully
From the pallid lips of a youth who lay
'Neath the prairie sky at the close of day.

And he wailed in pain until o'er his brow
Death's shadows fast were gathering now,
And he thought of home and his loved ones nigh
As the cowboys gathered to see him die.

"Oh, bury me not on the lone prairie
In a narrow grave, just six by three,
Where the wild coyotes howl over me,
And the buffalo paws on the prairie sea.

"It matters not, I've oft been told,
Where the body lies when the heart grows cold.
Yet grant, oh grant this wish to me,
And bury me not on the lone prairie.

"I've always wished to be laid when I died
In a little churchyard on the green hillside.
By my father's grave there let mine be,
And bury me not on the lone prairie.

"Let my death sleep be where my mother's prayer
And a sister's tear will mingle there,
Where my friends can come and weep o'er me.
Oh, bury me not on the lone prairie.

"Oh, bury me not," and he faltered there,
But we paid no heed to his dying prayer.
In a narrow grave, just six by three,
We buried him there, on the lone prairie.

    The squatters and settlers had their songs, too, and most of them gave a pretty accurate description of what it was like, proving up on a quarter of a section of land. A song that the settlers of old Greer County, Texas (now Oklahoma) remember well was "The Little Old Sod Shanty on My Claim," a parody of the sentimental minstrel song "My Little Old Log Cabin in the Lane." Some West Texas or Oklahoma settler with that popular song on his mind met the harsh realities of western sod busting and wrote new words to the old tune. The irony of the dream in the light of reality was emphasized by the contrast between the pastoral and ideal log cabin in the lane and the coldly uncomfortable and lonely sod shanty on his claim.

    One variety of the sod shanty on the plains of the Southwest was the half-dugout. The settler dug himself a room about four feet deep. Then he planked up the sides a couple of feet higher, laid a flat roof across it, and covered it all with dirt. My grandparents spent their first married year on their Greer County claim between the North Fork of the Red River and Prairie Dog Town Fork, and they spent it in a half-dugout, sleeping on the seed bin at the back. Like the sod shanty, the half-dugout had its disadvantages, the main one being that in a prolonged rainy spell it leaked and got muddy inside. They said it was fairly cool in the summer and not bad during the milder part of the winter, but the winter of 1898 spawned three blue northers—triplets, coming head to toe—that the settlers on the plains never did forget.

The Little Old Sod Shanty

I am getting mighty weary now while holding down my claim,
My vittles are not always of the best;
The mice play shyly 'round me as I lay me down to rest,
In the little old sod shanty on my claim.
The hinges are of leather and the windows have no glass,
While the door it lets the howling blizzard in,
And I hear the hungry coyote as he slinks up through the grass,
In the little old sod shanty on my claim.

Yet I rather like the novelty of living in this way,
Though my bill of fare is always rather tame,
But I'm happy as a clam on the land of Uncle Sam
In the little old sod shanty on my claim.
But when I left my eastern home, a bachelor so gay,
To try and win my way to wealth and fame,
I little thought I'd come around to burning twisted hay
In the little old sod shanty on my claim.

My clothes are plastered o'er with dough, I'm looking like a fright,
And everything is scattered 'round the room,
But I wouldn't give the freedom that I have out in the West
For the table of the eastern man's old home.
Still I wish some tender woman would pity on me take,
And relieve me from the mess that I am in;
The angel, how I'd bless her, if this her home she'd make
In the little old sod shanty on my claim.

And we would make our fortunes on the prairies of the West,
Just as happy as two lovers we'd remain;
We'd forget the trials and troubles we endured at the first,
In the little old sod shanty on my claim.
And if fate should bless us with now and then an heir,
To cheer our hearts with honest pride of fame,
O then we'd be contented for the toil that we had spent
In the little old sod shanty on our claim.

Sometimes the land was too tough to hold down. Old Greer County, Texas, provided a case in point. Greer County was that triangular piece of sandy prairie that lay between the North Fork of the Red River and the Prairie Dog Town Fork and was bounded on the west by the Panhandle. Texas had claimed this area since 1860 and fought a long battle with the United States and Oklahoma to keep it. My father's family and many other pioneers moved into this disputed land during the 1880s and 1890s, when Texas was trying to get it settled in order to enforce its claim. Texas finally lost the battle, the Prairie Dog Town Fork of the Red became its north boundary, and Greer County was cut up into several different counties and made a part of southeastern Oklahoma.

A traveling folk song that came out of the experience of settling Greer County was "The Greer County Bachelor." In the Texas-Oklahoma version Tom Hight is the bachelor's name, because that was the name of the singer that John Lomax got the song from. The Lane County, Nebraska, version of the same song has Frank Bolar as the bachelor. The characters changed with the settings, but the "Irish Washerwoman" tune that the song is sung to stayed the same, as did the sentiment, which has been voiced as long as people have been settling new lands and finding that the grass on the other side of the fence was not as green as they thought it was going to be.

> My name is Tom Hight; an old bachelor I am.
> You'll find me out west in that county of fame.
> You'll find me out west on an elegant plan,
> Just starving to death on my government claim.
> *Chorus*
> Hurrah, for Greer County! The land of the free,
> The land of the grasshopper, bedbug, and flea.
> I'll sing of its praises and tell of its fame
> And starve plumb to death on my government claim.
> My house it is built out of natural soil.
> The walls are erected according to Hoyle.
> Its roof has no pitch and is level and plain,
> And I always get wet when it happens to rain.
> (*Chorus*)
> My clothes are all ragged; my language is rough.
> My bread is corn dodgers, both solid and tough.
> And yet I am happy and live at my ease
> On sorghum molasses and bacon and cheese.
> (*Chorus*)
> How happy am I when I crawl into bed,
> And a rattlesnake hisses a tune at my head.
> A gay little centipede, all without fear
> Crawls over my pillow and into my ear.
> (*Chorus*)

Now come all you claim holders, and I hope you will stay
To chew your hardtack till you're toothless and gray.
But as for me I'll no longer remain
To starve like a dog on my government claim.
Final Chorus
Farewell to Greer County where the blizzards arise,
Where the sun never sets and the flea never dies,
Where the wind never ceases but always remains
To blow us all off of our government claims.

The settlers of Texas sang about subjects other than their particular adventures. The children had their own songs to sing and to play games to. Lovers, convinced that their joys and aches were the center of world movement, had theirs. They had songs to dance to and, when they were in a religious mood, songs that sent their prayers winging swiftly to a loving God. Most of these songs were the ones that had been around the longest and were a part of a traditional past rather than the specific happenings of settling Texas.

While the grown-ups were singing about their trials and conquests opening up the frontier, the children were singing their own songs. They came with a pack full of songs, many of them still bearing the stamp of the Old World. They sang songs about gathering at the king's levee, about the Grand Old Duke of York, and they sang a song about Old King William, who "had a star upon his breast / As big as any hornet's nest." They sang a version of "Froggie Went a'Courtin'," which their ancestors had sung when they were children in the reign of Henry VIII. A version of it was published in England as early as 1611, and the song has changed little since then. A southern version influenced by the blacks' style of singing became the most widespread in Texas. All sorts of nonsense syllables have served as the chorus, and one Texas version begins in an old-style, sober, minor key.

Froggie Went a'Courtin'
Froggie went a'courtin', he did ride,
  Rinktum-body-minchi-cambo,
Sword and a buckler by his side,
  Rinktum-body-minchi-cambo.

Kyma-nero down to Cairo,
Kyma-nero Cairo.
Straddle-addle-addle
Boble-adle-boble-linktum,
Rinktum-body-minchi-cambo.

He went down to Miss Mousie's house;
He said, "I'd like to see Miss Mouse."

He took Miss Mousie on his knee;
He said, "Miss Mousie, won't you marry me?"

"Without my Uncle Rat's consent,
I would not marry the president."

Then Mousie looked him in the eye,
Says, "Frog, I'll marry you by-and-by."

Where will the wedding supper be?
Way down yonder in a hollow tree.

What will the wedding supper be?
A fried mosquito and a roasted flea.

First came in was a tumble bug;
Under his arm was a whiskey jug.

Next came in was a bumble-bee;
He had a fiddle on his knee.

They all went sailing on the lake,
And they got swallered by a big black snake.
or,
Next came in was a brindle cat,
And she soon put a stop to that.

She gobbled them up—one, two, three,
The frog, the mouse, and the bumble-bee.

The Southwest frontier was great for men and dogs but hell on women and horses. Because there was a noticeable scarcity of women, courtable women were placed on a pedestal, and the relation between the sexes was not as casual and matter-of-fact as it ought to have been.

Meeting places for young men and women were scarce, too. Farm and ranch families seldom went to town, and when they did go, many went as strangers. Dances and play parties were as infrequent and far between in West Texas and Oklahoma as the scattered homes were. People sometimes came together for barn raisings, and in East Texas they met for log rollings. Probably more families had their beginnings at camp meetings than anywhere else. Held once a year and lasting for two or three weeks, the camp meetings were the social center, trading lot, and breeding grounds for the farmers and ranchers for miles around.

Even though lovers were scarce, love was still on the frontiersman's mind—strong lustful love, sweet idyllic romance, and just someone to live with to keep the "lonesomes" away. So they sang about their love with songs that went back generations before their families left the Old Country. They sang about hard-hearted Barbara Allen and about Lord Randall's ill-fated courtship as if these characters lived just down the road.

One of the first songs I ever learned by heart and saddened over was a mournful love ballad cast in dialogue form entitled "My Horses Ain't Hungry." It is one of a large family of songs that had its origin in Scotland in the seventeenth century. In the family are "Pretty Polly," "Rye Whiskey," "Some Say I Drink Whiskey," "Clinch Mountain," "Jack of Diamonds," and "The Wagoner's Lad," to mention a few. "My Horses Ain't Hungry" is closest to "The Wagoner's Lad" in story. The song is typical of many of the old-country ballads, such as "Edward," "Lord Randall," "Hangman's Tree," in its brief dialogue form. The introduction and conclusion have been cut away and only the climactic episode remains. The listener has to imagine what went before and what came after.

My Horses Ain't Hungry

"I'm leaving this country to stay for a while,
Across the wide prairie a many a long mile.
Well, dark, cold, and dreary, the moon sheds no light,
And my horses won't travel that dark road at night."

"Get down from your horses and feed them some hay,
And sit down beside me as long as you stay."
"My horses ain't hungry; they won't eat your hay,
So fare thee well, Molly, I'm going away."

"Your parents don't like me; they say I'm too poor.
They say I'm not worthy to enter your door.
So come with me Molly; together we'll roam
To some lonely little cabin and call it our home."

"I hate to leave Mother; she treats me so kind,
But I can't break that promise to that darling of mine.
Yes, I will go with you, though you're poor I am told.
It's your love I'm after, not silver and gold."

The British settlers of America brought with them an ancient tradition of dancing and a large number of tunes to dance to. They danced in rings and squares and in long lines facing each other. During the colonial period these dances were accompanied by fifes, bagpipes, and fiddles. After the Revolutionary War the bagpipe, which was associated with the losing Tory forces, was forced north into Canada, the fife got lost along the way, and the fiddle became the instrument to dance to in America.

Dance music in Texas was the sound of fiddles. There were exceptions, certainly. The Cajuns of the Texas Gulf Coast liked accordians; the Germans of Central Texas harkened unto the noise of sounding brass; and the religious fundamentalists sang the music for their play-party movements. But a respectable dance had a fiddle or two, seconded by mandolins, banjos, jugs, and anything else that could make a musical sound and strengthen the beat.

The American colonists soon put their stamp on the old jigs, reels, marches, and hornpipes that their people had brought over from the British Isles. Those hardy frontiersmen put fire in their fiddles and played their songs all the way from the tidewater to Texas. You can tell where they came from and where they stopped to rest along the way. Fiddlers haven't changed "The Irish Washerwoman" and "The Sailor's Hornpipe" much from what they were on the Old Sod, and one can almost trace the settlers' trails by the titles of the songs they picked up on the road and brought to the Southwest. They came from "Shady Grove" to "Cripple Creek" and found "Tennessee Wagoner" and "The Arkansas Traveler" before they got to Texas. Or they might have come the southern route and learned "Alabama Gals," "Natchez under the Hill," and "Mississippi Sawyer" on the long road through the South. However the fiddling tunes and songs got here, and there were many trails into Texas, they received a lot of handling in their journey. They were played on everything from a Stradivarius to a gourd with strings, and every fiddler doctored the song to suit his own musical tastes and talents. A few tunes became many through variations, and new tunes were born or borrowed from other musical traditions.

There was a lot of fiddling in Texas just for the fun of it, and sometimes fiddling became a part of a cowboy's work as he played a slow sad tune to keep the cattle quiet on night herd. Serious fiddling, though, was reserved for the dances, and there was no other social function that was looked forward to with as much excitement as a dance with a good fiddler or two.

The best square-dance fiddlers were also callers, but some lucky times when there was plenty of sugar in the gourd, there might be two or three fiddlers, guitar and banjo players, *and* a caller. The good caller was an expert, too, as he gave the turns, balances, and leads that the dancers were to follow. He had to have an imagination and enough tricks and turns to exercise the dancers and challenge their ability. The caller not only gave the directions for the dance; he frequently threw in verses, thereby making a song out of a tune.

The words that attached themselves to these old tunes were of American origin. They were incidental to the tunes and the dance calls, and this is the main difference between dance-music songs and folk songs in general. Some of these dance songs were no more than two- or four-line shouts, unconnected and without any narrative purpose, frequently comic and very simple, that were inserted at the whim of the caller or fiddler for variety's sake. "Fire on the Mountain" illustrates this kind of song.

Fire on the Mountain
Fire on the mountain! Run for home, boys.
Fire on the mountain! Run, boys, run.

Oh, my little Indian, don't drink whiskey.
Oh, my little Indian, don't get drunk.

Two little Indians sittin' on a log,
Looking at a hog in Arkansas.

Some dance songs are late enough in their creation to have their own histories. According to his family's tradition, Curtis Foley, father of the country-and-western star Red Foley, originated "Sally Goodin," the most popular of the present-day fiddling songs. He composed it to honor his sweetheart, a Texas girl from Leon County by the name of Sally Goodman. Fiddlin' Eck Robertson has another version of the song's origin. He said that a girl named Sally was being courted by two fiddle players, and she promised to marry the better fiddler of the two. The man named Goodwin won the contest with the tune that he later named after his new bride. Since then there have been thirteen generations of Good'ins, and Robertson finishes this bit of folklore by playing "Sally Goodin" thirteen different ways.

Sally Goodin
Had a little piece of pie
And a little piece of puddin'
And I gave it all away
To see Sally Goodin.

I looked down the road
To see Sally comin';
Nearly broke my neck
When I started out to runnin'.
   Chorus
   A long way home
   And the road's mighty muddy
   And I'm so drunk
   That I can't stand steady [pronounced "study"].

Gooseberry pie,
Huckleberry puddin'—
I'd give it all away
To see my Sally Goodin.

I ain't dead,
And I ain't wooden,
And I'm in love
With my sweet Sally Goodin.

I love pie,
I love puddin',
And I'm crazy about a gal
That they call Sally Goodin.

There was—and is, but it's rare—another folk song and dance tradition in Texas. That was the play party, or Josey party, as it is called in East Texas. Many of the settlers of early Texas were fundamentalists who held that the fiddle was the devil's instrument and dancing was the heathen's pastime, and they would have none of it. But they had an urge to dance that was strong enough to get them around the letter of the law, and they rationalized and came up with the play party.

The play party was religiously and socially acceptable to all but the hardest-shelled churchmen. There were no musical instruments present, and the dancers were considered to be players or marchers. Because of the religious ban against fiddles and other musical instruments, the only music they had was vocal. The music was supplied by one or two brass-throated, leather-lunged leaders, who could beller out thirty verses to "Old Joe Clark" with all the volume of a high-school band. The marchers usually sang with them or joined in on the chorus. An imaginative singer, just like an imaginative square dance caller, invented as he sang, pulling verses from one tune and modifying them to fit another, and changing names and situations to fit his own particular time and place.

This song-accompanied dance was acceptable also because it was considered a game and not a dance. Although the players marched in rings and reels, they didn't round dance and they didn't dance in squares, which was associated with sinful dancing. Players of the opposite sex kept a safe distance between each other. Crossing hands involved too much exciting proximity, as did waist swings, but hand swings were acceptable. At a Josey party the intricate maneuvers originated by an inventive square dance caller gave way to simpler marches and hand swings, but none of the vitality was lost. Josey is just as energetic a form of amusement as fiddle dancing, and in the faster pieces there is much foot stomping, prancing, yelling, and laughter.

"Old Joe Clark" is more popular and has more verses than any other play party song that I know about, and it is sung to a ring game of the simplest sort. Partners join hands and form a big ring. At large parties, especially those that are held in the yard or on the road in front of the house, these rings can be forty or fifty feet in diameter. When the singing starts, the players hold hands and march to their right. At the chorus, the boys turn back and begin weaving through the line of girls, swinging the first by the left hand, the second by the right, and so on until they reach their partners. Then they promenade through a verse and chorus and form the ring again. For variety's sake the boys change partners by dropping back to the girl behind them and then swing their ladies twice the second time around. With as many verses as most leaders know and can make up, "Old Joe Clark" can last a long time.

Joe Clark was a Virginian (and a preacher's son, so the song says) who fought in the War of 1812. In recognition of his services the state gave him a claim in the Blue Ridge Mountains. Clark settled there in 1815 and established the family name by siring twenty-four children. His influence over his family and the surrounding country soon made him the man to be reckoned with. From an imposing figure of a man, dominating a large hunting ground, he grew to be a legendary character with a song to continue his fame. The song is a teaser, however, as it gives few details about Joe Clark.

Old Joe Clark
Old Joe Clark was a preacher's son;
He preached all over the plain.
But the only prayer that Joe Clark knew
Was "high, low, Jack, and the game."

Chorus
Fare thee well, old Joe Clark,
Goodbye, Betty Brown,
Fare thee well, old Joe Clark,
I'm gonna leave this town.

I went down to Joe Clark's house;
He let me in the door.
He slept on the feather bed
And I slept on the floor.

I went down to Joe Clark's house;
He was eating supper.
Stumped my toe on the table leg
And rammed my nose in the butter.

I went down to old Joe Clark's,
Thought I'd go a-hunting.
I fell down and broke my neck
And came back home a-grunting.

Old Joe Clark he built a house
Sixteen stories high.
And every story in that house
Was filled with chicken pie.

Old Joe Clark has two girls,
Both are dressed in red.
Every time I see those girls
I wish my wife was dead.

I went down to old Joe Clark's,
Found he wasn't home.
Got in a fight with the oldest girl
And broke her tucking comb.

Joe Clark had a brindle cow
And she was muley born,
But it took a jaybird twenty years
To fly from horn to horn.

Old Joe Clark he had a mule.
His name was Morgan Brown.
Every tooth in that mule's head
Was twenty inches round.

> Old Joe Clark he killed a man,
> Killed him with his knife;
> I'm sure glad he killed that man
> 'Cause now I'll get his wife.

Old Joe Clark, for all his wealth and influence and dubious fame, evidently gained his notoriety as a result of a mean disposition rather than any enduring contributions to his society. One verse that is nearly always sung sums up the song's general attitude toward its hero.

> Old Joe Clark is dead and gone.
> He's gone down to hell.
> He made me wear a ball and chain
> Which made my ankle swell.
>
> (or)
>
> Old Joe Clark is dead and gone.
> I hope he's doing well.
> The last time I saw the man
> He was going down to hell.

If there is a common meeting ground for Texas singers it is in religious music. I don't mean just any religious music, but the old, traditional songs of our faith and of our fathers, and songs that were as much a part of our raising as the fire-and-brimstone preachers who helped nail them down in our memories. If there is a particularly traditional place for the sound of those old songs, it is under a brush arbor that provided some relief from the heat of a tin-roofed church house during the summer's Sunday sermons and revivals, protracted meetings, and annual associations. The brush arbor was also the center of all-day singings and dinners on the grounds and the place where modern gospel music spent much of its early life.

The music sung under the brush arbors in the early days of Texas were songs common to the southern Anglo-Saxon traditions, tunes brought over from the old country just a few generations back. Southern frontier preachers took popular tunes — the devil's music — put religious words to them, and sent their prayerful songs soaring to God through the wilderness. Many of these early religious songs were collected in 1844 by B. F. White in the shape-note song book called *Sacred Harp,* and "Sacred Harp" became the name of one kind of early religious music, the ancestor to modern gospel music. But this fasola music was still a long way from modern gospel. The world was harsh for the early settlers who came through the wilderness and survival was

Sacred Harp All Day Singing, Panola County.
Photograph © *Singin' Texas*.

difficult, so most of the songs they sang were mournful and in a minor key and directed the soul's eye across to the other side of Jordan and away from the troubles of this world.

Sweet Rivers
A few more days or years at most,
My troubles will be o'er,
And I shall join that Heav'nly host
On Canaan's peaceful shore.
    My happy soul will drink and feast
    On love's unbounded sea;
    The glorious hope of endless rest
    Is pleasing news to me.

A Sacred Harp song that illustrates the use of a popular folk tune to carry the burden of the sacred words is "Plenary," or "Hark! From the Tomb." This song is still used by some Masonic groups as a funeral dirge and is sung as a death march to the Scottish folk tune of "Auld Lang Syne."

Hark! From the Tomb
Hark! from the tomb a doleful sound
My ears, attend the cry:
"Ye living men, come view the ground
Where you must shortly lie.
    Chorus
    Where you must shortly lie,
    Where you must shortly lie,
    Ye living men come view the ground
    Where you must shortly lie.
Princes, this clay must be your bed,
In spite of all your towers;
The tall, the wise, the rev'rend head,
Must lie as low as ours."
    (*Chorus*)
Great God! is this our certain doom?
And are we still secure?
Still walking downward to the tomb,
And yet prepare no more!
    (*Chorus*)

> Grant us the power of quick'ning grace
> To fit our souls to fly;
> Then, when we drop this dying flesh,
> We'll rise above the sky.
> (*Chorus*)

The religious musical mood changed toward the end of the nineteenth century because the quality of life improved. In the battle between the people and the wilderness, the people had just about won, and their music began to express their joy in the victory and their optimism about life on earth. The tempo quickened and the mournful sounding minor keys shifted to the more positive majors, and religious music began to reflect the popular urban musical styles of the Gay Nineties and the turn of the century. This new, joyous, bouncy mood with a hint of ragtime was the beginning of modern gospel music.

Conventional gospel music became a musical fact in East Texas in the 1920s through the publications and the singing schools established by the Stamps brothers. It became big business in Dallas in 1926 with the foundation of the Stamps-Baxter Music Company. Regular gospel singing conventions with all-day singing and dinner on the grounds became traditional Texas gatherings, and the gospel sound was circulated out of rural East Texas through the South by radio and by the rapid proliferation of imitators of the Stamps Quartet.

The evolution of gospel music since 1926 has been synchronized with the musical and social movements of these last fifty years. Gospel music absorbed all the modern musical sounds at one time or another—jazz, swing, country and western, black rhythm and blues, and modern rock— and it brought into its fold all the musical instruments played by pop artists. It has spread far beyond the rural areas and brush arbors and its Texas origins and has become a popular religious musical medium for all ethnic groups, blacks doing more to integrate it with their musical sounds than any other group.

Academic folklorists label this "folk music" because its origin was some one or more of the anonymous "folk" and it was passed along traditionally in many versions. The music is also country music because Texas through the 1930s was basically a rural state and this music was the traditional music of the rural areas.

The change from folk-country music to modern urban country-and-western music began in the 1920s with the beginnings of mass-produced music on radio and records. Country music began its move into town and was established as a legitimately commercial form of musical ex-

Gospel singers,
Neches Valley Singing Convention, Woodville.
Photograph © *Singin' Texas*.

pression, even if it was not acceptable in the finer urban drawing rooms. The new country commercial musicians of the 1920s and early 1930s, like Gid Tanner and his Skillet Likkers and Vernon Dalhart, had one foot in the old traditional country sounds and the other pointed to the future where they might enjoy commercial success by mixing with the new urban pop sounds growing out of ragtime and jazz.

The first innovator to achieve stardom in the record-radio medium was Jimmie Rodgers, who blended black blues, a yodel, and some jazz with a large measure of hillbilly and became the Father of Country Music. In the mid-1930s Gene Autry became the first influential country singer to put the cowboy western touch on top of the country sound. About the same time Bob Wills and his Texas Playboys were mixing country with western and with modern swing and coming out with western swing. And all the while Roy Acuff and his Smokey Mountain Boys were keeping the old Anglo-Saxon mountain songs and ballads circulating from the Grand Ole Opry in Nashville.

These fairly dramatic changes in country music, brought about by widespread ownership of radios and phonographs, took place during the depression of the late 1920s and the 1930s, when the radio and phonograph were just about the only means of entertainment. Songs and song styles were spread some during that time, but not much. The Saturday western cowboy singers—Gene Autry, Roy Rogers, and the Sons of the Pioneers, among others—sent their own brand of slicked-up cowboy songs like "The Last Roundup" and "Don't Fence Me In" throughout the nation. And the Okies, Arkies, and Texans who dusted out took their music with them in their search for survival in California and in the valleys where some rain fell. But the southern, Texas country sounds remained at home and mainly in the rural areas during the depression years.

Country music, whether Old World or New, always leaned toward hard times and cheatin' hearts, and the depression years were the hardest of times. Poverty broke some of the strongest of family ties, and hard traveling in search of a dollar-a-day job, working "from can to can't," added to the troubles of those hungry years. Honky-tonkin' and honky-tonk music were a short sweet release from the harsh realities, and the music—still country—sang familiarly and realistically of the problems everybody knew.

This small-town-rural music was not only geographically restricted during the 1930s and early 1940s, it was also socially restricted. Townspeople with any claim to urbanity scorned it in favor of Benny Goodman, Tommy Dorsey, and the other great big-band jazz men of the

Country singers,
East Texas Bluegrass Festival, Rusk County.
Photograph © *Singin' Texas*.

Bluegrass banjo.
East Texas Bluegrass Festival, Rusk County.
Photograph © *Singin' Texas*.

day. "City people" didn't pick guitars or play fiddles or sing Stamps-Baxter gospel. That kind of music reflected a past and a poverty that most of them didn't want to think about.

Then the war in Europe began in 1939 and the whole social picture began to change. A farmer making a bare living on his eighty acres found out that somebody was paying a dollar an hour in the shipyards, and it didn't take him long to figure out that he could live better in the city—with paved streets, picture shows, and brick schools—than he ever thought about on the farm. World War II, and the industries that kept it going, signaled the end of the small subsistence farmers. They sold out and took their folks and their music to Houston and Dallas and the Golden Triangle. And they and their kids are still there, living city but thinking and singing country.

Servicemen in World War II took country–hillbilly–cowboy–honky-tonk music out of the South and the Southwest and spread it throughout the United States and the world. If a soldier had one drop of country in him, the songs that complemented his nostalgia were country and honky-tonk—"San Antonio Rose," "No Letter Today," and "Filipino Baby"—and he sang them and played them all over the U.S.A. and the battling world. The first sound after reveille in my barracks at Great Lakes Naval Training Station was a Texas boy yelling, "Turn on the brush music!" and the station that played Ted Daffan, Ernest Tubb, Roy Acuff, and their ilk stayed on all day long.

Honky-tonk singer Ernest Tubb spanned the war years, but the main bridge between the old prewar hillbilly music and the new electrified sound that was to become country and western was Hank Williams, the superstar of the early 1950s. Hank's "Cold, Cold Heart" and "Jambalaya," among many other songs, also closed the gap between country and popular urban music, as Tony Bennett, Bing Crosby, and other pop singers began to include honky-tonk music in their repertoires.

Since the 1950s the music that was to become country and western has put on some strange clothes in order to keep company with all the new musical styles of the last three decades. Elvis Presley, inspired by Hank Williams, began singing hillbilly but moved into a blues-influenced rock style that eventually spawned rockabilly. Rockabilly, country-pop, redneck rock, and the Austin sound were all part of the continuing evolution of a country sound that was hundreds of years old. The popularity—urban as well as rural—of the new country sounds brought international fame to Johnny Cash, Chet Atkins, Willie Nelson, and many others; and the music they played, as different as the

Raising Them in the Tradition.
Photograph © *Singin' Texas.*

A modern country music scene,
Backwoods Beer Bust, Nacogdoches County.
Photograph © *Singin' Texas*.

styles were, within the past decade or so was lumped together and called country and western.

Willie Nelson is not only the leading country-and-western singer today, but his music typifies the continual mixing of the country and urban styles. Willie sings the old, country-sentimental sad songs like "Blue Eyes Crying in the Rain," modern country-and-western kicker music like "Whiskey River," and—to finish the spectrum—he is now singing such urbane numbers as "Blue Skies" with full big-band orchestration. Willie also became the guru of a nation-full of romantic jet-set western wearers, tricolored cowboy booters, and ten-gallon hatters, be-plumed and be-tassled like cavaliers of old. Country kicker became a popular style in clothes and music, and Willie and the other heirs of the country music tradition dominate the radio air waves.

The recent pick-up on country-western styles and Luckenbach, Texas, is not the only thing that has shifted the focus of country music from the backwoods to big downtown business. From the late 1930s on, small towns have been getting smaller and many rural crossroads communities have completely disappeared. Populations have moved like iron filings to a magnet as pulp wood haulers have laid aside their chain saws and moved to the money of the big cities. Ask many Houstonians where they are from and they will tell you "Polk County" even though they've lived in the city for the past thirty years. Their hearts—and their traditions—are still rural. And so is their music, even though its style is as urbanized as they are.

Sometimes a listener is hard put to recognize the old country sound and style in modern country-and-western music, but it is usually there. Honky-tonk angels, hard times, careless love, the basic earthy scrapes people get themselves into: these are the same topics sung about in the folk ballads generations ago. Amplification has not changed that. And the styles and songs of Jimmie Rodgers, Roy Acuff, Hank Williams, and Willie are still the basic ingredients for any country-and-western band. But it all comes together with the strains of an old country fiddle and the guitar's rhythm as the band breaks into "Wild Side of Life." That's classic, whether country or urban.

Country-and-western music is folk music that finally became country music and then moved to town. Transportation is such that not many people live in the country any more. They live in town and commute to their farms and ranches. Or if they do live in the country, the way to town is so quick that their culture is as urban as it is rural. Modern "rural" music is like that road out to the pasture; it ties together the two ways of life, urban and rural. It sings of the soil and an ancient agrarian past in sounds that are as modern and urban as the brick-and-glass honky-tonks where it is played.

I am always amazed when I realize how close Texans are to the rural frontier. With the exception of the offspring of the settlers in the eastern part of the area, most Texans in their middle years are just two generations away from the old buffalo hunters and sod busters who were the first Anglo-Saxons to come to this land. Their grandparents were firsters: first to plow the land, cut the virgin pine, bring in oil fields, open new range. Through this hardy lot the children and grandchildren of this generation of pioneers have touched a piece of history that won't be repeated.

As close as we are — and as sentimental as we are inclined to be about our grandparents — it is difficult not to lapse into romanticizing about them and the past. But there is the other side to pioneering. The present generation is just now recovering from the destructiveness of some of our grandparents. They broke, planted, and exhausted the soil. They plowed and harrowed the dirt loose so that it could blow away during the grasshopper-dry years of the 1930s. They pumped the oil fields so dry that the earth caved in. They killed the game and left scant seed. And a person nowadays has to travel many a mile to see timber areas like the ones they turned into East Texas barrens at the turn of this century.

They came to a promised land that was all bounty and, with no better excuse (and no worse) than the Hebrews had, took it from a people who had held it for centuries. They came to a land of surplus soil, trees, water, and game, and got the idea that all this could never run out, no matter how much they used and wasted. Most of them lived to see what erosion could do, and most of them produced children who nursed the land back to health and strength.

The folk songs that the Texas pioneers sang show what they were, why they did what they did, and how they felt about it. These songs, in a way, are like the old worn-out Georgia stocks that still clutter up the corners of dilapidated sheds and pole barns. Like that old do-it-all plow, the songs are relics of the past, but unlike them, they can't be worn out. They keep popping up here and there, changing some in tune and word every time they come to the surface, but still surviving and still telling us how we feel about ourselves.

Running as a thread through several of the most prominent works in Texas literature is the sense of the land as a measuring reality. The land is often a borderland of conflicting cultures and heritages. Old values of those close to the land are endangered or perishing, and ancient foes become uneasy friends lamenting their lost world and estranged from the immediate. The integrity of land-centered values is affirmed even as the practice of such values is denied. Still absent from Texas literature is a convincing portrayal of the city and of characters whose lives are shaped by their urban context. Such omission from our writing may suggest the impersonal nature of Texas cities. But the fact that city settings remain less well defined may also imply that even in these days of lessening contact with the land as our natural and real estate, Texas writers and perhaps their readers hold the land as touchstone for much of our hope, our faith, and our values.

8
The Landed Heritage of Texas Writing

Betsy Colquitt

Awareness of the land is a reality in Texas writing from its beginnings, and Texas literature continues to draw upon this rural and landed heritage. To the Texas cities in which most Texans now live, Texas writing has been less attentive and, to this time, less successful when attention is so directed. Larry McMurtry has spoken of the "bitter love affair" that he and other Texas writers have had with this heritage; Dave Hickey's *Texas Observer* essay addresses the need to exorcise this elegiac strain.[1] Earlier than these comments are those of Katherine Anne Porter's autobiographically shaped protagonist Miranda, whose reverie concludes "Old Mortality."

> Her mind closed stubbornly against remembering, not the past but the legend of the past, other people's memory of the past, at which she had spent her life peering in wonder like a child at a magic-lantern show. . . . I can't live in their world any longer, she told herself, listening to the voices back of her. Let them tell their stories to each other. Let them go on explaining how things happened. I don't care. At least I can know the truth about what happens to me, she assured herself silently, making a promise to herself, in her hopefulness, her ignorance.[2]

However uneasy Texas writers may find their relation to the voices of this past, artistically sophisticated use of these materials comes only in this century when old farming and ranching ways were perishing or threatened. In its late artistic claim on these ways, Texas literary his-

---

1. Tom Pilkington, *My Blood's Country* (Fort Worth: Texas Christian University Press, 1973), p. 174; Dave Hickey, "Elegy and Exorcism: Texas Talent and General Concerns," *Texas Observer* 58 (Jan. 20, 1967): 14ff.

2. Katherine Anne Porter, *The Collected Stories* (New York: Harcourt, Brace and World, 1965), p. 221.

tory confirms Robert Frost's remarks in "The Gift Outright." In Texas, as elsewhere in America and in other cultures, "The land was ours before we were the land's," and settlement occurred long before the storying and literary enhancing of this pristine land.

> Such as we were we gave ourselves outright
> (The deed of gift was many deeds of war)
> To the land vaguely realizing westward,
> But still unstoried, artless, unenhanced,
> Such as she was, such as she would become.[3]

As John Graves observed of the Fort Worth of his youth in the 1920s, "It was dollar-crass, unscenic, newly sprouted, and short of both local color and what ladies call 'the finer things.'"[4] These "finer things," specifically the arts in their several manifestations, find little nurture in environments too newly sprouted or in cultures only vaguely realized. The domestic order of stable households, like that of Miranda's grandparents, must be writ large in the civic order for the arts to prosper. Through the nineteenth century, architecture was the art most seriously pursued in Texas, and testimony to its successful practice still exists in private houses adapting antebellum and, later, Victorian modes and in the numerous Texas courthouses fashioned from the granite abundant in the region. For the other arts, folk and popular expressions were their primary if not exclusive mode. Limitations on the formal education then available restricted the audience for serious writing, even as stringencies of settling in this new place required most energies. Frederick Law Olmsted, who traveled through Texas in the 1850s, commented on the lack of interest in literature and on the dubious accuracy of contemporary Texas newspapers: "In the whole journey through Eastern Texas, we did not see one of the inhabitants look into a newspaper or a book. . . . One evening I took up a paper which had been lying unopened upon the table of the inn where we were staying, and smiled to see how painfully news items dribbled into the Texas country papers, the loss of the tugboat 'Ajax,' which occurred before we left New York, being here just given as the loss of the 'splendid steamer Ocax.'"[5]

---

3. Robert Frost, *The Poetry of Robert Frost*, Edward Connery Lathem (New York: Holt, Rinehart and Winston, 1969), p. 348.

4. John Graves, untitled essay in *Growing up in Texas: Recollections of Childhood* (Austin, Tex.: Encino Press, 1972), p. 65.

5. Frederick Law Olmsted, *A Journey through Texas or A Saddle-Trip on the Southwestern Frontier* (New York: Dix, Edwards, 1857), p. 117.

Sam Redford.
Photograph by June Van Cleef.

Here as elsewhere, Olmsted's comments blend accurate observation with a tone of condescension. Yet Texas of the 1850s was mainly frontier, and frontier patterns remain durable and powerful aspects of Texas culture. That such patterns help to account for the tardy arrival of a serious Texas literature is probable.

A convenient date to place the beginnings of a Texas literature of a belletristic rather than a popular tradition is about 1930, just a few years after a similar though discrete literary development in the South. Why the South so long delayed or was delayed in developing a distinctive literature puzzles too. Speculations about the South's tardiness sometimes emphasize the Civil War and its aftermath of Reconstruction. For the antebellum South, the artful and perhaps art-fulfilling qualities of plantation life are mentioned, as are the morally and possibly artistically crippling effects of slavery (that the "peculiar institution" did not inhibit the arts in Periclean Athens or Augustan Rome may offer counterargument here). But whatever the worth of such speculations, the fact stands: an original and forceful literary movement in the South waited until the early 1920s to emerge.[6]

Like the South, from which so many Texans had come with their selective memories and shards of culture, Texas experienced a tardy literary blooming. Though plantation ways, the Civil War, and Reconstruction had less potent cultural effects here than in other parts of the Confederacy, other confrontations, wars, and skirmishes required attention, and always through the nineteenth century there was the settling in, the learning to live on the land, sometimes displacing its earlier inhabitants, sometimes accommodating to their presence. If until about 1930 H. L. Mencken's description of the South as "the Sahara of the Bozart" easily fits Texas, sensitivity to this accurate charge about our literary dearth is hardly justified: Texas was newly sprouted, and the arts take a while to root and grow.[7]

Yet nineteenth-century Texas offers a good deal of popular literature and has proved rich hunting for folkloric and regional materials. Popular novels and short stories of the time benefited by audience interest in the new and sometimes exotic subject matter that Texas offered. Mabel Major and T. M. Pearce point out the popularity in the 1840s and 1850s

---

6. See esp. Richard James Calhoun, "The Southern Renascence, 1925–1945," in *A Bibliography Guide to the Study of Southern Literature*, ed. Louis D. Rubin, Jr. (Baton Rouge: Louisiana State University Press, 1969), pp. 47–54.

7. H. L. Mencken, *A Mencken Chrestomachy, Edited and Annotated by the Author* (New York: Alfred A. Knopf, 1949), pp. 184–94.

of the dozens of "novels and books of short stories, many of the nature of juveniles, recounting the exploits of guides, hunters, rangers, and desperadoes of this new frontier."[8] Among these writers of popular fiction were two women: Augusta E. Wilson's *Inez, A Tale of the Alamo* and Amelia Barr's *Remember the Alamo* offer romanticized treatments of historical materials. Poets trying their hand at Texas materials include Mirabeau B. Lamar with his "The Daughter of Mendoza" and R. M. Potter with his "Ode to Texas." By the late nineteenth century, Larry Chittenden's *Ranch Verse* appeared.

Though of limited art, such writings are of interest both for their revelations of contemporary popular taste and for their early probing of literary use of Texas materials. It is perhaps incidentally worth noting that twentieth-century Texas writers have shown little interest in fictional treatment of major events and figures from Texas history. The turn of writers of the Southern Renaissance toward such historical materials (for example, the presence of the Civil War in William Faulkner's fiction and the historical currents of Robert Penn Warren's fiction and poetry) finds little corollary in modern Texas writing.

Of more intrinsic value and interest to Texas writers in this century are various autobiographical writings of the nineteenth century. Journals, travel accounts, chronicles, and letters—all of these literary forms largely free of artistic demands—authentically record the writers' experiences and responses in the Texas of the western frontier. The most noted of nineteenth-century Texas writers is John Crittenden Duval, whose *Jack Dobell: or A Boy's Adventures in Texas* and whose later *Adventures of Big-Foot Wallace* are slightly fictionalized treatments of chronicle-like material. *Jack Dobell* narrates Duval's experience as a survivor of Goliad and *Big-Foot Wallace*, the story of a friend in the Texas Rangers. Though both books are modest artistic achievements, they perhaps justify J. Frank Dobie's citing Duval as "the father of Texas literature."

First-person narratives continue in this century, not only in the work of many collectors of oral materials, such as J. Evetts Haley's recounting of Charlie Goodnight's story, but also in memoirs such as Sallie Reynolds Matthews's *Interwoven* and in the recent collection of autobiographical essays titled *Growing up in Texas*.[9] The value of these many

---

8. Mabel Major and T. M. Pearce, *Southwest Heritage: A Literary History with Bibliographies*, 3rd ed. (Albuquerque: University of New Mexico Press, 1972), pp. 81–82.

9. J. Evetts Haley, *Charles Goodnight—Cowman and Plainsman* (Norman: University of Oklahoma Press, 1949). Sallie Reynolds Matthews's *Interwoven* was first published by the Anson Jones Press in 1936.

autobiographical accounts has been noted by writers such as Elmer Kelton, whose western novels reflect his research in these and other materials, and John Graves, whose *Goodbye to a River* remarks on their worth: "[I]f the general run of folks want to believe that John Wayne and Frank Sinatra and Ricky Nelson and the Gabor girls made drama in the railheads of Kansas, they're going to keep on believing it. Read Andy Adams if you want to see cowhands right; read Teddy Blue Abbot, and Frank Dobie, and the groping-worded, utterly straight tales in *The Trail Drivers of Texas* and J. E. Haley's work on Old Man Goodnight."[10]

What emerges in these first-person accounts or recountings, their muse like Whitman's "installed among the kitchen wares," is the authentic voice of those who worked land and cattle and who knew this life as immediate reality rather than historical thesis or myth. Such postulates about the frontier as Frederick Jackson Turner explored and others later expanded are corralled in the autobiographical accounts of the dogged heroics of the everyday, with these heroics customarily phrased in litotes. Charlie Goodnight's recollections, for example, are consistently understatements, as his remembrance of a "doctoring" episode shows: "If left in, it [the arrow] was certain to kill him [Long Joe Loving], so nothing could be done but take a chance and extract it. The only instrument we had with us was an old-fashioned pair of shoe pinchers. Two strong men held him down and I succeeding in pulling it out.... Young Loving felt sure he would die ... but he fully recovered."[11] Goodnight was contemptuous of most writings about the West, which by his estimate were "a pack of lies," and his own straightforward narrative is persuasive of its truth. Like other first-person accounts, he rarely turns to literary or historical analogues and consistently avoids philosophical and metaphysical rationales. Such focus upon the immediate means that Goodnight and similar narrators are little touched by the romantic synthesis that generally colors nineteenth-century American literature and perhaps contributes to the depiction of the West that Goodnight condemned as "a pack of lies." Elmer Kelton too has noted the tendency of much twentieth-century western writing to "overromanticize" the cowboy "when his life was basically pretty hard and very often lonely."[12] Nor is the grandeur of the American West, which en-

---

10. John Graves, *Goodbye to a River—A Narration* (New York: Alfred A. Knopf, 1960), p. 198.
11. Haley, *Charles Goodnight*, p. 165.
12. Patrick Bennett, *Talking with Texas Writers: Twelve Interviews* (College Station: Texas A&M University Press, 1980), p. 197.

The Landed Heritage of Texas Writing

thralled numerous painters of the last century, given much heed in these accounts. Indeed, purely descriptive materials about nature are sparse, but respect for the natural and recognition of the beauty, power, and intransigence of nature are implicit.

More self-consciously literary and more purely descriptive than is usual in nineteenth-century Texas chronicles is Olmsted's observation of an area near La Grange.

> From Braunfels to the Colorado our road lay over long gentle swells, with an occasional creek of pure water and a patch of shade. The prairies were laughing with flowers in ravishing luxuriance, whole acres of green being often entirely lost under their decoration of blue and purple. Near Bastrop we entered a tedious sandy trace of post oak, a camp which, under our single blankets, I remember as one of the chilliest. To La Grange, a pleasant and busy village, the road keeps the pine-bearing sand, rarely descending into the Colorado bottoms, which are very fertile, and well stocked with old plantations.[13]

More typical of the chronicles is Goodnight's account. "Owing to the danger of Indians and stampede, I always got out of the settlements as soon as possible, for cattle that were scattered were much easier traced on the trail than in the settlements, and the danger of meeting Indians were less. . . . We always tried to reach water before sundown. This gave us ample time to have the cattle filled and everything arranged for a pleasant night. The herd was put in a circle, the cattle being a comfortable distance apart."[14]

Despite inevitable differences in emphases and in the particulars of the chroniclers—Olmsted as visitor, Goodnight as cattleman—common in both observers is the presence of the land with its small settlements. However appraised, these were the realities of Texas until recent decades, and it is hardly surprising that when a serious Texas literature developed, it relied heavily upon this heritage. Indeed, the gathering and use of oral and folkloric remains of this heritage were the lifelong interest of Dobie, and his publications and those of Walter Prescott Webb helped to initiate the Texas literary movement.

In 1929 Dobie first offered his course in literature of the Southwest and published his first book, *A Vaquero of the Brush Country*. Webb's *The Great Plains* appeared in 1931. Roy Bedichek, whose life has some-

---

13. Olmsted, *Journey through Texas*, p. 357.
14. Haley, *Charles Goodnight*, p. 179.

times been treated with biographical studies of his friends Webb and Dobie and whose book *Adventures with a Texas Naturalist* merits his description as our regional Thoreau, published his first book in 1947 and thereby stands apart from these Texas literary beginnings.

Dobie and Webb were fortunate in finding early the subjects and genres that remained lifelong interests: Dobie as regionalist and folklorist, Webb as historian of the West. Both found publication for their writings within as well as outside Texas. Both men enjoyed long and productive professional lives. For better or worse—and opinion vigorously divides on this point—Dobie became famed as the quintessential Texas writer, and his strong regional stress served to define Texas writing for several decades. As with Frost as The American Poet, Dobie by his looks and demeanor helped to popularize this Texas role as much perhaps as did his many books. Recent writings about Texas letters have intensely argued both for and against Dobie and the effects of his regional stance.[15]

Dobie's attitude toward the regional was not static, and the more embracing sense of history that Webb's second major study, *The Great Frontier,* shows finds correspondence in Dobie's measurement of the regional in the later part of his career. Tom Pilkington has compared changes in Dobie's attitude as shown in passages in the 1942 and 1952 editions of his *Guide to the Life and Literature of the Southwest.*

> In the first edition the author affirmed the necessity for Southwesterners to be versed in their own literature. He went further: he wrote that, if the Southwest had produced no literature at all, it would be more profitable for an inhabitant of the region "to go out and listen to coyotes singing at night in the prickly pear" than to read Cotton and Increase Mather, Jonathan Edwards, Anne Bradstreet and "other dreary creatures of colonial New England who are utterly foreign to the genius of the Southwest." But by 1952 his attitudes and emphases had changed considerably. He allowed the above statement to stand, but he added to the revised edition of his bibliography "A Preface with Some Revised Ideas," in which he said in part: "Hundreds of books listed in this *Guide* have given me pleasure as well as particles for the mosaic work of my own books; but, with minor exceptions, they increasingly seem to me to explore

---

15. See Larry McMurtry's "Ever a Bridegroom—Reflections on the Failure of Texas Writing," *Texas Observer* (Oct. 23, 1981): 1ff. Subsequent issues of the *Observer* include numerous responses to McMurtry's essay.

only the exteriors of life. . . . In short, these books are mostly only the stuff of literature, not literature itself, not the very stuff of life, not the distillations of mankind's 'agony and bloody sweat.' . . . Good writing about any region is good only to the extent that it has universal appeal."[16]

Though it is debatable whether Dobie's stay in England during World War II was crucial in reshaping his attitudes, most students of literature will agree with his revised judgment: regional literature per se is most often the "stuff of literature," and literature of wide, perhaps universal, appeal requires an artist rather than a chronicler. Katherine Anne Porter's first collection of short stories, *Flowering Judas,* has best claim to being the first distinguished fiction by a Texas writer.

With John Graves's praise of Porter as the "most realized artist that has ever come out of the state," few would disagree. Nor is disagreement possible with his qualification that "it's hard to say whether you should call her a Texas writer. Her important stuff has a Texas background to it, but she has certainly never wanted to identify herself with the state particularly." Porter's nonfiction offers at least partial support to the claim that historians and critics of the Southern Renaissance make upon her writing. "I am the grandchild of a lost war," she writes, "and I have blood-knowledge of what life can be in a defeated country on the bare bones of privation."[17]

Yet if like her Miranda she was a grandchild of the Old South, she was a child of Texas. Despite her ambivalence about her birthplace and its literary traditions, both her biography as well as fiction and nonfiction justify her being claimed and honored as a Texas writer and as the first fiction writer who met Dobie's criteria of universality and of art. Her unease about the emerging literary community in Texas may have come by her recognition of the excesses of regional stress and of the artistic dangers inherent in this emphasis. Her character and personality also played their parts in her reservations, as do the characters and personalities of others who were comfortable in the Texas literary community.

Porter's essays, however, generously acknowledge her Texas past. Remarkable among these is "*Noon Wine*: The Sources," one of a small

---

16. Pilkington, *My Blood's Country,* pp. 186–87.
17. Bennett, *Talking with Texas Writers,* p. 85; Katherine Anne Porter, "Portrait: Old South," *The Collected Essays and Occasional Writings of Katherine Anne Porter* (New York: Delacorte Press, 1970), p. 160. See also Joan Givner, *Katherine Anne Porter: A Life* (New York: Simon and Schuster, 1982).

number of excellent writings on the creative process of the fiction writer. What she elsewhere calls her "usable past" derives from her growing up in Texas and from those she knew or was aware of in her early years.

> Someone asked me once where I had ever heard that conversation in "Noon Wine" between two men about chewing tobacco—that apparently aimless talk between Mr. Hatch and Mr. Thompson which barely masks hatred and is leading toward a murder. It seems that I must have heard something of the sort somewhere, sometime or another; I do not in the least remember it. But that whole countryside was full of tobacco-chewing men, whittling men, hard-working farming men perched on fences with their high heels caught on a rail, or squatting on their toes, gossiping idly and comfortably for hours at a time. I often wondered what they found to say to each other, day in day out year after year; but I should never have dared go near enough to listen profitably; yet I surely picked up something that came back whole and free as air that summer in Basel, Switzerland, when I thought I was studying only the life of Erasmus and the Reformation.[18]

Vignettes of funeral processions, of callers to her grandmother's house, of "a bony, awkward, tired-looking man, tilted in a kitchen chair against the wall of his comfortless shack . . . blowing away at a doleful tune on his harmonica" are important sources for Porter, as is the natural world she remembers from her childhood.

> This summer country of my childhood, this place of memory, is filled with landscapes shimmering in light and color, moving with sounds and shapes I hardly ever describe or put in my stories in so many words; they form only the living background of what I am trying to tell, so familiar to my characters they would hardly notice them: the sound of mourning doves in the live oaks, the childish voices of parrots chattering on every back porch in the little towns, the hoverings of buzzards in the high blue air—all the life of that soft blackland farming country, full of fruits and flowers and birds, with good hunting and good fishing; with plenty of water, many little and big rivers.[19]

---

18. Porter, *Collected Essays*, p. 473.
19. Ibid., p. 470.

Though Porter's fiction obviously draws on materials other than those provided by "that soft blackland farming country," these Texas materials appear in short stories throughout her career and provide substance for some of her best fiction. Porter's stories with Texas settings support the accuracy of Flannery O'Connor's observation that "what she [Porter] does have aplenty is the ability to make things actual. She can create the sweating stinking life out of anything."[20]

In general, Porter's Texas characters come within two categories: there are transplanted Southerners, with possible similarities to Porter's own family, whose dream is to shape the frontier to their memories of the Southern past and whose descendants would, like Miranda, escape these bonds of heritage. And there are the lower-class country folk, the poor whites and ne'er-do-wells. Though probably too of Southern stock, they have legend neither of the South nor of the frontier to inform their luckless tries at life in Central Texas.

Because "this living background" is familiar to her characters, extended descriptive passages like those in the "Noon Wine" essay are rare in her fiction, which evokes place by incidental though incisive details. Her characters perceive physical setting only as context for their actions, but Porter stories create an unusually credible locus in which "things are made actual." Exactitude of detail conjures for the reader the farm of the Whipples in "He" and the dairy of the Thompsons in "Noon Wine," for example. The Whipples' impoverished farm mirrors other poverties, especially those of love for the son who is "not right," and the coldness, which is a persistent detail, has spiritual counterparts. The disorder of the dairy speaks to other disorders and testifies to Mr. Thompson's convictions about work, both "woman's work" and man's.

For these characters, land and livestock are crucial to their well-being. For the chief characters of the Miranda stories, dependence is less immediately on the natural world than on the world of the family. Though "The Grave" and other Miranda stories that create her childhood importantly use the natural world, domestic settings are more important. From stored-away trunks come photographs, old wedding dresses, and other relics to summon past lives to present harrowing. The adult Miranda of "Old Mortality" seeks in her hopefulness and ignorance to escape this composite of the past—of persons and actions, things and settings.

20. Flannery O'Connor, *The Habit of Being: Letters of Flannery O'Connor*, ed. Sally Fitzgerald (New York: Farrar, Straus, Giroux, 1979), p. 481.

In these Central Texas stories, the land and those who live upon it provide Porter important sources, which she realizes with artistry and authenticity, and her Texas characters belong among the most complex and credible that her fictional gallery presents. To compare, for example, Mr. Thompson's portrayal with the sketch of the Swede Mr. Helton is to recognize that the fullness of Thompson's depiction reflects both aesthetic choices as well as Porter's security in her awareness of her Texas folk. By such characters, Porter warrants comparison to Joyce and his Dubliners and to Faulkner and his Yoknapatawpha genealogies, and with few exceptions, literary critics have affirmed the quality and importance of these portions of Porter's canon.

Even as Dobie's predilections affected Texas letters generally, Porter's initiation of the serious tradition in Texas fiction affected subsequent writers, and important among these effects is her choice of rural materials. Towns and cities of Texas are notably excluded from her fiction, even though she knew such environments in her childhood and in her years as journalist. Yet for her, as for many later writers, the most usable Texas experience proved to be the rural and its people.

The quality of Porter's early writing is the more apparent by comparison to Dorothy Scarborough's *The Wind,* which was published in 1925 and enjoyed a greater commercial success than any of Porter's fiction prior to *Ship of Fools.* To the recent edition of *The Wind* from the University of Texas Press, Sylvia Ann Grider provides a foreword that describes the furor initially occasioned by the novel. Set in Sweetwater, the Scarborough home for a few years during the novelist's youth, *The Wind* is the story of Letty Mason, who comes to live with a cousin and his family. As Letty travels across Texas, she finds that her Virginia background little prepares her for the Texas landscape (mesquites aren't peach trees, for example) and for small West Texas towns. Uninformed about the West, Letty is equally shocked by the harsh land and by the impoverished culture.

Though Wirt Roddy acts as the human agent to destroy Letty's fragile hold on moral order and sanity, her real antagonist is West Texas. The natural world is her menace, and the inhospitality of nature is epitomized by the wind, which she finally associates with her murder of Roddy and with her own self-betrayal.

In a 1926 letter, Scarborough notes the "real origin" of her novel out of her "mother's vivid accounts of her struggles with the climate of the West. . . . So in the back of my mind has been for a long time the purpose to write a story which would show the effects of the wind and sand on a nervous, sensitive, woman of the type not prepared to cope with it . . . and to make sure nobody should take the idea, I hurried up and wrote the novel myself."[21]

Granted that Scarborough's comments come in a letter and that Porter's earlier quoted remarks on her sources are from a carefully developed essay, Scarborough's words obviously lack the perceptiveness and stylistic grace of Porter's, and *The Wind* suffers by comparison with Porter's Texas fiction. Simplistic and polemical, the novel earns little admiration for its art. Yet as Grider points out, the book has historical interest "because it was written by a woman and about a woman" and because its subject of the "parched frontier" was "unusual in the early chronicles of the cattle industry. Furthermore, *The Wind* is one of the first novels to deal realistically with the negative aspects of the great myth of the West."[22] The immediate popularity of the book also directed national attention to Texas writing.

Social and historical actualities that shape the emergence of Texas writing continue to have forceful effects. The size of the state and the large population required for settlement help to account for the presence and the endurance of the frontier heritage, and the developing Texas cities, perhaps because of the rural and small-town origins of most of their denizens, evince small-town qualities even after their population size reaches city proportions. Though the oil discoveries of the 1920s altered the economic structure of the state and brought other immediate meanings and values to the land, Texas literature has rarely explored such changes, and the older rural uses of the land provide the private heritage of many Texas writers. To list Texas writers whose fiction has been published since about 1940—George Sessions Perry, Tom Lea, Fred Gipson, William Humphrey, William Goyen, Bud Shrake, and Elmer Kelton, for example—is to recognize the persisting dependence on these rural materials. The East Texas world of Humphrey and Goyen necessarily differs from the West Texas of Lea and Kelton and from the Central Texas of Perry's sharecroppers. But central in such fiction is the rural heritage in its meanings to diverse characters.

More surprising is the persistence of this subject matter in recent novels by writers a generation younger. R. G. Vliet and Allen Wier, with their novels of Central Texas in its rural and small-town aspects, exemplify this pattern. So too does a large body of recent small-press publications in Texas. Though lacking the reputation and prominence

---

21. Dorothy Scarborough, *The Wind* (Austin: University of Texas Press, 1979), pp. 8–9.
22. Sylvia Ann Grider, foreword to *The Wind*, pp. 15–16.

of Goyen, Lea, Humphrey, and others, writers such as Warren C. Miller and James P. White contribute valuably to contemporary Texas fiction. Miller's short-story collection of 1980, *A Small Town Is Best for Waiting*, is set in Lone Star, a composite of Buna and other East Texas towns in which Miller grew up.[23] His characters are often those would-be farmers whose livelihood is newly and uneasily tied to the refineries, which encourage depression-born hopes for a steady job. White's *Birdsong*, his first novel (1977), slightly fictionalizes the Grand Prairie of White's youth. The coming-of-age discoveries of White's protagonist are the more trying because they occur in a small town that claims private experience as public property.[24]

Perhaps because Texas fiction has characteristically turned to materials of declining social immediacy, Texas writers have rarely been experimenters with fictional techniques. Of contemporary Texans, only Donald Barthelme, whose fiction is little connected to Texas subjects, explores and works within post-modernist fictional modes.

As yet, the achievements and abundance of Texas fiction find no parallel in drama and poetry by Texas writers. Summer theatricals at places like Albany and Canyon have for some years presented West Texas as pageantry, and Larry King's musical *The Best Little Whorehouse in Texas* successfully commercializes another Texas lore, but playwrights remain few, in Texas as in contemporary American writing generally. Preston Jones's *Texas Trilogy* stands as the most distinguished example of drama using Texas materials, and that his plays draw upon the rural, small-town sources fictional writers have long employed reinforces the thesis of the persisting presence of these sources for our native writers.

Though a serious tradition of poetry in Texas is also recent, contemporary Texas poets are many, and their writings are lively. Here too, the Texas past marks the writings of the most prominent of these contemporary poets. William Barney, whose subjects reflect his roots in north central Texas, knows this region by persons who have shaped the patterns and values of this locale. Traditionalist in poetic methods, Barney is inevitably compared with Frost. His four collections, published over two decades, confirm his continuing interest in Texas subjects.[25]

23. Warren C. Miller, *A Small Town Is Best for Waiting and Other Stories* (Athens, Ga.: Climate Books, 1980).
24. James P. White, *Birdsong* (Providence, R.I.: Copper Beach Press, 1977).
25. Barney's collections from the 1950s are *Kneel from the Stone* and *Permitted Proof.* Prickly Pear Press issued *The Killdeer Crying* in 1977, and in 1982 Thorp Springs Press published *A Little Kiss of the Nettle.*

Important too in Texas poetry is Walter McDonald, whose reputation, like that of Barney, extends well beyond this region, yet McDonald's several poetry collections point to an increasing interest in Texas materials. McDonald's Texas, of Lubbock and the high plains, provides the immediate reference for some of his best poems.[26]

The most prominent of contemporary Texas writers remain, however, those whose works are in prose, and with little debate the best known and most highly regarded among these writers are acknowledged to be Larry McMurtry and John Graves, both of whom have explored rural Texas materials. Though McMurtry is a distinguished essayist and Graves an accomplished writer of short fiction, McMurtry is chiefly identified with the novel and Graves with his special brand of nonfiction prose.

Patrick Bennett remarks that McMurtry's Texas is "recognizably that of Dobie, Kelton, and Lea, but the time is fifty to one-hundred years later."[27] Predictably perhaps, McMurtry's treatment of ranching and of Thalia, the fictive town suggesting his native Archer City, is often elegiac and nostalgic, especially in his early novels. *Horseman, Pass By, Leaving Cheyenne,* and *The Last Picture Show* are structured around the conflict between old values shaped by frontier ways and new values that in their materialism and selfish emphases betray old and honorable patterns. The conflict is most explicit in *Horseman*, McMurtry's first novel, which shows the grandfather Homer Bannon and his stepson Hud battling before the innocent and awakening protagonist. Though Lonnie knows that with his grandfather's death "nobody would slow Hud down," Lonnie anachronistically holds to old values, though his appreciation fails to ensure their enduring and Hud's energies forecast their demise. And like characters in McMurtry's later novels, Lonnie finds himself displaced in the contemporary.

Such alienation also occurs in McMurtry's fiction in which the city, often Houston, is primary. His principal characters generally come from ranching and small-town backgrounds to an urban setting in which the physical world is only restrictive and mainly ugly, and an axiological contest is inchoate. For Danny Deck, protagonist of *All My Friends Are Going to Be Strangers,* the city is his setting, but the "only good

---

26. McDonald's poetry collections since 1976 include *Caliban in Blue* (Lubbock: Texas Tech University Press), *One Thing Leads to Another* (New Braunfels, Tex.: Cedar Rock Press), *Anything, Anything* (Seattle, Wash.: L'Epervier Press), *Working against Time* (N. Hollywood, Calif.: Calliope Press), and *Burning the Fence* (Lubbock: Texas Tech University Press).

27. Bennett, *Talking with Texas Writers,* p. 9.

things" in his second novel—his treatment of Granny and Old Man Goodnight—come from his ranching past. *All My Friends* concludes with Danny's Prospero-like drowning of his book, with his literally submerging the manuscript into the Rio Grande, and his reverie following this action ends the novel. "I looked up the river north and west, to where the Sorrows lay beneath the same pale stars. A hole opened in the night, and I didn't see the great scenes anymore, the Old Man riding, the Old Woman standing on the ridge, the wild scenes from the past that I usually saw when I was walking some border on my own at night. Maybe that was over. All I saw through the hole in the night were the bright windows of the hospital, yellow in the Houston drizzle."[28] The reverie is of course a blessing of the past and of the future, which has little to do with the world of Old Man Goodnight and grandmothers.

More than most contemporary writers, McMurtry has spoken and written on his own writing and on the writings of others among his contemporaries with connection to a Texas milieu. Of his own career, he comments:

> Obviously in the first three [novels] there's the large social action that I observed as I grew up, which was the move off the land toward the cities and the gradual disintegration of the rural way of life. . . . The first three books attacked that theme from a country and small-town perspective, and the next three attacked it from the perspective of people who have left the country and found themselves in the city, a sort of transitional generation. I think that *Horseman, Leaving Cheyenne* and *The Last Picture Show* have a common concern. The next three do too—*Moving On, All My Friends,* and *Terms of Endearment.* The last book, *Somebody's Darling,* is apart from that. I finished that movement so far as I'm concerned. I don't think I'm going to write about that anymore, at least not for a while. I'm not quite sure what I will have my say about next.[29]

Like Porter's Miranda, McMurtry has sought to allay this past in his early novels and, the past dispelled, is able to turn his talents to other materials. McMurtry's comments about Texas writing, including his own fiction, strongly support the necessity of such a turning. Yet like Danny

---

28. Larry McMurtry, *All My Friends Are Going to Be Strangers* (New York: Simon and Schuster, 1972), p. 285.
29. Bennett, *Talking with Texas Writers,* p. 27.

Deck, McMurtry compels by his authentic treatment of materials drawn from the "great and wild scenes" of this past when challenged in the inhospitable present, and despite McMurtry's arguments to the contrary, his characters born only of the present often lack the resonance that requires the reader's belief.

John Graves, with his shift from city to country life, reverses the transition of characters in McMurtry's most recent novels. Born in Fort Worth and resident for several years in New York City and in places abroad, Graves returned to Fort Worth, and briefly to teaching, during the 1950s. For more than a decade, he has made his home on a hardscrabble farm near Glen Rose. Graves's reputation as writer is supported by several works of short fiction, of which "The Last Running" is the most notable, and most importantly by his several nonfiction books, of which *Goodbye to a River* and *Hard Scrabble* enjoy the most acclaim.

In these latter two books as well as in *From a Limestone Ledge*, a collection of essays first published in *Texas Monthly,* Graves responds sensitively and judiciously to places, people, history, and the changing ways that his writings record. Like McMurtry, Graves sometimes evokes nostalgia, yet his view is determinedly realistic: If engineers with dreams of dams lamentably modify rivers, so too a century of injudicious farming and pasturing wipes out what once—and naturally—was rich and flourishing land along the Paluxy and the Brazos and elsewhere. Graves aims his particulars toward the universals, and his aim is made accurate by his realism as well as by his knowledge and wit. Like Bedichek, he is a naturalist; like Dobie, he is steeped in the regional and its lore; like Webb, he measures against history, and he measures too against a good deal more.

The people created in Graves's nonfiction have the authenticity of fictional creations of Porter and later Texas writers. And best among Graves's characters is Graves himself. As persona, Graves speaks with Horatian clarity and, like Horace, affirms the virtue and interest of the rural. Like Thoreau, with whom he, like Bedichek, has been compared, Graves as persona links the disparate subjects of his nonfiction into a graceful whole. Among other artistic achievements, the easy and pliant movement of Graves's prose suggests his masterful handling of structure and style.

For Graves and for most other contemporary writers who can be immediately associated with a Texas literature, the rural as heritage and as present reality continues to be a vital subject and to exert a tenacious hold on current writing. Whether writers should be labeled as Texas

Texas Still Life, Redford House.
Photograph by June Van Cleef.

writers presents another sort of question, and examination of the merits and restrictions implicit in such literary dependence on a now-vestigial pattern of life raises more issues. But to survey writing out of Texas is to encounter the powerful presence of these rural materials, and with Texas writing, as with all works of art, judgment has be to made upon such works as exist and not upon the postulated works that critics may envision.

A survey of our writing makes clear that, to this time, Texas literature lacks a convincing portrayal of the contemporary Texas city and of characters whose lives are shaped primarily by their urban context. Perhaps the recency of the development of Texas writing, the accidents of biography that connect present Texas writers to the rural, and the newness of Texas cities partially explain such omission in this body of writing. As McMurtry has noted, Texas writing has not produced the equivalent of a Dickens or a Balzac to present contemporary experience in a consistently urban reference.[30]

Whatever truth such speculations carry, contemporary Texas writing affirms the importance of the rural, and for the most representative Texas writers, this landed heritage proves a more compelling subject than does the contemporary city. Of the puzzle and mystery of the connections—literary and not—between present and past, John Graves writes with understanding and compassion.

> If a man couldn't escape what he came from, we would most of us still be peasants in Old World hovels. But if, having escaped or not, he wants in some way to know himself, define himself, and tries to do it without taking into account the thing he came from, he is writing without any ink in his pen. The provincial who cultivates only his roots is in peril, potato-like, of becoming more root than plant. The man who cuts his roots away and denies that they were ever connected with him withers into half a man. . . . It's not necessary to like being a Texan, or a Midwesterner, or a Jew, or an Andalusian, or a Negro, or a hybrid child of the international rich. It is, I think, necessary to know in that crystal chamber of the mind where one speaks straight to oneself that one is or was that thing, and for any understanding of the human condition it's probably necessary to know a little about what the thing consists of.[31]

30. McMurtry, "Ever a Bridegroom," p. 9.
31. Graves, *Goodbye to a River,* p. 145.

Even a highly selective and fragmentary sampling of Texas folk groups yields a unique portrait of Texas as a place apart—an island in the land. The view from the other side of the furrow continues to enrich or to defy the mainstream rural life in Texas. Continuity of conflicting cultures and heritages is assured by the fact that we are, once again or as ever, a land of migrants. As farmworkers flee from the fields of Vietnam, Mexico, or Pakistan and settle in the communities along the Trinity, the Brazos, and the Rio Grande, their experience will add other dimensions to the image of Texas. Even though the open fields are all occupied, these folk groups will nudge or jolt as they, too, assume their dual identification as Texans. They, too, will mingle among us as our sample groups have done.

9
From the Other Side of the Furrow: A Folk-Group Sampler

Dona B. Reeves-Marquardt, Karl Weigand, Joe S. Graham, and Joseph Wilson

The wise writer backs away from Texas, in the knowledge that it has been analyzed, observed, organized, illuminated, explained, probed, poked, and all but branded by the best and the worst of the lot. Describing Texas is a risky business, at best, because of its clichés: its mythic proportions, its troublesome familiarity, its awesome past, and its cantankerous present. It is an ill-tempered subject that won't stand still, won't be counted, can't be tamed, has all the stability of quicksilver and as many facets as a sphere. But anyone who has ever been to Texas, even for a short visit, becomes an expert and expects to share an accumulated enlightenment with others. Furthermore, writers seem never overwhelmed enough by any topic to retreat. We go on examining, defining, searching. Here we take the risk, possibly because Texas, the land, is now mapped and settled, and we still have the need to discover.

As stage director Lee Abraham wrote in a program note introducing a brace of Texas plays, "When we dreamed ourselves large, we dreamed ourselves as Texans." Such are its heroes in the pulp novels, the epic western movies, and the television soap operas. A topic such as the rural scene limits us to a back forty of Texas and has little if anything to do with heroes, but the ground here is also shifty, even when we strike such fences as rural politics, rural women, and rural habitats. Each post would have ideally multiple folk group braces, for we tend always to overgeneralize and oversimplify, judging the light from one facet to be the light of the whole, even though warned to weigh the "outsider" carefully as a cornerpost of mainstream culture and cautioned to add regional, gender, and ethnic diversity to any interpretation of a Texan values system or life-style. The task is multidimensional, multicultured, multifarious.

Without entering into a discussion of what an ethnic group is, as contrasted with a "plain Texan," we will use as a working definition any folk group that followed the lure, "Gone to Texas," forced or voluntary, displacing the native American and having some sense of common identity that caused them to perceive themselves—or be perceived by others—as distinctive. Such a definition by its very breadth is dangerous and can lead to every group's being considered a "folk" group, even such a group as the University of Texas alumni chapter in Washington, D.C. A flexible definition, however, has advantages over a more narrowly defined identity, for it allows us all to belong to an ethnic group. The recent *Harvard Encyclopedia of American Ethnic Groups* graciously includes articles on southerners and Appalachians, as well as on Afro-Americans and Zoroastrians.[1]

Aside from the native Americans, every settler in Texas went through —and continues to go through—an immigrant experience, even when moving from one rural region of Texas to another. That experience is perceived in the literature, in the music, and in any variety of expressions and manifestations. Folk culture goes beyond national or racial origin. Each national group, settlers of each geographical region, found its own response to the change from a wagon to a train to a pickup or eighteen-wheeler economy.

Our discovery of the rural Texan must include a consideration of folk groups. Our sampling is small, designed more to arouse than to exhaust, to interpret by reflection rather than to describe historically. We have chosen four groups. Two of them are major folk groups, more or less politically organized and contrasting sharply in a number of ways with mainstream culture: the Brazos Valley blacks and the South Texas Mexican Americans. The remaining two are much smaller groups, the Hurnville Germans from Russia, fiercely aware of their folk identity, and the Wends, no longer preserving their historical origin but adamant in accepting their dual heritage.

We might have chosen any of dozens of folk groups, for most arrivals became farmers in the beginning. Most held landownership as a sacred goal; most had large families simply because that was part of growing up in rural Texas. Unfortunately, landownership did not always lead to financial security, social acceptability, or the upward mobility brought by money, prestige, and education. Forty acres would

---

[1]. Stephan Thernstrom, ed., *Harvard Encyclopedia of American Ethnic Groups* (Cambridge: Harvard University Press, 1980).

neither allow nor support the super-tractor with its air-conditioned cab designed for fenceless expanses. Retreat from cotton to synthetics would neither allow nor support the sharecropper. More work could be accomplished with more machinery; debts and installment payments could lead to greater machinery inventory; land did not beckon to be owned, but to be leased. Younger sons and daughters moved to the city, intermarried with the outsiders of a more uniform society. Sharecroppers might become migrant workers or join the growing percentage of municipal labor force with supplemental income from a few acres. The family homestead of the early 1900s, whether a proud little frame house on the prairie or a private, unplumbed tenant farmer's hovel, gave way to the mobile home, symbol at once of transience and modular conformity.

Fathers and mothers might regret the loss of a language, a "simpler" way of life, a more fundamental value system, but they would send their children to a consolidated school, hoping that Friday night football mania in the local community would replace the neighborly fun of the lost ice cream social and that a high-school football star might attain the upward mobility that race or folk group might limit. Folk perception gives way to a degree, but only to a degree, to something else akin to a regional or community identification. Social pressures combined with a sense of uniqueness have reinforced and continue to reinforce folk perception, even as that perception changes and no longer reflects what it was in 1880 or in 1910.

The transition from tenant farmer with a mule and wagon to mechanized agribusiness aiming for sterilized soil that can be replenished chemically has left nowhere more heartbreak than among the South Texas Mexican Americans. Early land records attest to prevailing landownership—many of the original land titles of the state of Texas were held by Spanish-surnamed Texans. Mexican Americans were the first to settle here, and they named the rivers and towns. "The South has the Civil War and slavery as its unique heritage; the Southwestern motif is distinctly Spanish. The Indian occupies the tragic center of Southwestern history and fiction, but it is the Spanish culture that marks the area with its particular regionalism. Spanish words are a part of Southwestern language; Mexican food is almost as pervasive as pizza and hamburgers. . . . The Indian was obliterated; the Chicano merely went underground."[2]

Mexican Americans lost their land, or at least the vast acreage they

---

2. Max Apple, ed., *Southwest Fiction* (New York: Bantam, 1980), p. xvi.

once held. They became tenant farmers, but when mechanization expanded and cotton was no longer chic, they turned their knowledge of land and skills of harvest to the migrant trail. Home was still Texas; hope was still a piece of land, a garden in a small town, or an acre or two at its edge. In spite of more or less rigid social, economic, and political exclusion, they asserted their culture and self-worth in their language, their music, and their food. The *vaquero* became the model for the Texan allomorph of a cowboy. Even the Longhorn was basically Spanish.

If retreat from a cotton economy and the growing industrialization deprived the tenant farmer of livelihood and homestead, the developments of the first half of the twentieth century drove many South Texas Mexican Americans into small towns, but these changes did not turn Mexican Americans away from agriculture. Neither did many abandon Texas for more profitable work in the big cities of the North and East. More often, they became migrant laborers, following the harvest trucks and the markets, but most returned to Texas after the harvest.

Today, their situation resembles the old European farm-village system in which the farmer lives, buys, and worships in the village and travels from his house to his fields each day to tend his crops. Rural Mexican Americans may, of course, live on the land they till; just as often, they live in a small town. Wherever they live, they still supply most of the work force for Texas agriculture. Indeed, as we shall read in the following essay, it seems that Mexican Americans in the past fifty years have been a more stable element in the shifting population of this part of Texas than the Anglo-Americans. Whatever the condition of their homes, they are compelled by a mysterious folkloric urge to own the ground it is built upon. On the one hand, it may have to do with the sun's ripening the fruits of Texas before it ventures northward; to an outsider, however, it might seem that the Mexican American harvesters first reap at their doorsteps, taking care of Texas homeland before setting out on the migrant trail.

If Texas cities are new, barely unwrapped from their expressways, rural South Texas remains old in its core. Flocks of tourists swarm through the Winter Garden area every winter; military bases alternate with truck farms, fishing ports, endless ranchland, the packing houses. "Some inhabitants have not even learned to eat Mexican and wear cowboy boots. But they will. The superficial will point to the central, the Spanish heart and the frontier soul of the area. In such ways do manners aspire to the universal."[3]

3. Ibid., p. xix.

Bedroom with altar.
Photograph by June Van Cleef.

The South Texas Mexican American
Karl Weigand
Translated by Ingeborg R. McCoy

Rural South Texas can hardly be imagined without the Mexican Americans because they are the main labor force in various agricultural enterprises. Villages and small towns with names like Santa Rosa, Zapata, La Gloria, Agua Dulce, and Rio Hondo attest to the presence of this ethnic group. These places are characterized by the Mexican-American life-style and culture: extended families living in small homes, little neighborhood stores selling *cabrito* and displaying *tortillas* and *pan dulce,* small gardens overflowing with flowers, cars and trucks displaying on the dashboard a figurine representing the Virgin Mary, Low Riders parading their sumptuous cars, and at every street corner the Tex-Mex dialect heard in animated discussions. Many Mexican Americans of the Southwest are migrant farmworkers following the harvests in Texas and in the northern United States.

Today, the Mexican Americans continue to form a rather cohesive group, while outsiders, namely Anglos, frequently perceive them in common, stereotyped notions and ideas. This study illuminates two pervasive aspects of the Mexican-American community—segregation and home ownership—two facets about which the average reader may have only incomplete knowledge or differing impressions.

It is difficult to obtain a good overview of the history of the "Mexican migrants" because of the abundance of studies. During the past few years, dozens of reports on migrants have been published by various federal, state, church, and private institutions that have attempted to better the destitution of the migrants through so-called poverty programs. My own studies were, by necessity, limited by time and space, and so I concentrated on an empirical investigation for which only a few prior statistics existed. They were conducted in 1975 and 1978; earlier studies from 1950–51 and 1968 enabled me to make certain comparisons. The problems of the Mexican Americans can be understood only against their cultural background. Their history and current problems are probably well known in the United States, but several facets of their situation were especially noteworthy to this German visitor.

To begin, I shall examine the segregation and differing life-style of Mexican Americans during the recent past in San Marcos, Hays County, and Dilley, Frio County. Spatial segregation and the distinctive life-style of the Mexican American were for many years after World War II facts that were rarely discussed. San Marcos, a traditional, small college town, presents a good example. At the close of the 1960s, every third inhabitant was a Mexican American; in 1951, 57 percent of the Mexican-American families were migrant workers; and even in 1968, one-third of the Mexican-American population still followed the harvests in various regions of Texas and the United States, to return only during the winter months to their home base in South Texas.

The sections of San Marcos where the Mexican Americans lived were almost hermetically separated from those inhabited by Anglos. Naturally, the migrants settled only within the residential section of their Spanish-speaking compatriots. In 1968 I classified all of the 3,500 houses of the town according to their condition: substandard, bad to average, average to good, and good to very good. The result demonstrated a sharp contrast between the Mexican-American barrios and the Anglo sections of town because the barrios were part of the urban poverty areas, as were the black sections. A survey conducted during the General Neighborhood Renewal Project at that time revealed 314 family homes without sanitary facilities — 310 of the families were Mexican American. Needless to say, during relocation that was necessitated by new construction in 1960–62, 65 families connected with the college avoided moving into the barrio. After all, at the college, which had been part of the town for nearly half a century, there were very few Mexican-American professors and students.

The Mexican Americans lived outside the mainstream, their lifestyle completely different from that of the Anglos. This fact became apparent in a study investigating the mobility of the two ethnic groups. During the 1960s San Marcos changed from rural college town to small city when a wave of new people arrived from far beyond the Texas borders. Just as in other developing Texas cities, mobility of the Anglo residents became the rule rather than the exception. In 1968 the new suburbs of San Marcos had an Anglo population, two-thirds of whom had lived less than eight years in the city, and only every seventh person had been a resident for more than twelve years.

The reverse was true of the Mexican-American population: 83.6 percent had been citizens of San Marcos for more than twelve years, and every third person had lived in the town for more than twenty-eight years.[4] During more than half of the year the small houses of the migrants were closed and the school in their area had low attendance,

---

4. Karl Weigand, *Stadtgeographische Studien in Südwesttexas und ausgewählte Untersuchungen zur Mobilität der Spanisch sprechenden Wanderarbeiter* [Geographical Studies of Towns in Southwest Texas and Selected Investigations about the Mobility of Spanish-Speaking Migrants] (Wiesbaden: Steiner Verlag, 1973), pp. 84–85.

for the children went with the parents to help with the harvest.[5] Both of the population groups were mobile, but the mobility of the Mexican American was special since it was seasonal and because, as a rule, these migrants all returned to their home base.

The barrio represented a completely homogenous group differing from the Anglo group even in the shopping habits of the people. The Mexican Americans bought only in the small neighborhood stores where Spanish was spoken and where the "confusion" of the big supermarket could be avoided. The Anglos, however, were not satisfied with what the small stores of the city offered; rather, they met their greater consumer needs through purchases in Austin and San Antonio. A study of 1968 revealed that 75 to 80 percent of the Anglos but only 10 to 15 percent of the Mexican Americans made such shopping trips. In 1968 the small city of San Marcos still offered the typical picture of a segregated society, an image that then characterized most South Texas towns.[6]

During the last decade, the situations of many of the Mexican Americans in the United States have changed in a way that former generations would have never even dared to dream of. Just as remarkable as the changes in political participation and activism is the new level of education apparent in the younger Mexican-American generation. As in the entire state of Texas, San Marcos also offers complete schooling for all Mexican-American children, even for the migrants, whose children under the age of sixteen now remain at school while their parents go north for the harvests. Thus, the fluctuations in school attendance apparent during the years just following World War II are now unthinkable. No difference in school attendance exists any longer between Mexican-American and Anglo children; the higher dropout rate during high school, however, is still a Mexican-American phenomenon. Nevertheless, Mexican-American students are very much in evidence on the campus of the big university, where they now constitute 18 percent of the entire student population. Political participation by and educational opportunities for Mexican Americans are new and positive developments.

It is doubtful, however, whether ethnic segregation has disappeared with such changes. Now, as before, exclusively Mexican-American resi-

---

5. Karl Weigand, *Das amerikanische Schulwesen in San Marcos, Texas* [The American School System in San Marcos, Texas], Lehrerprüfung [Thesis] (Hessen, 1951).
6. Weigand, *Stadtgeographische Studien*, p. 112.

dential sections, or barrios, exist. The political involvement of Mexican Americans in the administration of the city, as well as their activities in other institutional organizations, does not compensate for the fact that, even at the close of the 1970s, the Rotary and Kiwanis clubs—surely representative of the structure of civic society—still did not have a single Mexican-American member.

Dilley, a small town in Frio County, is situated in the Winter Garden area, where, as in the Rio Grande Valley, the Spanish-speaking population exceeds that of the Anglos. The town itself had about twenty-four hundred residents in 1975; 70 percent were Mexican Americans, and of these, every third person was a migrant worker. In Dilley, just as in San Marcos, I categorized all of the 632 homes in the town's residential center according to their condition; I included sixty-six trailers. The results showed that the poor housing in the northeastern part of town was inhabited almost exclusively by Mexican Americans (60 percent of the houses); the "good" Anglo section on the west side of the railroad tracks accounted for 25 percent of the homes. Only 15 percent of the homes are located in the so-called mixed section where both ethnic groups reside.[7] The most pertinent factors of the study are the following: in the barrio, each third house can be called substandard, whereas in the Anglo section only each twelfth house is substandard. Conversely, every third house in the Anglo section is "good and better," but only every tenth Mexican-American home can be classified as such. Only in the small mixed area, where most affluent migrants live, is there no great difference in the quality of the homes of the two ethnic groups.

This study reveals the persistence of spatial, ethnic separation well into the very recent past. Segregation—although well known in all metropolitan areas—becomes especially evident—and depressing—in the small South Texas towns. The structure I found in the barrio of San Marcos is repeated in Dilley: the migrant workers are completely integrated into the Mexican-American group and not separated along socioeconomic lines. Moreover, an obvious characteristic of the barrio in Dilley (and probably in most other South Texas small towns) is the close side-by-side location of good and poor homes. Between them stand many dilapidated shacks and vacant lots overgrown with weeds.

---

7. Karl Weigand, *Chicano-Wanderarbeiter in Südtexas: Die gegenwärtige Situation der Spanisch sprechenden Bevölkerung dieses Raumes* [Chicano Migrants of South Texas: The Contemporary Circumstances of the Spanish-Speaking Population of this Area] (Kiel: Geographisches Institut, 1977), pp. 58–63.

In 1978 many Mexican Americans of South Texas were still migrants following the historical routes, but their socioeconomic circumstances had changed.[8] Many federal and state programs, such as welfare funds, schooling for migrant children, and Head Start programs, allowed mothers to participate in the harvest. Working conditions had changed as well. Risky, temporary work that pays less than the legal minimum wage still is the lot of the illegal alien, but for Mexican Americans with U.S. citizenship such conditions belong to the past. Such changes, however, do not alter the fact that the average Mexican-American migrant still lives in poverty.

I should like to consider next the ties of the Mexican-American migrants to their residences. I believe that we can no longer speak of "free migration" in the strict meaning of the word, but rather of "long-distance commuting." In general, these long-distance commuters are different from other commuters only in the distance their home lies from their job. More and more, commuting to stable though distant work takes place in modern cars, trucks, and vans; 42.5 percent of these, too, are owned by the migrants, according to a study conducted in 1977.[9] If we ask why most Mexican-American migrants regularly return to South Texas, we find that the security within their ethnic group is important to them, as is a shared language and a common life-style. Further, they seem to lack the ability to integrate into the environmentally and socially different industrial regions of the North and Northeast. I have attempted to assess one factor in the large spectrum of ties to South Texas more concretely, namely, the factor of home ownership. The studies of San Marcos and Dilley indicate that most of the time only small houses and small lots are owned. Although the property is often in sad condition, it nevertheless is of great importance to the migrant.

A study conducted in La Grulla, Starr County, reveals some special characteristics of migrant homes. La Grulla is situated on the banks of the Rio Grande, about fifteen miles from Rio Grande City. Mapping the 354 houses in 1975 revealed the old Spanish land distribution pattern along the river: small strips of land, *porciones,* a mile wide along the river and fifteen miles deep. *Porciones* 94 and 95, as well

---

8. Karl Weigand, *Veränderte Lebens- und Migrationsformen der Chicano-Wanderarbeiter in Südtexas auf dem Hintergrund der allgemeinen Situation der Spanisch sprechenden Bevölkerung dieses Raumes* [Different Life and Migration Styles of the Chicano Migrants of South Texas, against the Background of the General Circumstances of the Spanish-Speaking Population of this Area] (Bonn: Deutsche Forschungsgemeinschaft, 1979).

9. Weigand, *Veränderte Lebens- und Migrationsformen,* p. 26.

as part of a bend of the river, still determine the borders of the residential section of La Grulla. Irregular lines characterize streets and property boundaries and present a classic contrast to the typically rectangular Anglo-American settlement patterns with the railroad tracks in the center of town.

Only Mexican Americans live in La Grulla. The study conducted in this community is, therefore, especially valuable for answering the question of how the migrants have merged with their own ethnic group. Once again, the settlement pattern of the Mexican American is confirmed; small groups of good and poor houses, as well as small migrant groupings are found in some sections of town. Principally, however, there is no strict separation between rich and poor inhabitants, and the migrants do not live segregated from the other Mexican Americans. Furthermore, sixty-one abandoned houses on untended lots were encountered, located on all streets. Two-thirds of all houses needed repairs and should be considered bad to average quality. Only every fifth house could be called in good condition, and only every tenth house as very good; the Anglo standard is, on the other hand, average to good. Very good Mexican-American houses were found only outside of the residential sections; the owners were also migrants, but their migrations led them to Mexico to purchase contraband.

Of the houses in La Grulla, 182 belonged to nonmigrants and 172 belonged to migrants; 57.7 percent of the population was residing in these. The migrant families were younger and had more children. Many of the nonmigrants included retired people, and therefore the absolute number of their homes is likely higher. Of the migrants, 58.8 percent lived in homes that can only be called bad to average—a considerable number. And yet, this is 10 percent less than nonmigrants living in such homes. In fact, 30 percent of the local workers, the nonmigrants, are living in substandard housing. In 1975, as many migrants as nonmigrants owned homes in the category termed "good." This fact is especially noteworthy since migrants generally live only on the income that they earn during the harvest season. Even the inclusion of farmers and businessmen in the group of nonmigrants living in relatively good homes does not change the overall statistics from 1975. Some of the migrant homes had been renovated, painted, and maintained well.

When I returned to La Grulla in 1978, many changes had occurred. Numerous houses had been repaired and renovated to such a degree that now half of them could be considered average, and 23 percent of the homes were classified in the good to average category. The trend of 1975 was completely confirmed: the migrants used part of their income to improve their residences. On the other hand, it was clear that the number of substandard houses had also risen; every fifth house belonged in this category.

These manifestations are typical of many other small towns and villages of rural South Texas that continue to be the embarkation point for the migrations. Basically the same situation exists in other rural places as in La Grulla: 20 to 40 percent of the migrants live in very poor housing. They belong to the poorest of the poor, and their conditions are not changing. The rest of the migrants, however, are intent on upgrading their homes. It is difficult to count all of the migrant homes that have received interior as well as exterior renovations, but their large number is obvious. Some of these homes count among the best in the barrio and can withstand comparison with the average Anglo homes. All of this clearly indicates that for many migrants home ownership is of great importance.

For a statistical comparison of migrants who rent with those who own their home, it should be stressed that home ownership frequently cannot be defined clearly. In many cases inheritance rights have not been determined; in other situations taxes have not been paid in decades, making sale of the property highly questionable. A breakdown of renting and homeowning residents in three towns is presented in the accompanying table.

	La Grulla	Dilley	San Marcos
Migrants in 1975 lived:			
in their own homes	70%	63.4%	62.1%
in the homes of children or other relatives who own their home	12	7.7	6.1
in apartments or rent houses	18	28.9	31.8

The large percentage of migrants in San Marcos who rent can be explained partly by state-supported housing programs there for the poor, and partly by the fact that many single migrants live there, as well as families who rent only until they buy their own homes. San Marcos also presents a good case study of Mexican Americans who leave the migrant life when they find work in town or nearby, but who are quick to return to the harvests as soon as working conditions in town deteriorate for any reason. In many cases, some members of the family work in town while other members find work in the harvests. In any event, the parents are not necessarily the first members of the family to cease being migrants because they often lack sufficient education to find work in town. Town jobs fall to their children, whose education has improved greatly. Because they are unskilled, uneducated workers, the older ones must continue to pursue seasonal field labor.

Of course, there are many families who head north in order to find better working opportunities, whether in agriculture or not. But it should be stressed that the majority of these people do not leave completely. They return to their familiar environment and attain a satisfactory economic level, normally evidenced by home ownership. I was able to discover that in 1975, thirty-two former migrants were able to establish their own businesses in San Marcos; these businesses included twelve grocery stores, two bakeries, six filling stations, five construction companies, three taverns, two flower shops, and two body shops. These facts furnish evidence that a significant number of the migrants become well integrated into the social structure of their environment. From records of the health department in San Marcos, it became evident that thirty-seven families had ceased being migrants during the previous five years. Of these families, twenty-two own their own homes; other family members hold the following jobs: five as employees at Southwest Texas State University; two as employees at the Baptist Academy and in the school district; four as workers in small businesses; two as owners of small stores; two as farmworkers in Hays County; and six as construction workers (five in Austin, one in San Antonio). Only one family was living on welfare.

In 1975, an additional investigation of 2,190 migrant households in Laredo demonstrated that home ownership had been attained by only 55.5 percent of those migrants whose family members were born in Mexico. These migrants had parents who had immigrated to the United States—legally or illegally—only recently, in order to join the migrant stream. The study encompassed mainly young families; many of them had been unable, so far, to buy their own home. In the other migrant group, whose family members had been born in the United States, 79.1 percent had attained home ownership.[10]

In summary, about 70 to 75 percent of the Mexican Americans living in South Texas own their homes, according to my studies. As diverse as their life-styles might be in other ways, in this respect, at least, they are no different from the Anglos for whom home ownership is significant. Although the homes differ in quality, they nevertheless constitute a possession that the migrants cherish and to which they return year after year. In this respect, the situation is comparable to that

10. Weigand, *Chicano-Wanderarbeiter in Südtexas*, pp. 64-65.

of the European migrants, the "guestworkers," who come from Mediterranean areas to work, by permit but without change of nationality, in countries like Germany and France.

Finally, even today, 30 percent of the interstate migrants belong to the poorest of the poor. This group is constantly replenished by new illegal immigrants from Mexico. For most of the migrant group, however, the initial faraway job, characterized by extensive travel and unstable working conditions, has turned into regular seasonal work, just as in Europe. The ownership of a home, no matter how small or modest, creates the link to hometown and home state.

The social status of these migrants remains inferior to that of Anglos because of continuing segregation. Many migrants, however, have been demonstrating a new political consciousness; they are contributing to a different situation for the Mexican-American population in the United States. It might be interesting to find out how many of the politically active Hispanic leaders of today are former migrants.

Though conditions were far from happy for Mexican Americans, they held historical and cultural ties with Texas and prided themselves, at least among close acquaintances, in being *tejanos*. Historically, their destiny had been to decline before rising. Their roots have been in Texas since the Republic, or perhaps only since the Mexican revolution; the *tejanos* have felt the inconvenience or the danger of their resemblance to Mexican nationals, and the woe of pursuit by the Texas Rangers. They have resisted assimilation and held to their own special life-style, firmly established in the church, extended family solidarity, and language. Pressures of modern life have brought change, but change has brought little loss of identity.

On the other hand, Texas blacks were never able to share the private self-esteem of the Mexican Americans, since they found themselves from the very beginning totally dependent upon the attitudes of the dominant society. Brought here as slaves, even in freedom they found themselves bound to the land and a standard of living scarcely above subsistence level. Set apart by race and education, they found few employment opportunities beyond farm or domestic service. With the exception of those who migrated to the metropolitan areas of Dallas and Houston, the highest concentration of blacks in Texas remains in the fertile former cotton land of East Texas, in the valleys of the Trinity, the Sabine, and the Brazos rivers, where they still compose a generous portion of the rural labor force.

Ethnic cultural images may not be understood by the dominant society and may simply be overlooked. But appearances that cannot be overlooked have accounted for countless instances of discrimination and persecution. Whites—of whatever national origin—still own the land, and their regard for field help has changed only imperceptibly. "There can be no doubt that the Anglo has a higher regard for the Latin than for the Negro. . . . Anglos regard the Latin field hand as superior to the Negro although they sometimes complain about the unreliability of the Latin."[11] Such unflattering perceptions contribute to continuing isolation, segregation, and cultural misunderstanding. There can be little doubt that the dominant society, the Anglos, have persistently denied the blacks equal education, under the guise of "separate but equal," principles, or enfranchisement, under the aegis of the poll tax. As the political mechanism changed in the 1950s, the apparently harmonious social caste system had to rearrange itself; such shifting brought about a cleft in the familiar value system felt within the black rural community. In the city, the cleft was less manifest because of the inevitable assimilating factors that assail an urban labor force. That is not to imply that urban destitution is no less disillusioning than rural. But it does imply that expressions of frustration differ. Shattered hopes in Houston do not differ much from shattered hopes in Saint Louis, but the Brazos Valley response to political, educational, and social change is different, fastened as it is to soil and seasons.

Rural Blacks in Texas: A Culture in Transition
Joe S. Graham

When black Texans were freed, their lives changed in many ways. Many who were freed migrated to urban areas through the late 1890s, only to find that towns were not the havens they were seeking.[12] Many retreated to rural areas, only to be met with the most blatant forms of prejudice and racism. They returned to the only occupation many of

---

11. William Madsen, *Mexican-Americans of South Texas* (New York: Holt, Rinehart and Winston, 1973), pp. 13–14.

12. James Smallwood, "Black Texans during Reconstruction: First Freedom," *Eastern Texas History: Selections from the East Texas Historical Journal,* ed. Archie P. McDonald (Austin: Jenkins, 1978), p. 133.

them knew, tilling the soil, and to the lands they had once worked as slaves. Some were fortunate enough to buy their own land, but the 1900 census reported that only 8.0 percent of all farms in the five major cotton-producing states were owned by blacks (only 6.5 percent of all farmland). A number of factors may help to account for the situation, but two economic historians have concluded that "the freedman was systematically denied the opportunity to become an independent farmer *because of his race.*" Thus, as they had done in slavery, most rural blacks lived by tilling someone else's land. One historian points out that studies of migration to the north have obscured the fact that "the vast majority of black people were farmers until the Great Depression of the 1930s."[13]

The 1930s saw the beginning of the end of farm labor for most blacks, particularly sharecroppers, as labor-saving technology began taking its toll on the labor force in all of agriculture. In ever-increasing numbers, blacks were forced to leave, as farmers and plantation owners turned more and more to machines. Their fate was shared by whites. The net result was the exodus of 17 million people from U.S. farms.[14] The change came in two stages: from rural farm to rural nonfarm, and from rural to urban. This shift had profound implications for black culture and society.

This brief study is an attempt to examine some of the changes as seen by an elderly black couple now living in Calvert, Texas. Both were born and reared on sharecropper farms and were themselves sharecroppers for much of their lives. They express a point of view held by many rural blacks I have interviewed in East Texas—especially in the Nacogdoches and San Augustine areas—and the Brazos Valley from Calvert to Anderson. Since the data for this paper are based on interviews, the perceived changes in values may be partially due to an idealization of the social rules of the earlier period and to the "good old days" syndrome. But whatever the actual changes, the informants believe that there has been a significant change in the quality of life and in the value system.

Eugene Bullard was born on April 6, 1902, near Lexington, Texas, the second of sixteen children born to Ada McDowell and Chat Bul-

13. Richard Sutch and Roger L. Ransom, "The Ex-Slave in the Post Bellum South: A Study of the Economic Impact of Racism in a Market Environment," *Journal of Economic History* 33 (1973): 131–48; Manning Marable, "The Politics of Black Land Tenure 1877–1915," *Agricultural History* 53 (1979): 142.
14. Richard H. Day, "Economics of Technological Change and the Demise of the Sharecropper," *American Economic Review* 57 (1967): 428.

lard, a freedman. He was reared on a forty-acre farm near Doak's Spring by his grandfather and grandmother; both had grown up in slavery. Eugene moved to Calvert in 1932 and has worked most of his life as a sharecropper and laborer on plantations and farms in the area. Almost eighty years old, he still looks after several dozen head of cattle, fixing fences and doing whatever needs to be done. Both Eugene and his wife are highly respected in the community, by both blacks and whites.

Anna Mae Parks Bullard was born on May 15, 1910, on a farm ten miles from the small East Texas town of Jewett. The fourth of seven children of Adde Brewer and Andy Parks, Anna Mae grew up in a sharecropper's cabin and spent most of her life on a farm. "I ain't been nothin' but a sharecropper all my life," she said. Like Eugene, Anna Mae was reared by her maternal grandparents, both of whom had been slaves. She came to Calvert in 1952. Eugene and Anna Mae were married in 1963, the second marriage for both, their first spouses having died some time earlier. Both have children by previous marriages. At seventy, Anna Mae still cleans house for a white family twice a week and takes in ironing and sewing. Her handmade quilts bring a good price, and she can't keep up with the demand.

The Bullards (and many of my other informants) offered extensive commentary about changes they have observed in their own culture over the past seventy or eighty years; rural blacks have seen changes in occupations, in social relationships, in family relationships, in attiudes toward religion, and in a sense of independence.

Occupation
One of the most obvious changes in black rural Texas over the last seven or eight decades has been in the way blacks have made their living. The depression of the 1930s brought an exodus from the farm by both blacks and whites. Then, as was noted above, improved technology and the desire of landowners to maximize profits led to further drastic reductions in the numbers of laborers used to plant and harvest crops. Where there had been tens of thousands of black men and women tilling the soil—as sharecroppers, farm owners, or wage earners—prior to 1950, blacks suddenly found themselves looking for employment elsewhere, and the transition was not easy. Eugene gives this insight into the transition.

> When Mr. Billy Anderson said, "We're going to quit having crops or sharecroppers," he said, "I'm gonna raise your salary

and let you fool with the cows." "Mr. Billy, now you raise my salary, and all these other hands here, all these years, been workin' crops, and all like that. The first thing you do—you just can't turn them loose." That's what I told him. "You can't just turn them loose, just like a bunch of cows, just say 'go.' They're lost. They don't know how to look out for themselves. . . . Give them about half a pension [salary], about half what you was givin' them when you was workin' a crop." So he did that.

The next year, then, things began to go up a little bit. And I went to 'em and began to talk to 'em about it. They hadn't gone then; they just stayed out there on the farm, wandering around, trying to decide what to do. They would go and chop and pick around for different folks. . . . They finally got used to it. When they got used to it, they all left. I said, "All you can go on away from the farm. I want to still stay on the farm." I say, "I don't know where to go to make a living. . . . Y'all goin' to town. Where you gonna work? You gotta go back to the farm to work. And so I just as well stay out here on the farm where I can make me a good, independent living." And that's what I did.

Some blacks stayed to work on farms as wage earners, but the majority sought work elsewhere, usually in nearby towns. Some continued to live in the small rural all-black communities and to drive to work in the larger towns. Most, of course, moved to the towns, where they met with varied measures of success. Tom Bradley, mayor of Los Angeles, is the son of a Calvert, Texas, sharecropper.

Social Relationships
The move from the farms and plantations into the towns and cities resulted in many changes, one of the most profound of which was the loss of the earlier sense of community. Over time, of course, new alliances were formed in the smaller towns, but these alliances never took on the same meaning for the older folks. One can still find that sense of community in the small settlements consisting of five to twenty or more families scattered along the Brazos Valley. Of all aspects of change in their lives, this change in the sense of community is most frequently noted and almost universally lamented by my informants in East Texas and in the Brazos Valley.

Willingness to share and to help one's neighbors characterized this sense of community. The person who butchered a hog or beef shared with his neighbors, who would reciprocate when they butchered. They

From the Other Side of the Furrow

helped neighbors in trouble. Their willingness to help is described by Anna Mae Bullard.

> I always did say that there was better times back yonder than it is now. It is to me. It was hard work, but it was still a better time . . . because of the people.
>
> People back there that we growed up with, they was so friendly and helped one another, you know. You get in a tight, well, folks would help you. But now, if you get in a tight, they'll walk off from you. Everybody's on his own, and nobody for nobody else, you see. Now you take us when we was comin' up—well it was like if this man over here got sick and his crop needed work. Well, Daddy would take us and go over there and work that crop, you see. But they won't do that now. And us children, we'd go over there and chop [cotton] just like we was in our own field—we had to 'cause our parents would lick us good. And we was willin' to do it, you know. But now, children they'd go hollerin', "I ain't gonna do so-and-so for so-and-so. You gotta pay me." But they didn't pay Daddy nothin'.

This informant, like many others, sees that move from the farm to town as the primary cause of this lost sense of community. Even those who are happiest that the "good old days" are gone share in this sense of loss of community that has occurred. However, not all of the changes in social relationships have been negative ones.

Though not to the extent they were in slavery, black sharecroppers were greatly dependent upon plantation owners for their very existence.[15] As with slaveholders, some plantation owners were better to work for than others. Sharecroppers usually had the option of changing landlords if conditions became unbearable. Anna Mae describes the situation. "Back in them days and times, you just had to humble yourself, and just take a whole lot that you wouldn't take now, you see. You had to take a whole lot back there in them days and times because if you didn't, if you'd kinda buck up, you know, they'd whip you or kill you or something or another like that." This submissive behavior was reinforced by the stories Anna Mae had heard from her grandmother, who had been a slave in Louisiana.

> She [Anna Mae's grandmother] had one brother get killed over there in Louisiana. They was pickin' cotton, she said, and they

---

15. Smallwood documents in great detail the treatment that blacks in Texas had at the hands of whites following emancipation.

didn't allow 'em to get on their knees. They had to stand up and pick cotton all the time. And her brother—and, you see, the guard, he'd ride around with a gun all the time, and he [the brother] just got so tired until he just had to get on his knees. And she said the man told him to get up off his knees, and he wouldn't get up, and she said he shot him right there in the field—killed him right there in the field. He was just a slave there on the plantation.

Even though many blacks sought accommodation with whites, they sometimes found themselves in a situation where conflict was unavoidable. Eugene describes such an instance in the life of one of his cousins, who had bought a span of mules from a white man and had mortgaged his cotton crop to pay for them. The man paid a visit.

He looked out; here came that white man. "Hey. Ain't you got that cotton out?" "Naw suh. It's been rainin' and I ain't got that cotton out." He said, "Just as soon as it dry out, and I can get that cotton, I'm gonna get it picked, and I'll bring it on in, Mr. Brown." The white man said, "If you ain't got it, I'm gonna whip ya." My cousin [Ed] said, "Mr. Brown, now you brought that lariat rope there to rope your cows. Now, don't you come whippin' me with that rope, hittin' me with that rope, 'cause I ain't goin' to stand it." So his wife went to the door and got a double-barrel shotgun. He [the cousin] begged for her not to shoot him [Brown]. So finally he [Brown] got that lariat rope down, doubled it, and hit him across the shoulder, twice. Big white feller, weighed about 250 pounds. My cousin was a small hard-time man. He had a wife with hair about [five inches] long, brown-skinned woman. She looked at him, and she said, "Hey," she said, "Spit on him, if you don't do nothin' else." He wouldn't spit on him. And when Brown did that [hit him with the rope] he got mad. He said, "Well, Lord, I got to. I got to battle with him now. But what I got, I got to go up against him." The deputy sheriff was with him and he had a pistol on. He said, "I got to go up here and fight here. Course they gonna kill me. I know they gonna kill me." He said, "but I got to defend myself." He jumped him, downed him, got on top of him, taken that rope and hit him two licks. That white man say, "Ed," say, "I got enough now." Say, "Quit now." When he got up, he say, "Ed, when you get that cotton out, you bring it on, carry it on to town and sell it, and come on by my office, an' I'm gonna give you a clear receipt for the mules." He was scared to do it. [Ed] got the cotton out, and he was scared to sell the cotton 'cause it was mortgaged. He say, "Come on. Come on by. Go to the gin and gin that cotton, gin that cotton," he say. He stand at the door, lookin' at him. "Come here, Ed." So he went on over there. Said, "Well," say, "I know the man gonna kill me," said, "but I'm goin' over there." And he took a sample of the cotton, you know. He said, "Mr. Brown, I got that cotton out, and here's a sample here." Say, "You can take it." He said, "Ed, carry that cotton home and sell it, and put the money in your pocket, and come in the office here. I'm gonna give you a clear receipt." He say, "I didn't have no business comin' out there tryin' to whip you." He say, "You got mad at me and taken the rope from me, and hit me two licks," and say, "it's all over with, and I'm goin' to give you a clear receipt." So he went on back home, and carried the money back to his wife. . . . Now, you know good and well that if Ed stood up there, that man'd whup him. How is he goin' to live with his wife? If she say something out of turn, and then if he haul away and tell her to hush, "You didn't do that to that white man. That white man whipped you like you was a baby, and you stood there and taken it." Cousin said that it scared him half to death. Say he didn't know what to do. That man haul away and hit him, and man! that double of the rope hurt him across the back there. The man weighed about 250 pounds.

The law offered little or no protection for the blacks, and to the question "What could a black man do when a white man did something to him?" Eugene answered, "Naw suh. Couldn't go to the law [for help]. Go to the law? Naw suh. I was here in that day when they used to just get out there and hit us and beat us and do anything they wanted to us, and you couldn't go to no law, see. I always say they [the whites] was the law. I still say they are the law." Anna Mae observed that things are not nearly so bad now: "I'll say one thing. It's gettin' better. It's gettin' better, a whole lot better. . . . It wasn't no cakes and pies all the way through the sharecroppers, you know. It wasn't no cakes and pies. It had some ups and downs, too. But it is gettin' better, a whole lot better. We ain't got all what belongs to us yet, but we is on our way."

Older blacks, particularly those from rural areas, still tend to be formal and polite in their social relations with whites, whom they address as Mr. and Mrs., and say "Yes, sir" or "Yes, ma'am" in conversation.

Such habits, developed over a lifetime, are hard to break. But in many instances there is genuine respect or affection behind this verbal behavior. A great source of irritation for many of the older blacks is the tendency of the younger generation to be disrespectful toward older folks, black and white. A black janitorial supervisor on the Texas A&M University campus recently complained that although the white students usually speak to him when they pass him on the campus or in a hallway, the black students don't. "They don't want no truck with the likes of me," he said.

Thus, though my informants lament the loss of the sense of community once so strong among rural black folk and now greatly altered even in the smaller towns, they are, nevertheless, proud of the progress that blacks have made in moving toward a social and economic equality with whites.

Family Relationships

Among the rural blacks I have interviewed, the feeling has been almost unanimous that the younger generation—the grandchildren generation, especially—does not enjoy proper upbringing, and that the reason is the weakening of family ties, the loss of religious values, and the growing dependence on government for one's livelihood.[16]

In comparing family relationships during her childhood and those of the present generation, Mrs. Bullard was very critical. "But in them days and times, parents was raisin' children. But now they are just growin' up. They're not raisin' children now. The children are just growing up." The parent-child relationship was based on obedience, punishment, and respect. The Bullards gave the following responses to the question "What kind of relationship existed between children and their parents?"

> *Eugene:* They loved their parents then. There's a hatred done grown up between the parents and the children now. "You can't tell me nothin'. I'm my own boss."
>
> *Anna Mae:* Children loved their parents then, and children would mind their parents, too. I don't care what they tell you to do, you had better do that. They didn't tell you but one time. They didn't make a song out of it. We all had jobs to do. They'd give all seven of us a job, and they told us just one time.

---

16. Though it is clear that informants often tell the interviewer what they think the interviewer wants to hear, this observation about the welfare system is consistent with the philosophy of many of these independent rural blacks.

> *Question:* What about religion in the home?
>
> *Anna Mae:* Yes suh. Family prayer every morning at the table.
>
> *Eugene:* When you went to the table to eat supper, you went to the table there and my grandaddy, well he was goin' to pray, say the blessing before he eat. But *now* the people, the people go in there and the children go in there, and when they get to the table, you go in there and start eating. The children don't wait till you say the blessing. And used to have Sunday morning prayer around the table in the morning. Now? "I don't want to get up right now." They don't get up and go to the table and eat. They get up about 10 o'clock.

Anna Mae and Eugene described their own religious upbringing. They were expected to say their prayers every night, and parents often listened in to make sure they did. They went to church every Sunday, a brush arbor church.

According to Anna Mae, children don't get the religious upbringing they once did. "Oh, we don't have no religious children now, hardly at all. . . . 'cause the parents don't bring them to church, and it's too much [bad] environment now. . . . The parents done let them get loose. Our parents didn't let us get loose that way. You had to be a Christian in them homes. If you didn't, you couldn't stay there."

Another reason why the younger generation is out of control is that they have too much free time. Anna Mae claimed that the only free time she had as a child was after church on Sundays. The parents saw that they were busy all the time. Nowadays, young people are not happy unless they are walking the streets, going to parties or to dances.

Like their white counterparts, many of the older rural blacks are confused, frustrated if not angry, about the "new morality" among young people today. The Bullards give their own perspectives on earlier approaches to courtship among rural blacks. Anna Mae offered the female perspective.

> Well, you had to be sixteen [to begin dating]. You couldn't [go] out here at no fo'teen. You had to be sixteen. And you had a certain time to go and a certain time to come in. See. And you leave at eight, you had to be back by nine. And [if] he pick you up here at this doorstep, that's where he had to bring you back. That's what they had to do. They had to bring you right back there. And, if it is well with the girl, that's the only boy she goin' to go with, too. She ain't goin' with this 'un and that

'un. That's the only one she goin' to go with. And if she got spoiled, that boy had to marry her. See what I mean? They wouldn't let her go with this boy and that boy. They had to go with that one boy. And they'd tell you quick. Say, "Now you takin' company with so-and-so, and no other boy. Because, now, if you get spoilt, we can protect you, 'cause we know who goin' with you. But if you hittin' here and yonder, we don't know. And you can go out and stay out, then come back home, and that boy better bring you right back there and help you in that house, on that porch there." They'd be standin' at the door lookin.'

If a girl did get "spoiled," she was no longer a girl, but a woman.

And if the girl got spoiled, well you [as a girl] couldn't associate with her. "I [mother speaking] can, but you can't." That's just the way, that's just the difference in them then than it is now. You see what I mean? We thought probably they was kinda mean and hard, but they wasn't. They just only made mens and womens out us. Sho did. They come up, raised up pretty tough, and they wanted to raise us up, not in, you know, under the bad conditions they were, but they wanted to raise us up in the right way. That's what they wanted to do. Where the folks would respect us, and we would respect the folks, you see? They wanted to raise us up as respectable children.

And what about today?

[The young people] sho is footloose now. But we wasn't footloose. The children is footloose now. They go anywhere they want to and do anything they are big enough to do. . . . Now, people don't care nothin' about respect, themselves. My mother and father, I ain't never seed them take a drink of nothin', but water. They didn't go to no parties; they didn't go to no dances. See, in them days and times, that was for them to go to, you know. But they wouldn't go. They wouldn't drink, and nothin', but water. Now, how many children can you find in this town today that say they ain't never saw they mother and father drink? They mother and father drink *with* them.

In another interview, Eugene describes courting from the male perspective.

Well, you'd take a girl to different places, all right, but you had to be back with her at a certain time. And then, and if you went with that girl and you treated her like you wanted to marry her, you know, sort of like that, well, that was different. You had to respect her. If you went to a dance or something or another, you didn't go out and stay all night like the boys do now. Naw suh! You could go to church [with her] all the time. If you was bad about goin' to church, you get that girl and go to church, and go to where you brought a horse and buggy, why you'd carry the girl to church and then carry her back home after church was over with. But you brought her back home at a certain time, and then when you got there, you sat there and talked a little while. Then before long she'd go on in the house and you'd go on alone. You didn't go there and sit out like they do now. Some of them [girls] had to get married, but that's pretty rare.

Finally, Anna Mae was very critical of a welfare system paying young women to have babies, which she called "bush babies."

Religion
Many of the rural blacks I interviewed lamented the changes that have taken place in the religious services themselves and among the people who lack Christian virtues. Active churchgoers, the Bullards worry that people are too self-centered now, especially the preachers, who are more interested in a good salary, a nice church, and a large membership roll than they are in Christian principles. Eugene was especially critical of the preachers, saying there would be more preachers in hell than any other group. Anna Mae compared the earlier church experience to that of today.

> Oh Lord! A prayer meeting back then, them days and times, whenever people go to prayin', make the hair rise on your head. Them there good old hymns! Boy, you ought to hear them folks sing them good old hymns! And they'd go to havin' prayer service before we got there, and people would go to runnin' to get there. And anytime that a sinner would come to that arbor, he couldn't stand on the outside, like he do now. He had to come in there. Them prayers would bring him in there, and come on in there and join the church. It ain't like it is now. Man, back there in them times they used to have some prayer services. They could make the hair rise on the back of your head. It was good, now I'm tellin' you. You see, *now,* I call them [songs currently sung in church] these little ole jumped up ditty songs.

> But back then there was them spiritual songs, the Old One Hundred Hymns. That's what make the spirit, the Old One Hundred Hymns. And then let some old sister or some old brother get down there and pray. Man, you couldn't stay there. I'm tellin' you. Oh, Lord, that spirit would make you go. I'm tellin' you the truth. It was really good. Whole lot different now than it was back then. They don't nearbout have church now like they used to have. . . . And the preachers could preach, too. . . . Yes suh. Preachin' ain't nothin' now 'side preachin' was when I came on. And it was all outdoors. . . . And people were servin' God better than they do now. . . . They recognized God back there, but they don't recognize Him now, you see? They off on they own, now, but people back there was on God; they's lookin' to God. But people now lookin' to man. . . . They gone to servin' man.

As to living the Christian teachings,

> There's so much difference now and back then when I was comin' up that it's pitiful. And you take—people get sick in the community, Momma and Daddy would take us and go to work they crops while they were sick. Now if the sister was sick, Momma would take us and go clean up the house, go clean her yard, and all like that. Now if the brother was sick and he was workin', had his crops started, well the group of mens would get together and go work there—go plow the crop; and then a bunch of sisters would take their family [food] and then we'd go chop cotton for them. That's what you call Christian. But it ain't nothin' like it now. It's all indifferent.

Independence

Contrary to the white stereotype of blacks, many of the rural folk were and continue to be fiercely independent, looking with anger on those who could work but prefer to rely upon government assistance. They would no more accept a handout than many of their white counterparts. Although advanced in years, both Bullards still work and refuse to accept food stamps or other welfare assistance. Anna Mae had this to say about the welfare system.

> I call it a bad program. Now, I says the old people, it's good for the old people, 'cause I know old people can't work, done worked theyselves to death, and they can't work and they's sick—I say,

give them something. But this young generation, I say don't give them *nothing*. Let them come on and work like I did. The government didn't give us nothin'; the government didn't give our foreparents nothin'. We had to work for what we had. And I think the government done a wrong thing when it went to puttin' these young folks on the welfare. That's just encouragin' them to steal, and kill, and rob folks. 'Cause if they had to get out there and work for that, they wouldn't do it, 'cause they'd be on the job workin'. The government give 'em money; they got nothin' to do but walk the street, day and night, breakin' in folks' homes, breakin' in stores and things. . . . That's what the government made the world like it is today with the young people, by given' them money.

Even as sharecroppers, many blacks took advantage of opportunities offered by some plantation owners to raise gardens, pigs, and sometimes a milk cow. Some of the finest gardens in the Brazos Valley are raised by rural blacks. Many who moved into towns continue to raise gardens as well.

Rural blacks are masters at making the best of what they have. Many of the older blacks had little chance for education and specialized training for skilled jobs. Those skills they had mastered on the farm were in little demand in the towns. Paper sacks and other such modern miracles of technology replaced the marvelously wrought split-oak baskets once so common in rural areas; working blacksmiths are a rarity, though there are still a few, like Frank Green on the Terrell Farms at Allentown, near Navasota; and though it is rare, some blacks still raise their own cane and make their own syrup, as the Devault family does in the Clay community near Somerville. Many rural blacks at the bottom of the economic ladder "make do" with what they have. Whites often look down their collective noses at the signs of near poverty and attribute them to lack of initiative, rather than lack of opportunity.

As we have seen, older rural blacks have witnessed great changes in their society and culture over their lifetime: changes in the way blacks make their living; changes in social and family relationships; changes in their religious experience and in their sense of independence. Many of these changes were also experienced by whites, who underwent similar dislocation from their rural roots. But, given the nature of our society, poor blacks found the move more traumatic because so many opportunities were closed to them. But their ancestors had survived slavery, and they, themselves, had survived the miseries of Reconstruction and

Fort Worth laborer, 1979.
Photograph by June Van Cleef.

the Depression. These rural blacks have not only survived the changes, but also have made what they see as significant progress: they are better off materially, for the most part, and have moved significantly toward equality with whites. This progress mitigates, to an extent, the effects of the perceived changes in the quality of life brought about by the changes in life-style discussed above.

Most Europeans coming to urban America managed to pass as Americans within one generation. In the city, they quickly learned to shed the quaint, distinctive features of the homeland, foremost among them the language and dress. They conformed to a new life-style, generally reserving old country habits and values for the privacy of their homes or churches. In the country, however, things are quite different. Immigrants may cherish vestiges of their home culture, marking the cadences of nature with the unique sound and structures of the native tongue, knowing that the neighbor over the hill—provided he doesn't burn them out—will understand the concern for a good crop and a fine herd even if he doesn't understand their language.

Language and culture seem to reflect each other. Wilhelm von Humboldt first asserted that "man lives with the world about him . . . exclusively as language presents it to him." In order to understand a culture, first one must determine how language shaped a people's construct of the surrounding world.[17] Language measures and dignifies the life-order of mankind; too often, not understanding the one has led to a breakdown or the extermination of the other. In a pluralistic society such as in the United States, one group dominates smaller, subordinate groups to the degree that the smaller groups allow. When a group says "no" to efforts to subordinate heritage, culture, and life-order, language often remains that part of the baggage brought across the Atlantic that persists.

Early European immigrants recognized the good soil and healthful climate of Central Texas between the Brazos and the Colorado rivers. The area nurtures a rich ethnic mixture that today tolerates intermarriage across national and religious lines. That easy tolerance tends to swell the number of inhabitants with dual or multiple ancestries, the dominant group that tends to think of itself as "plain Texan." But "no" has been heard in a variety of languages. Enter the country church at

---

17. John T. Waterman, *Perspectives in Linguistics,* 2nd ed. (Chicago: University of Chicago Press, 1970), p. 67.

Serbin and find a Texan who yet regards the church as a bastion of culture; it supported grandparents in an alien country; it divided when they sensed their identity changing; it preserves the cyclical documents that mark life—baptism, marriage, death; it accepted their remains into its cemetery and marked graves in the language of the European homeland. Each generation sought its own identity in this quiet countryside, at a pace measured in decades rather than in years. The questions each generation of this tiny folk group asked would have been inaudible in a city.

Wendish to German to English: The Texas Wends
Joseph Wilson

The Wendish Germans of Texas are in many ways unique. Typically, the immigrant communities in America maintained their language and their identity for a few generations and then accepted English and merged with the mainstream. The Texas Wends are different in that they first completed a transition from Wendish to German before starting the transition to English.[18] At the same time, they were making the transition from agrarian Europe to farms in Central Texas.

The main immigration of Wends into Texas took place in 1854, when nearly six hundred made the hazardous voyage together on one ship, the *Ben Nevis,* under the spiritual leadership of their pastor, John Kilian. The Wends (also called Sorbs) had been an ethnic minority group in Germany: Slavs who had been encircled by Germans centuries ago, and who over the centuries were being assimilated into the "German melting pot" (which had absorbed Poles, Czechs, Danes, French, and others) in the same way that ethnic groups were being assimilated in America. In the Germany of 1850 most of the Wends had long since become Germanized: they had given up their Slavic language for German, they had intermarried with the other Germans, and in general

---

18. The same is true of the Wends who immigrated to other places, mainly Australia, Canada, and South Africa. The major difference is that these other Wends went in smaller groups and simply joined German communities, whereas the Texas Wends were numerous enough to form their own community and thus to use and preserve Wendish longer. See George R. Nielsen, *In Search of a Home: The Wends (Sorbs) on the Australian and Texas Frontier,* Birmingham Slavonic Monographs, no. 1 (Birmingham, England: Birmingham University Press, 1977), pp. 2, 56ff, 99ff. This book is the most detailed and accurate source of information on the Texas Wends and the other Wendish immigrations.

they had become indistinguishable from them. Sometimes their surnames might offer a clue as to their original Wendish origin, but usually even the name was no evidence. For one thing, intermarriage naturally brought purely German names in. And some originally Wendish names had been germanized. Even left in their Wendish form, the surnames "looked German," because Wendish was written with conventions of German spelling, and because German surnames, like American ones, have varied origins. However, in 1850 there were still about 150,000 unassimilated Wends in Germany who still spoke Wendish principally and had preserved some of their original folklore and customs.[19] Even among these, naturally, the German language and German customs had made many inroads. Just as, in this country, English is the key to education, business success, and many other facets of life, in Germany, German was the key to upward mobility. Consequently, even these remaining "unassimilated" Wends were bicultural and largely bilingual. They felt the mixed loyalties any minority group feels. On the one hand, they felt that they were Wends and different from the Germans among whom they lived, but on the other hand they felt that they, too, were Germans, in a broader sense. That the Wends considered themselves to be Germans is clearly demonstrated in many ways: for example, by the fact that in every instance of Wendish immigration, into whatever country, the Wends always joined the other Germans.[20] This kind of double identity should be easy enough for us in America, with our many ethnic groups, to understand, but it was an even more natural situation in the Europe of the nineteenth century, when nations often contained the most varied ethnic and linguistic groups within their borders, so that there frequently was an ethnic and linguistic difference between the village and the nation.

The Wendish Germans, who spoke Wendish at home and had to learn German for higher purposes, were not in such a very different position from most other Germans who spoke a dialect at home and standard German in school and business. And, like our Yankees and southerners, north Germans will often, even today, express contempt for Bavarians—and vice versa—but then unite against a common foe, realizing that they are both Germans. In very much the same way, a Wendish German might be angry with a non-Wendish German one day and join with him as a fellow German the next day.

As is unfortunately to be expected with any minority group, there

19. Nielsen, *Search*, p. 11.
20. Nielsen, *Search*, passim.

was at times discrimination against the Wends and overt pressure on them to give up their language for that of the majority, but there was apparently little, if any, discrimination against them in Germany at the time of the immigration to Texas, contrary to what is sometimes stated.[21] There is a similar, persistent, pious myth that the Wendish Lutherans who immigrated to Texas did so for purely religious reasons because they were being forced to join the amalgamated church of the Prussian state. George Nielsen in his work on Wendish migration has called attention to the fact that, at the time of the immigration to Texas, religious minorities in Prussia had the freedom to form "free churches," and the Wendish Lutherans had long since done so.[22] This is not to say that a desire for greater religious freedom played no role in the migration, merely that this role has been overstated. Similarly, in regard to their economic situation, the Wends surely hoped for improved opportunities in America, but it is wrong to say that they had been living in virtual slavery in Germany. Even a casual glance at the passenger list of the *Ben Nevis* will show that there were landowners, mill owners, and master blacksmiths among them.[23] Most were, to be sure, not so well off as these, but poverty was, after all, the general state of the masses in Europe. Pastor Kilian would hardly have applied to return to Germany to reassume a position in a Wendish congregation, as he did in 1864, if there had been significant religious oppression and ethnic discrimination.[24]

When they came to Texas, the Wends naturally continued to consider themselves a subset of the Germans. As a matter of fact, they even still considered themselves Prussians and Saxons, respectively, depending on which of these two German kingdoms they had come from. Their first official action as a congregation, after boarding the ship for Texas, was to elect their leaders; for this they divided into two groups, Prussians and Saxons, and each group elected its own proportionate number of leaders. The minutes of this action were taken in German, and German continued to be used for most such official written purposes (baptismal records, marriage certificates, and the like) for the next hundred years in Texas, as it had been in Germany.[25] Wendish was, how-

---

21. Gerald Stone, *The Smallest Slavonic Nation: The Sorbs of Lusatia* (London: Athlone Press, 1972), p. 19; Anne Blasig, *The Wends of Texas* (San Antonio: Naylor, 1954), p. 11.
22. Blasig, *Wends*, p. 11; Nielsen, *Search*, pp. 60ff.
23. The list is reproduced in English in Blasig, *Wends*, pp. 92ff.
24. Nielsen, *Search*, p. 90.
25. Serbin Papers, Archives of the Texas District Offices of the Lutheran Church—Missouri Synod, Austin, Tex. (hereafter referred to as Serbin Papers).

ever, used for the minutes of the early congregational meetings. After a long and grief-filled voyage, the Wends were met in Houston by the German pastor, Caspar Braun, and members of his congregation, who helped them find food and shelter and passage onward. They made the ox-cart trip from Houston into the interior in small groups, making stopovers on the way at other German settlements such as Industry and New Ulm. Some stayed temporarily, and a few permanently, in these places; however, within a few months, most had gathered at or near what came to be called Serbin, in what is now Lee County. At that time, the area was part of Bastrop County, and for about two years, before the word *Serbin* was coined, the community simply called itself the Wendish Settlement. Although the region was largely wilderness, most of the geographical features already had English names—Low Pinoak Creek, Rabb's Creek, Bullfrog Creek, Knobb's Branch—and these names were used for giving the location of a person's farm, naturally adapted into Wendish or German, *Farmarja pschi Bullfrogu,* or *eines Farmers am Bullfrog,* "of a farmer on Bullfrog Creek."

Wendish was naturally written with the conventions of German spelling.[26] Wendish books were printed in the standard ornate old German type, and handwriting was in the old German style. But, as was also the standard German usage of the nineteenth century, "Latin" print and handwriting, quite similar to those used for English today, were also often used for special purposes—proper names, foreign (not Wendish or German) words, and the like. The spelling of Wendish in Germany today has been changed radically, in a way that makes it look less like German and more like Czech; the Texas Wends, of course, never used this spelling. As examples, the surnames that were, and still are, spelled (in Texas) Pietsch, Schelnik, and Zieschank, would be Pič, Šelnik, and Cišank according to the new orthography, and would look very strange to the Texas Wends who bear these names.[27]

When they settled in the Serbin area, the Wends continued their intimate relationships with the other Germans nearby. Some organized German Methodists, whose more emotional preaching and services at-

---

26. There also was a system of spelling Wendish with a Czech-based orthography, which was used by the Catholics; Stone, *Slavonic Nation,* p. 120. Both systems have their relative advantages; the German-based system was easier, since the Wends had to be able to use both languages, and thus could use the same spelling system for both.

27. In Germany today, either spelling may be used for such proper names; Stone, *Slavonic Nation,* p. 163. Undoubtedly, most people will continue to use the traditional German form.

tracted a few of the Wends away from Kilian's stately Lutheran services, were a major cause of the first split of the congregation.[28] On the other hand, Kilian served for years as a kind of circuit-riding minister to various groups of German Lutherans nearby and even as far away as New Ulm and Industry, some forty miles away. These other Germans were evidently mostly not Wendish. Each year thereafter, more Germans—Wends and others—joined the group. The pastor's records, all in German, make no distinctions between Wends and others or between members of the Serbin congregation and nonmembers.

The following is a typical random sample of the surnames of settlers mentioned in the early records as being from the Serbin vicinity: Gröschel, Schulze, Matthiez, Kappler, Miertschin, Wünsche, Urban, Lehmann, Melde, Menzel. Presumably all these people were Wends, but the surnames give no direct indication. Nor do the given names, which are all standard German names: Magdalena, Andreas, Hanna, Matthäus, Dorothea, August, Johann, Carl, Ernst. The germanization of the Wends had already proceeded to the point that they were voluntarily using German names almost exclusively. Only a few names still had double forms, such as Jan for use in Wendish and Johann for use in German, or Jurij and George. In the great majority of the cases even in a Wendish context the German form is used, naturally with the necessary Wendish inflectional suffix, if required, as Ernstej, "to Ernst."[29] And even in those cases where there was a different Wendish form available, the people themselves evidently preferred the German form, perhaps because it was too much trouble to keep up with two different forms. Pastor Kilian, a learned man, always signed his Wendish documents as Jan Kilian and his German ones as Johann Kilian, and his English ones as John Kilian, and similarly shifted between, for instance, Jurij and George, when he was listing people's names, and when there was a different Wendish form available. But in the few cases in the Serbin records where the people signed their names themselves, they almost always used the German form, even in a Wendish document. To sum it up again: it is impossible to tell from the Serbin records whether any individual person is Wendish or "pure" German. The

28. Nielsen, *Search*, pp. 87ff.
29. The *-ej* is a dative suffix. Wendish is a highly inflected language; the person who does not understand how to interpret the many suffixes and other inflectional changes will make false interpretations of Wendish words and names. Thus, the title pages of Pastor Kilian's Wendish printed works sometimes give his name in genitive form as *Jana Kiliana,* but the uninflected normal Wendish form is *Jan Kilian.*

linguistic preference, Wendish or German, of the individuals cannot be determined from the records either. Presumably in the majority of the original families, the normal home language was Wendish, but in some it was German, and it is quite clear that nearly all were bilingual.[30]

Since they quite naturally joined the other Germans in Texas, their German-Wendish bilingual world, with German the culturally dominant, more official language, continued in Texas as in Germany. They joined the conservative German Lutheran church of the Missouri Synod, all of whose dealings were in German—its church services, schools, seminaries, books, newspapers, and correspondence. As in Germany, the tendency of Wendish to die out and be replaced by German continued—indeed, it accelerated. Any bilingual situation like this was going to produce squabbles—and, of course, all kinds of other disputes—in Serbin. But the complicated struggles there, which twice resulted in the split, and later reunification, of the congregation into Saint Peter's, which was more "German," and Saint Paul's, which was more "Wendish," revolved about the most varying factors; they were not at all simply the result of "ethnic-German" opposed to "ethnic-Wend," as is sometimes stated.[31] This is abundantly clear from the fact that at the time of the second split (in 1870, which involved more of a Wendish-German clash than the first one had), both congregations conducted services in both languages—Saint Paul's continued its practice of German and Wendish services every Sunday, and Saint Peter's did so for several years, before discontinuing the Wendish because of the difficulty of finding a pastor able to preach in it. Both churches continued to consist of both Wends and Germans.[32] When language usage did materially enter into the dispute, as in regard to the language of the congregational meetings, many of those favoring exclusive use of German were ethnic Wends, who felt they were being progressive in giving up what seemed to them to be a useless dialect. And even those Wends who clung most tenaciously to their Wendish wanted their children to be educated in German.[33] Clearly, it was only a matter of time before German would replace Wendish altogether.

By the 1880s the use of Wendish in the homes had largely been re-

30. Nielsen, *Search*, p. 91.

31. Thus while admitting a multiplicity of factors, W. H. Bewie, *Missouri in Texas* (Austin: Texas District Offices, Lutheran Church—Missouri Synod, 1952), p. 11, says that the "real cause" of the 1870 split was "a language question."

32. Kilian letter to Buenger, Nov. 25, 1873; Kilian's declarations read to the congregational meeting of Jan. 16, 1870, Serbin Papers.

33. Kilian's notes for the congregational meeting of Aug. 8, 1869, Serbin Papers.

placed by German, even when both parents spoke Wendish. From then on, Wendish was relegated almost exclusively to the older generation; although Wendish services were still held until 1920, the Texas Wends had been completely germanized. Until approximately 1940 their world was almost totally German. Not only were their churches, their schools, their festivals, and their weddings completely in German (with the marriage certificates and other such documents in German), but even their local newspapers were in German.

All this time—during the "first transition," to German—the use of English was practically nil among the Wends, except for the geographical terms (*creek, branch*) and new concepts (*Smokehaus, Fence*). Nevertheless, after about 1890, most people began to learn some English, because, after all, there were Anglos and blacks around who did not speak German, although a surprising number of both categories did. The "second transition" was beginning, although English was not to become dominant until the 1950s and 1960s. Nearly all of the Wends born between 1890 and 1940 became fluent in German and English, with German their originally stronger language, and those who still heard Wendish at home became trilingual—truly a remarkable situation.

The most eloquent and visible testimony to the Germanness of the Texas Wends is given by the cemetery in Serbin. All the older grave inscriptions, from the 1860s on, including the graves of the original old settlers from Germany, are in German, usually with lengthy Bible quotations or hymn verses. Only one, from 1889, is in Wendish; like the German ones, it is in beautiful Gothic letters. The cemeteries of such daughter congregations as Fedor, Warda, and Winchester are similar. Besides the one Wendish inscription at Serbin, the only use of Wendish I have found on a gravestone is in a single bilingual German-Wendish inscription in the Old Warda (Holy Cross) cemetery. The inscriptions naturally also bear witness to the rigors of pioneer Texas and to life's continuing ironies. One stands over the common graves of three young brothers and sisters, who all died within a week, undoubtedly from one of the yellow fever or other epidemics; two others honor young World War I soldiers, both killed shortly before the end of the war, fighting for their new homeland against their old homeland, now resting forever beneath beautiful stones, one in English, one in German. The gravestones also graphically depict the second transition, to English. The one soldier's stone is among the earliest in English, although there is a beautiful bilingual English-German stone from 1891. There are a number of English stones from the 1930s, but German continued its dominance until the 1940s and 1950s; it was used extensively even during World War II and long after. The latest German inscription, to my knowledge, in Serbin is from the year 1963 — 108 years after the immigration.

German was used as the exclusive language of the congregational meetings at Serbin from the mid-1860s until 1966, long after the other German congregations of the area had gone over to English. For the next three years, both German and English were used, with the minutes kept in both languages. Since 1969, only English has been used. This amazing language-loyalty to German at Serbin is the reason I have often referred to Serbin as "the most German place in Texas."

The German-Wendish surnames have, of course, been retained by the descendants of the Wends, usually without any changes except for the normal anglicization of the German umlauts, as in Groeschel for Gröschel. The names have always been pronounced in German fashion; this is becoming a problem now that many of the younger generation have little knowledge of German, and because dealing with non-German-speakers has become common. In the 1920s a few people began giving their children English first names, even in instances where the family language was still German. Serbinites and others from the area born in the 1920s and 1930s, who were nearly all raised in German, will have either English names like Leonard or Milton or Victor, or German ones like Christoph, Helmut, or Hedwig. After the late 1930s English names predominated, but even in the 1940s and in some cases much later, some children were still being given German names.

Old Wendish and German Bibles, hymnbooks, and prayerbooks are common family heirlooms, but the bilingual catechisms — the basic books of religious instruction — offer especially visible witness of the two transitions in Serbin. From the time of the immigration through the early 1900s, bilingual Wendish-German catechisms were common; throughout the book, facing pages give the Wendish and German versions of Luther's explanations of the Lord's Prayer and the sacraments. Since some of the children were confirmed in Wendish and others in German, the same books could be used for both groups. In the 1930s these were replaced by bilingual German-English versions, as some children began to be confirmed in English. Nowadays, they are simply in English.

Another such cyclic repetition is seen in the language usage of the family. In the 1880s and 1890s, when Wendish was being displaced, parents bilingual in Wendish and German raised their children in German, but often used Wendish with older people and between themselves, frequently as a kind of secret language to keep the children from understanding—which ensured, of course, that the children learned some Wendish.[34] A generation or two later, from the 1940s right down to the present, this family scenario was being and continues to be repeated, but now with the roles being played in German and English.

The end of the second step of this historic integration process is still in progress. We are fortunate to be able to witness the living use of German in Texas. Serbin and five other churches in the area still conduct German services regularly every other Sunday or once a month; these are well attended, although naturally mostly by middle-aged or older people. Before and after the services the people talk together in German or English. Many still prefer German at home. There is even at least one person, Carl Miertschin, left in Serbin who is still fluent in Wendish, as well as in German and English. The use of German is still taken for granted in these communities. Even to the young people who speak only English, it seems natural to hear their elders speak German. However, in the not-too-distant future, when all the German speakers in the area have died, their descendants will surely marvel that their forebears—on this same Texas soil—spoke German, and before that, in many cases, Wendish.

Hurnville probably never did exist as a village. Try as one may, it cannot be found on the map today. A church, a school, a filling station, clustered not so closely together—that is all it ever had been, and now the church and school are gone. The group of Germans from Russia who settled there were not pioneers; they bought their land from others who moved on, rather than wresting it from wilderness, Indians, or the Land Office of the state of Texas. They were too few to change dynamically the course of farming or of history on the Red River. Their compatriots had brought hard winter wheat to the prairie to the north a quarter of a century earlier. They lived apart from their neighbors, separated by language, values, traditions, a multitude of variations that make up a culture. In a greater sense, Hurnville was a *community*:

---

34. My late mother-in-law, Emma Zoch Herbrich, born in 1885, grew up in this typical family setting. My father-in-law, Paul Herbrich, also born in 1885, heard little Wendish at home because his father, Ernst Herbrich (Herbrig), spoke only German, even though he was as a child one of the original Wends who came over on the *Ben Nevis*. Both always considered themselves German; if asked about the Wends, they would typically reply, "Oh yes, those were the old people; my parents were Wendish."

everyone there shared a common background traced through more than 150 years of cluster migration through three continents. The quality of flour for baking was important enough to trek over the Red River to Oklahoma to replenish supplies. For a while, stucco rock adobe set their buildings apart from the clapboard or brick of the area. Their children wore the dark fur caps of their homeland until ridiculed in a language they could not understand. These few families offer a microscopic view of the similar folk experiences of a collection of other groups in Texas. To a great extent, however, this group is overlooked or wrongly counted by ethnologists of Texas; in public statistics, they are figured among the Russian-born, and that is far too simple.

The Hurnville Germans from Russia
Dona B. Reeves-Marquardt

Early settlers claimed there were no trees. The wind swept in from the north in the winter to freeze man and beast. In the summer, breezes from the coast to the south might withhold rain for months and bring with them hordes of insects. Spring can send tornadic winds and storms to devastate the land and to plant primeval fear in the hearts of the children. Trees grow now, even fruit trees, but they testify to the tenacity of the men and women who till the soil and reap its harvests. These cultivators are God-fearing worshipers for whom religion, predominantly of the Protestant varieties, is as bread and water. They live in a seemingly limitless landscape, with only enough knolls and rises to keep the earth from being flat, an occasional stream that varies in size with the seasons and, now, a light network of roads to facilitate the transport of surprisingly abundant agricultural products.

So might read the physical description of two distant parts of the world: Clay County, Texas, bordering the Red River near Wichita Falls, and the Kherson-Beresan region of Russia, north of Odessa, bordering the Black Sea. Clay County lacks the visual beauty and felicitous climate of more attractive areas of Texas. To love this land, to feel at home in it, provides a description of the people who live, who endure here: Anglo-American pioneer stock who moved west when the county was created late in 1857. Its settlement could repeat the history of many of the areas that stretch across the division of farm-ranch economy in Texas, but it would seem an unlikely locale for one of the most cohesive folk groups of Texas, the Germans from Russia. The physical similarity of the two regions may account for the island of these immigrants that centered around the now extinct village of Hurnville. Relatively few Germans from Russia settled in Texas; most sought the easier farming regions of Kansas, Nebraska, and the Dakotas. In Texas they are concentrated today primarily in Clay and Lipscomb counties.[35] The Hurnville Germans from Russia came, by and large, from the Russian village of Rohrbach, about sixty-six miles northeast of Odessa, and arrived in Clay County beginning about 1890. To understand this folk group in general, the Rohrbach-Hurnville group in particular, and the success of their transplant to this seemingly alien environment, we must examine the historical and religious background of the group. In this background may be found an explanation for the unusual retention of language and traditions of the group and their continuous adjustment to new living and farming patterns.

In 1763 when Catherine the Great invited the first German settlers to participate in her plan to cultivate and Europeanize her then remote hinterlands, she did not foresee the pioneers' necessarily agonizing adaptation to drastically new living conditions, removing from an organized and orderly, albeit politically capricious, community to a frontier environment already sparsely populated with a suspicious, if not hostile, folk group. The experience is examined here because of its similarity to the resettlement by descendants of these migrants to the "steppes" of Clay County. The attraction of free, or at least cheap, land and favorable terms of transport and initial subsidies was more than people recovering from the War of Succession and the Seven Years War could resist. German settlements sprang up first along the Volga. Later German pioneers streamed into "New Russia," beginning about 1804 in the Black Sea area near Odessa.

Continuing his grandmother's invitation to European settlers, Alexander wisely avoided some of the mistakes of the earlier colonization attempt. For *his* New Russia along the shores of the Black Sea, he accepted only experienced farmers and craftsmen. Again, certain benefits were promised: a degree of autonomy, religious freedom, and a generous grant of productive land for each family. Although the entire colonization effort was far better organized and genuine attempts were made to guarantee a safe voyage, to ease the necessary quarantines en route, to provide housing upon arrival and sufficient food and medical attention, hardship and tragedy were more often than not the traveling companions of the early migrants, either through their own blun-

---

35. Richard Sallet, *Russian-German Settlements in the United States*, trans. LaVern J. Rippley and Armand Bauer (Fargo: North Dakota Institute for Regional Studies, 1974), pp. 198ff.

dering and the mismanagement of their leaders or through the miscalculations of the administrators.

Settlement names of the villages they founded in the Odessa area, 1804–10, echo place names of their homeland: Speier, Landau, Rastadt, Karlsruhe, Rohrbach, Baden, Elsass, Mannheim, and others. The immigrants came almost exclusively from Baden, Alsace, Württemberg, and the Palatinate. Later arrivals, 1816–19, would include Separatists, Stundists, Sabbatists, Chiliasts, and a variety of other religious zealots primarily from Württemberg. These pietists suffered to an even greater degree on their journey; plague, fever, and unsanitary conditions cost in the year 1817 alone from thirteen hundred to three thousand lives. When the remaining families finally reached the Odessa area, most were so decimated and disheartened they decided to remain there and joined earlier settlers in Grossliebenthal, Alexanderhilf, and Neuburg, among other villages in the Beresan district. Only the hardiest and most fanatic reached their original destination of the Caucasus. The new influx of Pietists in the Odessa area added a significant dimension to the predominantly Lutheran villages in which they settled, a dimension that was later to be felt particularly in Rohrbach and that ultimately was transplanted in Texas.

The area of southwestern Germany from which they had migrated to Russia relied largely on agriculture to support the economy, typically a mixture of grains, livestock, viticulture, and forestry. The German pattern was and is yet primarily a village pattern, farmers grouping their farmsteads in small irregular villages from which they proceeded to cultivate their scattered fields. Cultivation was intense, and vestiges of Roman law brought smaller and smaller landholdings to ever larger families. But it is also tempting to examine the spirit of the farmers of this area, beginning with the uprisings here in the Peasant's War, the incubation here of the Protestant Reformation that resulted in the patchwork of Reformed, Lutheran, and Catholic villages, and the rich commercial heritage brought about by the easy transportation of the upper Rhine and the young Danube rivers. The religious and political history of the area simply adorns the devastating effect that a conquering army, a crop failure, a millennialist fanatic, or an avaricious prince might have on the destiny of a farm family. At the same time, one must remember that the majority of the original settlers around Odessa came from an area some fifty miles wide by eighty miles long. Rohrbach/Odessa, founded in 1809, lists thirty-three families from Baden, forty-four from Alsace, twelve from the Palatinate, four from Württemberg, and seven from Poland in its census of 1816. Among the original settlers we find the names Faijok (Feiock), Herdt, Reichert, Zimpelmann (Zimbleman), Gemar, Bachmann, Wiest (Wüst, Wiist), Fuhrmann, Moser, Trautmann, and Baumgärtner.[36] We find these names again in the 1900 census of Clay County or in naturalization records on file in Henrietta or in Wichita Falls. Cohesion, family ties, and steadfastness of faith and purpose account for cluster migration, but it is unusual at best to find such a spirit of togetherness extending over three continents and two centuries.

Although landscape features of Rohrbach/Odessa and Hurnville, Texas, are astonishingly similar, the initial shock of migrating from the richly forested, intensely cultural landscape of Germany to a boundless, treeless, but nonetheless fertile steppe in Russia must have posed some problems for the German pioneers. On the other hand, farming practices were similar, and Rohrbach/Odessa served as a training stage in the transfer from Germany to Texas. In Russia the settlers could continue residing in villages that sheltered the farmer, his animals, and his produce. Rohrbach, and for that matter almost all other Black Sea German villages, was a *Strassendorf* or village established along a central street, the farmstead a single, one-story stone building, long and narrow, with its gable side to the street and its entrance on the side in the farmyard. Summer kitchens were the rule.

At first, breaking the prairie ground in Russia was difficult, but with the introduction of a better plow around 1848 and, as the chronicler notes, more temperate habits of the farmers, most families had 100 to 160 acres in crops.[37] A different land distribution system allowed farmers here to acquire larger landholdings than might their compatriots along the Volga. This, along with the fertile nature of the soil, allowed many landholders to attain a considerable degree of wealth. Oral tradition recalls that each child of some families boasted its own Russian *Kindsmagd,* roughly the equivalent of the Anglo-American nanny.[38]

---

36. Karl Stumpp, *Die Auswanderung aus Deutschland nach Russland in den Jahren 1763 bis 1862* [Emigration from Germany to Russia in the Years 1763 to 1862] (Tübingen: privately published, 1974), pp. 788–94.

37. Adam Giesinger, "Villages in Which Our Forefathers Lived," *Work Paper of the American Historical Society of Germans from Russia* 22 (Winter, 1976): 28–29.

38. Frequent references will be made to a series of interviews conducted among the Hurnville Germans from Russia by Joe S. Graham for Glen E. Lich of the Institute of Texan Cultures in September, 1978. The author is indebted to both Graham and Lich for making transcripts of these tapes available to her. The wealth of the family in Russia was described in an interview with Edward and Rosie Wust Moser, in Clay County, Sept. 15, 1978.

Eventually the German farmers would be driven to church in fine carriages by their Russian servants, who then had to wait outside for their masters, winter and summer. The stark contrast of German master and Russian servant, the dominance of German culture and the contempt the Germans held for the less adroit Russians, gave cause for concern among the descendants.[39] Perhaps because of their own insights as a minority folk group in Texas, they regret that the Germans and Russians had not mixed or sought more productive cooperation. However, the fact remains that very few colonists learned Russian, and the German language was used exclusively in homelife, church, school, and even government. Year and family cycle traditions were preserved as they had been in Germany. Villages had been established as Protestant or Catholic; colonists rarely mixed with the other denominations, and generally marriages were arranged within the same village or in a neighboring or allied village. Marriage between a Protestant and a Catholic would be unthinkable, but marriage between a Rohrbach swain and a Waterloo maid not more than five miles away might be considered shaky as well.

Life on the steppe was monotonous, emphasizing the importance of year and life cycles. Routine was not broken by any blossoming cultural development; no first-class poet, writer, or playwright was produced, even though nearly every child could cipher and read and write German. No composer or virtuoso performer of international fame stemmed from the Black Sea villages, although musical instruction was highly prized and nearly every village had its band. Life centered on planting, tilling, harvest, and in the winter months, the relaxation brought by weddings and the Christmas festival. Focal point of all life beyond the field was the church. Hermann Dalton found in about 1868, "Politics, literature, industry, art, insofar as they relate to a rural popu-

---

36. Karl Stumpp, *Die Auswanderung aus Deutschland nach Russland in den Jahren 1763 bis 1862* [Emigration from Germany to Russia in the Years 1763 to 1862] (Tübingen: privately published, 1974), pp. 788–94.

37. Adam Giesinger, "Villages in Which Our Forefathers Lived," *Work Paper of the American Historical Society of Germans from Russia* 22 (Winter, 1976): 28–29.

38. Frequent references will be made to a series of interviews conducted among the Hurnville Germans from Russia by Joe S. Graham for Glen E. Lich of the Institute of Texan Cultures in September, 1978. The author is indebted to both Graham and Lich for making transcripts of these tapes available to her. The wealth of the family in Russia was described in an interview with Edward and Rosie Wust Moser, in Clay County, Sept. 15, 1978.

39. Interview with Leon Moser and Esther Louise Linstaedt Moser, Hurnville, Sept. 12–14, 1978.

lation, have entirely receded to the background, while all church and religious questions occupy most of the colonists in their leisure hours."[40]

In an investigation of the church and its continuing effect upon the Germans from Russia in Texas, we must appraise the peculiar religious tapestry of the Odessa area. On the surface, there were Protestant—after 1832, Reformed and Lutheran—villages, Catholic villages, and Mennonite villages. Religious freedom had been guaranteed, but each church cherished its own and guarded against infringement from any other, and all united against the Russian Orthodox, which was never really a serious threat, serving as it did only the Russian inhabitants. Even today in Germany, any faith beyond Catholic, Lutheran, and Reformed is nominally considered a sect. However, in 1909, Rohrbach claimed three prayer halls: a Lutheran, a Reformed, and a *Baptist*.[41] The Baptist prayer hall deserves some explanation. We have already seen how the Swabian influx of 1817–19 had established a Pietistic base, even if the former Separatists had joined Lutheran or Reformed congregations. Then in 1824 the Basel Evangelical Missionary School sent a born-again Christian of considerable persuasive rhetorical power, Johannes Bonekemper, to the flock at Rohrbach. After some initial discouragement, he soon began prayer meetings, Bible reading, and revivals in his home or wherever spirit and crowd found it convenient, and he was to become in a short time the "Father of Stundism" of south Russia. "Under his guidance religious awakenings, beginning in Rohrbach, spread to all the colonies in the surrounding region. In fact, the movement became so strong in Rohrbach that this village soon stood out as the stronghold of Stundism in south Russia. . . . Bonekemper had great talent for preaching and was an outstanding revivalist. . . . [T]housands of people gathered to hear his words. . . . He was working among Germans, some of whom had lived under Pietistic influence in their homeland, people who had brought with them a deep religious fervor."[42] Bonekemper remained until 1846, building the framework for the next evangelist.

Americans brought the first Baptist church to Germany. The first Baptist congregation was founded in Hamburg in 1834 by Johann Gerhart Oncken, who had been baptized by Americans in Berlin. German

---

40. Hermann Dalton, "Reformed Colonies in South Russia," trans. Theodore Charles Wenzlaff, *Work Paper of the American Historical Society of Germans from Russia* 3 (Feb., 1970): 20.

41. Giesinger, "Villages," p. 29.

42. George J. Eisenach, *Pietism and the Russian Germans in the United States* (Berne, Ind.: Berne, 1948), pp. 48–49.

Baptist missionaries appeared in both the Volga and Black Sea areas from about 1860, and Oncken himself, the leader of the German Baptists, followed them, visiting south Russia in 1869. By 1879 the Baptists were nominally recognized and condoned; Odessa became the center of missionary activity, and by 1897, Baptists numbered about twenty thousand.[43]

Although the nonconformity of the Baptists caused some friction and hostility at home, it would be wrong to suggest that religious convictions or the practice of religious freedom caused the migration of a cluster of Germans from Russia from the Black Sea to Hurnville beginning about 1890.[44] Nor was the cause hunger for land, for these migrants were accustomed to relative wealth, successful farming practices, and servants when they departed. Indeed, they exchanged the role of a dominant folk group, imposing its culture upon a more or less alien host, for the role of a suppressed and misunderstood minority group, whose initial survival depended upon solidarity of the group confronting the dominant "Englischer." To be sure, friends and relatives who had gone to America beginning in about 1872 and who had settled primarily in the Dakotas extolled the new opportunities of a fruitful land in their letters back home, and the quest for something better and the urge to be near loved ones contributed to no small degree to the migration of the Hurnville group.[45] But the single most significant factor leading to their emigration was a bold Russification policy since the ukase of 1874, the vulnerability of the young men to draft into the dreaded Russian army, and the fearsome prospect of having to serve six years. Coupled with the death of Czar Alexander III in 1894, the unsettled political climate aggravated the danger of such service, and the outbreak of war with Japan in 1904 ensured that there would be a tide of emigrants seeking to escape military service. Essentially the

---

43. Adam Giesinger, *From Catherine to Khrushchev: The Story of Russia's Germans* (Winnipeg: Marian Press, 1974), p. 191.

44. Douglas Hale, *The Germans from Russia in Oklahoma* (Norman: University of Oklahoma Press, 1980), p. 49. Pietistic tendencies are still evident in America among the people from Rohrbach. Enough settlers converted to Seventh Day Adventists to support a church near Hurnville a short while. Other Rohrbach natives, settling in Sutton, Clay County, Nebr., share the same family names as those in Hurnville. According to an interview with Mrs. Hugh Dobler in Lincoln, Nebr., May 10, 1980, the Hofer church in that community is distinguished by the fact that its beloved Pastor Hofer died early in the twentieth century and the congregation honors his memory by having lay members read Pastor Hofer's sermons and conduct church services themselves rather than calling another pastor.

45. Giesinger, *Catherine to Khrushchev*, p. 230.

tide exhausted itself by 1906. Indeed, first- and second-generation Germans from Russia in Clay County recall that they left only because of military service. They retain a good image of their life in Russia, where "everything you stick in the ground growed."[46]

Probably the first arrival of a German from Russia in the Hurnville community was George Wiest (Wüst); his family arrived in New York on the *Normannia* in September, 1890. Other early arrivals may have included Heinrich Schaffner, Adolph Oster, Fred Wohlgemuth, and John Forsch. There were already a few *Reichsdeutsche,* German nationals, in Clay County at the time, and quite naturally, Germans from Russia were prevailingly thought of (if they were noticed at all) as "Germans."[47] More often they were called "Dutchmen," in contrast to other parts of the United States, where they became known as "Rooshians." There may have been some advantage in this double concept, for George Wiest reported to the census in 1900 that he was born in Germany, as were his parents, wife, and two children, but naturalization records bear out his Russian birth. Census records of 1900 register 110 persons born in Russia in the county, of which 77 resided in precinct two, the Hurnville-Petrolia area.[48] Others were scattered throughout the county, including several Catholic families settling in the Windthorst community who migrated from Landau and Catharinenthal, both, like Rohrbach, in the Beresan enclave. In such a high concentration, it was easy enough to continue German traditions: the language, the tacked goose-down comforters instead of the quilts of the Anglo-Americans, the foods, viticulture, summer kitchens, field work from dawn till dusk, women working alongside men in the field, and the peculiar style of stucco rock adobe structures.

Even though the new landscape looked familiar, many of the early arrivals could not cope with the climatic extremes or other threatening factors; they left and joined kinsmen or compatriots in Oklahoma, Nebraska, or the Dakotas. Although the transplant called for sizable ini-

---

46. Interview with Alexander and Teenie Moser Bachman, Sept. 13–14, 1978, Clay County.

47. Even more recently, descendants of some German-born settlers were thought of as Germans from Russia. Taylor groups the Obermier family, actually *Reichsdeutsche,* with the Hurnville German-Russians. William Charles Taylor, *A History of Clay County* (Austin: Jenkins, 1972), pp. 78–79. This volume contains several interesting photographs from the Leon Moser collection, including one of the Moser homestead in Russia.

48. U.S. Census, manuscript schedules of population, 1900, Clay County, Tex. Also U.S. District Court, Naturalization records, Clay County, Tex.

tial adjustments (such as planting after the rain in Texas instead of before the rain as in Russia), hard work, large families, and frugality brought a portion of prosperity, so that by 1915, some families could boast sturdy bank accounts. Diversified farming, including small grains, cotton, and dairy cattle, brought success that was largely ignored but generally respected by the dominant Clay County Anglo-American leadership. The English language was limited to communication with that dominant group for commercial purposes; little note of the Germans from Russia appears in the Henrietta newspapers of the time, and the immigrants in their turn learned of the outside world from the German language newspaper, *Dakota Freie Presse*.[49] They established their own German Baptist church in 1894.[50] Its founding members include Germans from Russia as well as *Reichsdeutsche*. The church is not unique in any way; the first German Baptist church in Texas had been established long before in Washington County, and the German Baptist conference was organized in 1884.[51] It is, indeed, very likely that the early establishment of a Baptist church lent acceptability to the otherwise so different group. In Russia, Baptists had been set apart, if not persecuted, but in Texas they are the norm, and in Clay County they outnumber all others.[52] Among the Hurnville Germans from Russia, this church continued to be a uniting and preserving element in the lives of the group until it was dissolved in the 1950s. It offered a haven in the war years, when the superpatriots of Clay County found no distinction between *Reichsdeutsche* and Germans from Russia, and both were likely enemies, targets for public hatred. In 1914 the church was sealed off and an edict forbidding German worship posted at its door, an edict that was promptly ignored.[53] The critical attitude is made clear by no less than the editor of the Henrietta *Independent*, who wrote on November 15, 1918, in an editorial entitled "God Won the War," "God is against German kulter [sic] and will not let it prevail." Other German-Texan communities endured the same experiences, but they did not respond with the same degree of unity and cohesion, as they were not fostered by the same lasting historical bonds of this group

---

49. Interview with Leon Moser and Esther Louise Linstaedt Moser, Apr. 3, 1980, Hurnville, Tex.
50. Taylor, *History of Clay County*, p. 109.
51. Minnie Knispel, *Establishment and Development of the Kyle German Baptist Community* (N.p.: privately published, 1969), p. 19.
52. Taylor, *History of Clay County*, p. 109.
53. Interview with Magdalena Graf, Wilhelmina Graf Hoeffner, Leon Moser, Edwin Koeffner, and Vondee Hoeffner, Sept. 15, 1978, Henrietta, Tex.

nor the religious foundation of their immigrant experience. This unity served continuously to bind the group not only through the political buffets but through the agricultural metamorphosis of the North Texas heartland, as it changed from cotton-based economy to petroleum and wheat, from dairy to beef cattle. Fortunately, these changes came easily, for the gently rolling banks of the Red River offered no obstacle to ever-larger mechanized farm equipment, and fields were limited only by the amount of land a farmer-rancher owned.

The uniqueness of this group is further underscored by the special self-image it holds: literally all of the descendants of the original settlers who came from the Black Sea are aware of their heritage. After a few moments of reflection or a glance at a treasured document, most can even come up with the name of the village their parents and grandparents left. Shared language and traditions have supported a folk identity, but without the institutional bulwark of their common religious experience from Rohrbach and related villages, this sense of uniqueness might have been lost. It becomes poignantly striking when a present-day rancher comes in from a day of working cattle to share his letter from a cousin in distant Siberia, written in German. It sustains a tenuous thread of communication with the homeland that has been broken or forgotten by many immigrant groups of Texas.[54]

Although some farms are still intact and some descendants are still living in the area, as one settler stated, "the young people flied and the old people died." The process is inevitable. It was hastened by the sale of the church and the scattering of the flock. But the landscape, the economy, and the social structure of this part of Texas have been touched by the Black Sea.[55] It became something different than it would have been, had Alexander not allowed his Germans to leave.

Conclusion

Our sampling of Texas folk groups has been highly selective and fragmentary; it is intended to be so, providing in this manner some in-

---

54. In comparison, the German community of Windthorst, only twenty or so miles distant, has preserved some of its heritage but has lost the German language, for the most part. Interview with Edward Moser and Rosie Wust Moser, Sept. 15, 1978, Clay County.

55. An interesting consideration of the German-Russian building and architectural style has appeared in Terry Jordan, "A Russian-German Folk House in North Texas," *Built in Texas,* ed. Francis Edward Abernethy, Publications of the Texas Folklore Society 42 (Waco: E-Heart, 1979), pp. 136–38.

The gravestone in Texas of a German from Russia.

sight into possibilities for research more than access to or instruction concerning the group. In each case our view has been from the other side, from the group as outsiders. Whether our groups came voluntarily as immigrants in quest of land, or whether they came by force of slavery or with new territory acquired by conquest or purchase, they maintained a separate role through commitment to their own identity or through rejection of the mainstream. In conclusion, we might reaffirm the benefit of folk-group research for its own sake and for contributing to a more thorough understanding of Texas as a place apart.

Of fourteen features recently recommended for the study of ethnicity, the combination of internally or externally perceived distinctiveness, religious faith, and ties that transcend kinship, neighborhood, and community boundaries seems most salient for rural Texas groups.[56] In some instances, distinctiveness is bound to birth, such as color or language, features that powerfully resist assimilation. In others, distinctiveness is ascriptive, harnessed to history or to place. In each of our samplings we have implicitly or explicitly described the cohesive unifying force of the church. A breakdown in faith, even the dissolution of a community church, may lead to a revised folk-group integrity. Furthermore, as Texas transforms progressively from a rural to an urban scene, folk ties will adjust, relax, reform, and perhaps in some cases disappear. In whatever form, however, folk ties will continue to be a part of any definition of Texas.

At a time when we might be tempted to contrive an "ethnic Texan," set apart by a conceived folklore, tradition, or other distinctive features, we might also examine those forces that lead us into such scrubby range. The first of these forces is assimilation, the unifying tendency to make us all alike, absorbed, and uniform. It is nourished by technology, urbanization, public school education, and the urge to "manage"—even agriculture students are required to study "range management," "agribusiness," and animal "science." It is the same tendency that views people as "human resources," something to be used, classified, and, if possible, improved.

56. Thernstrom, ed., *Harvard Encyclopedia*, p. vi. The features recommended are (1) common geographic origin, (2) migratory status, (3) race, (4) language or dialect, (5) religious faith or faiths, (6) ties that transcend kinship, neighborhood, and community boundaries, (7) shared traditions, values, and symbols, (8) literature, folklore, and music, (9) food preferences, (10), settlement and employment patterns, (11) special interests with regard to politics in the homeland and in the United States, (12) institutions that specifically serve and maintain the group, (13) an internal sense of distinctiveness, (14) an external perception of distinctiveness.

The other force is acculturation, or the process of learning a second culture. It is the process that causes us to examine our own values when they conflict with another culture, to appraise our role in society when confronted with diversity, and to make choices based upon such examination and appraisal of our surrounding reality. It is also the process that lends a degree of authenticity to our "ethnic Texans," as they seek in the role of slightly ridiculous urban cowboys to retrieve a perceived loss. It is discovery of identity in a climate of change, a statement conditioned not so much by nostalgia as by societal conviction.

Afterword
John J. McDermott

The story of Texas is replete with the presence and adventures of those who came from elsewhere in this nation and abroad, and who built a legendary and prosperous community. These immigrants to Texas were of multiple racial, religious, ethnic, and political origins. They built a state while faced with the stubborn and arid land, the vagaries of weather, the enormous distances between settlements, and the complex and challenging ecological variety of flora and fauna. Conflicts with the native Americans of Texas, who were rightfully enraged by these incursions, provided still another major difficulty. Immigrants to Texas saw their move as both a challenge and an opportunity. This dialectic between possibility and disappointment is a central theme in the present book.

Readers of these essays confront a series of emergent themes. Taking them in order, we find the rural-urban dichotomy, hard times or "hard scrabble" as the lot of most Texans, the self-made or "macho" version of Texan success, and the plurality of peoples but the narrowness of opportunity for many of them. These themes of loss and gain have significance for the Texas of the twenty-first century.

The shift in Texas urban and rural population figures is most startling. From less than 10 percent urban population in 1870, we have moved to 90 percent urban population in 1980. Thus, in slightly more than a century, Texas life-style has reversed itself. The obvious daily environment for Texans of the nineteenth century has become the object of nostalgia for the late twentieth century. These figures connote more than a mere geographical or demographical realignment of the Texas population. The distinction between coming to consciousness in a genuinely rural environment, as in historical Texas of the past, is as different from growing up in a suburb of Houston or Dallas as it would be to have been nurtured in a foreign land.

This demographic development is paralleled in the rest of this nation. Some 90 percent of Americans now live on 10 percent of the land. Government and absentee ownership account for most of this inequitable distribution of our population. Virtually all of the forty-eight continental United States have experienced an extensive growth of urban population and a decline of rural population. Yet, the Texas experience is different. First, Texas has a tradition of vastness that renders the term *rural* almost equivalent to cozy. Texas was not rural in the sense of New England or Kentucky or even Colorado. Texas was the epitome of the West—storied, frightening, endless, a haven for escapees from previous failure or cultural claustrophobia and mavericks of every persuasion. Actually, Texas was what Europeans thought, incorrectly as it turned out, America to be. Texas fulfilled the exotic dream Europeans had of America and eastern Americans of the West.

One could disappear into Texas. The great western films portrayed Texas as endless, nay, infinite space, in a finite earth. No matter the source of discontent or flight from the past, Texas had room for anonymous presence, and, indeed, structured its early government and institutional life on the protection of just that precious anonymity.

The awesome space of Texas generated two characteristics: hard times and a determination to "make it" on one's own abilities, against the elements, unhindered by the trappings of civilization. This was especially true of West Texas. Listen to Larry L. King in his essay on "The Lost Frontier."

> The land is stark and flat and treeless, altogether as bleak and spare as mood scenes in Russian literature, a great dry-docked ocean with small swells of hummocky tan sand dunes or humpbacked rocky knolls that change colors with the hour and the shadows: reddish brown, slate gray, bruise colored. But it is the sky—God-high and pale, like a blue chenille bedspread bleached by seasons in the sun—that dominates. There is simply *too much* sky. Men grow small in its presence and—perhaps feel diminished—they sometimes are compelled to proclaim themselves in wild or berserk ways. Alone in those remote voids, one may suddenly half believe he is the last man on earth and go in frantic search of the tribe. Desert fever, the natives call it. . . .
>
> The summer sun is as merciless as a loan shark: a blinding, angry orange explosion baking the land's sparse grasses and quickly aging the skin.[1]

1. In *The Old Man and Lesser Mortals* (New York: Delta, 1975), p. 207.

Afterword

Well into the twentieth century, most Texans had hard times, but many of the early Texans regarded these obstacles as the stuff of life. They resented subsequent generations who attempted to tame Texas and make it like the other states. Indeed, this obdurance with regard to the importation of so-called civilization into Texas is a strand of folk music and tall tales, and, although severely diluted in our time, remains an important ingredient of contemporary Texas culture. This book is rich in detail about these features of Texas history—covering song, prairie life, and housing. Hard times, indeed, but always accompanied by a provocative and evocative version of the human condition, Texas style, complete with an original and intense aesthetic context.

One theme remains to be discussed: the difficulty many settlers had in being accepted. In the instances of women and ethnic minorities, this problem remains today, as the compelling essays by Martha Allen and Dona Reeves-Marquardt witness. Despite the political tolerance of Texas and its populist tradition, women and ethnics found assimilation, acceptance, and possibility for growth difficult to achieve. Some ethnics have long since made their way into the fabric of Texas life. Women, propelled by a national movement, have slowly begun to crack the male chauvinist attitudes so endemic to Texas manners, politics, economics, and life-style. Mexican Americans have closed the gap, somewhat, but proportionate to their long-standing role in Texas history, they are, to this day, still struggling for proper recognition.

The plight of black Americans in Texas is quite another story. Long segregated in schools and housing, they have not prospered in contemporary Texas. As several of the preceding essays chronicle, the demise of the family or small farm in Texas has worked to their severe disadvantage. The rapid and almost total urbanization of Texas has served to disenfranchise black Americans, whose cultural history in Texas was distinctively and creatively rural. More than in any other state in the Southwest, black Americans in Texas have become a *Lumpenproletariat* deprived of their rural heritage and systemically excluded from the spoils of the booming, new metropolitan urban areas.

Other contemporary Texans, liberated from the hard times, can look back at the positive aspects of the lives of the early settlers. Song and story, stripped of the harshness of reality, embellish the past and render the present jejune and boring. Yet, recent events plead for recognition. The question before us, as Texans, is just how we choose to grow, to develop, to make our distinctive mark on the United States. Economically, because of agriculture and energy, Texas is at the center, not only of the national but of the international ecosystem. This may,

Afterword

or may not, continue. One thinks, for example, of the fragility of the energy market or the dire warnings pertaining to the water crisis facing West Texas.

More to the point, Texas, understandably nostalgic about the precious conquest of hard times and hard scrabble, has failed to identify a newer and more insidious enemy that emerges with the rise of urbanization. Sentimentality about our space, prairies, Longhorns, and bluebonnets has blocked us from acknowledging that we have the most inept, inefficient, and even absent urban transportation system in the nation. Even though Texas has three of the ten most populated cities in America, we seem to know very little about how cities function: their ambience, their charm, their dangers, and their needs. We rank atrociously low in money spent for public libraries, teacher salaries, social services, and cultural amenities in the public sector. Texas now faces different hard times, urban rather than rural. By the year 2000 Texas cities will confront social, educational, and racial problems of an intense and even inflammatory nature. The "scrabble" then will be different than the "scrabble" of this book. The challenge, however, will remain identical. Texans, whatever their origin, are once again called upon to act with courage, imagination, and above all, tolerance for diversity. Texas is fast becoming the flagship state of the nation, replacing New York and California. It is our biggest challenge, and our finest hour. We cannot allow nostalgia for our legendary past to prevent us from having a momentous and path-setting future.

The Contributors

FRANCIS EDWARD ABERNETHY is professor of English at Stephen F. Austin State University, the executive secretary and editor of the Texas Folklore Society, and a member of the Texas Institute of Letters. He is the editor of *Tales from the Big Thicket, Built in Texas, Legendary Ladies of Texas,* and eight other volumes for the Texas Folklore Society. He has published poetry, short stories, a folk music book entitled *Singin' Texas,* and a book of legends entitled *Legends of Texas' Heroic Age.*

MARTHA MITTEN ALLEN serves as professor of history and director of the American studies program at Southwestern University in Georgetown, Texas. Her doctoral dissertation was based on travel accounts by women in the West in the nineteenth century, and subsequent publications have focused on western travel and women's history.

BETSY COLQUITT is professor of English at Texas Christian University and editor of *Descant,* a literary quarterly. Editor of several books, including *A Part of Space: Ten Texas Writers,* and *Honor Card,* a poetry collection, she has published essays, fiction, and poetry.

JOE B. FRANTZ teaches now at Corpus Christi State University. For many years he taught at the University of Texas, where he was the first Walter Prescott Webb Professor of History and Ideas. He has published widely in oral history and been visiting professor at universities throughout the Americas. He has also served as historical advisor of the National Aeronautics and Space Administration and consultant in history to the White House.

JOE S. GRAHAM is a specialist in the folklore of Texas, particularly Texas-Mexican folklore. He is assistant professor of English at

The Contributors

Texas A&M University. From 1977 to 1979 he was the Folklorist-in-Residence at the University of Texas Institute of Texan Cultures in San Antonio. He has published one book and a number of articles in folklore.

GLEN E. LICH teaches English and German at Schreiner College and is the author of *The German Texans*. He is the editor of *German Culture in Texas: A Free Earth* and of *The Cabin Book*. His areas of specialization are regional American studies, German-American cultural relations, and visual aspects of history and literature.

AL LOWMAN is a longtime resident of Stringtown, Texas, where he grew up and still lives on the family ranch with his wife and two children. Since 1968 he has been a research associate at the University of Texas Institute of Texan Cultures at San Antonio. He has published several books and articles dealing with the history, folklore, and art of Texas and the Southwest. His latest book is *Printing Arts in Texas*.

INGEBORG R. MCCOY, educated in Germany and at the University of Texas at Austin, is professor of modern languages at Southwest Texas State University. She specializes in women's studies and German-Texan culture.

JOHN J. MCDERMOTT is Distinguished Professor of Philosophy and Humanities and professor and head of Medical Humanities at Texas A&M University. He is editor of scholarly editions of the writings of Josiah Royce, John Dewey, and William James. He is cofounder and advisory editor of a critical edition of *The Works of William James* and author of more than thirty essays in scholarly journals and collections of essays.

DONA B. REEVES-MARQUARDT is professor of German at Southwest Texas State University. She has published translations, articles, and books on German Renaissance drama, foreign language teaching, ethnicity, and multicultural studies. She has served as president of the Texas Foreign Language Association, was a founder of the German Texan Heritage Society, and was elected to serve on the National Executive Council of the American Association of Teachers of German and the International Board of Directors of the American Historical Society of Germans from Russia.

CLARENCE C. SCHULTZ served on the faculty of Lee College in Baytown, Texas, where he taught history, sociology, and political

The Contributors

science, and he is now professor of sociology at Southwest Texas State University. In 1976 he was named a Piper Professor by the Minnie Stevens Piper Foundation.

J. B. SMALLWOOD, JR., is associate professor of American history at North Texas State University. He is the author of numerous articles and papers concerning southern and environmental history.

JUNE VAN CLEEF, photographer, has completed advanced study in photography at the Visual Studies Workshop in Rochester, New York. She teaches photography at the college level. Her prints have achieved distinction in exhibitions and shows throughout Texas, and her recent work includes documentary photography of vanishing Texana—landscape, architecture, and people.

KARL WEIGAND is professor of geography and director of the Research Institute for Regional Studies at the Flensburg Teachers College, and he has held an appointment at Kiel University since 1970. He has published in Germany on the cultural geography of South Texas, and in 1977 he published *Chicano-Wanderarbeiter in Südtexas: Die gegenwärtige Situation der Spanisch sprechenden Bevölkerung dieses Raumes,* the only book-length study in this field in the German language.

DEL WENIGER chairs the Department of Biology at Our Lady of the Lake University in San Antonio. He is the author of *Cacti of the Southwest, Cacti of Texas and Neighboring States,* and *The Explorers' Texas: The Lands and Waters,* and has published articles on botany and ecology.

JOSEPH WILSON is professor of German at Rice University. Most of his publications have been concerned with the Texas Germans, especially the Wendish Germans in Lee County; others have dealt with Old Germanic, computerized lexicography, and Texas archeology. He has spent research leaves at the universities of Kiel and Marburg with the aid of grants from the Humboldt Foundation.

Index

Abbot, Teddy Blue, 176
Abilene, Tex., 54, 57–58
Abraham, Lee, 191
acculturation, 241. *See also* assimilation
Acuff, Roy, 162, 168
Adams, Andy, 176
Adventures of Big-Foot Wallace, 175
Adventures with a Texas Naturalist, 178
agriculture, 245; commercialization of, 78, 84–85; labor force and, 206; Mexican Americans and, 194; Old World, 231, 232; and rural life, 127; specialization in, 67, 69, 109
Agua Dulce, Tex., 196
Aguayo expedition, 46, 49
aircraft industry, 88
airports, 84
Albany, Tex., 56, 184
All My Friends Are Going to Be Strangers, 185–86
Allen, George N., 145
Allen, W. B., 51
Allentown, Tex., 217
Allison, John, 59
Allred, James V., 83
Alpha, Tex., 58
Alpine, Tex., 64
Alsace, Germany, 231
Alvarado, Tex., 51
Amarillo, Tex., 48–49, 132
America in Search of Itself, 12
American Farm Bureau Federation, 80

American Songbag, 142
Anahuac, Tex., 39
Anderson, Tex., 206
Anderson County, 56
Andice, Tex., 131
Angelina County, 46
Angelina National Forest, 18
Anglo Americans: discrimination by, 205; housing of, 104; immigration to Texas of, 95; as landowners in West Texas, 133; musical heritage of, 157, 162; place names chosen by, 38, 41, 46–47, 53; political affiliations of, 73; in San Marcos, 197, 198; towns established by, 39, 55, 201; transiency of, 194
Anson, Tex., 60
Antelope, Tex., 53
Anthony, Tex., 42
Antioch, Tex., 53
Apache tribe, 40, 46
Apple Springs, Tex., 52
Aransas Bay, 38
Aransas Pass, Tex., 38
Archer City, Tex., 185
architecture: basic plans for, 102–103, 111; folk, 92–116; government plans for, 111–12, 113; Victorian, 107, 172
"The Arkansas Traveler," 152
Arlington, Tex., 10
art, 233
Arthur, John, 51
assimilation, 204, 219, 220, 221, 226, 240, 241, 245. *See also* acculturation
Atascosa, Tex., x

250

Index

251

Atascosita (later Liberty), Tex., 42
Athens, Tex., 56
Atlanta, Tex., 56
Austin, Stephen F., 27, 43
Austin, Tex., 24, 60, 72, 198, 203
Austin County, 43, 60
Austrians, 77
automobiles, 78, 83, 196, 200
Autry, Gene, 41, 162
Avalon, Tex., 57

Baden, Germany, 231
Bailey, Joseph W., 78
Bailey County, 59
Balcones Escarpment, 93
Bandera, Tex., 46
Bandera Pass, 46
banks, 73
Banquete, Tex., 50
Baptists, 235, 237
barbed wire, 75, 109
Barney, William, 184
Barr, Amelia, 175
Barthelme, Donald, 184
Bastrop, Tex., 60, 177
Bastrop County, 27
Bean, Judge Roy, 60
Beaumont, Tex., 82, 87
Bebe, Tex., 58
Bedichek, Roy, 177–78, 187
Bee County, 39, 51
Bell, Peter Hansborough, 60
Bells, Tex., 53
Belton, Tex., 60
Benavides, Placido, 47
Benavides, Tex., 47
Ben Bolt, Tex., 62
Ben Ficklin, Tex., 44
Bennett, Patrick, 185
Ben Nevis, 220, 222
The Best Little Whorehouse in Texas, 184
Bethany, Tex., 53
Bethel, Tex., 53
Bethlehem, Tex., 53
Bettie, Tex., 130
Bexar County, 39
Birdsong, 184
Black, Reading W., 46

blacklands, 17, 95
blacks, 74, 130, 131, 134, 192, 204, 205, 219, 245
Black Sea, 229, 230, 233, 238
Blanco County, 128, 131
Boerne, Ludwig, 57
Boerne, Tex., 58
Bogata, Tex., 56
Boggess, I. H., 54
Bonham, Tex., 60, 80
Borden, Gail, 60
Borden County, 60
Bosque County, 56, 59
Bosqueville, Tex., x
Bovina, Tex., 50
Bowden, Velma, 130
Bowie, Tex., 60
Bowie County, 58, 129
Bracht, Viktor, 27
Bradburn, Col. Juan Davis, 25
Bradley, Tom, 208
Braun, Caspar, 223
Brazoria County, 60
Brazos River, 25, 27, 30, 39, 187, 190, 192, 205, 206, 208, 217, 219
Brazos River Conservation and Reclamation District, 82
Brazoswood, 64
Broadway, Tex., 49
Bronte, Tex., 57
Brooks County, 50, 131
Brown County, 55, 77
brush country, 95
Bryan, John Neely, 60
Bryan, Tex., 131
Buckeye, Tex., 56
Buda, Tex., 48
buffalo hunters, 142–43
"The Buffalo Hunters" ("Caledonia"), 143
Bullard, Anna Mae Parks, 207–208, 212–17
Bullard, Eugene, 206–207, 212–16
Bullfrog Creek, 223
Buna, Tex., 184
Burkburnett, Tex., 62
Burleson, Edward, 38, 60
Burnet, David G., 60
Burnet County, 131

Index

Burrowes, Jack, 29
business, 66–91, 119, 203
Bustamante, Anastasio, 47
Bustamante, Tex., 47
Bustillo y Cevallos, Juan Antonio, 43
Butterfield Overland Mail Route, 45

The Cabin Book, 5
Cactus, Tex., 52
Caddo, Tex., 38
Caddoan tribe, 39
Cadiz, Tex., 51
Cajuns, 136
Calallen, Tex., 62
Calhoun County, 95
Calvert, Tex., 206–207, 208
Cameron County, 43, 49
Camp County, 129–30
Canaan, Tex., 53
Canary Islanders, 42
Candelaria, Tex., 47
Cañon de Ugalde, 46
Canyon, Tex., 184
Carrizo (later Zapata), Tex., 46–47
Carson County, 132
Castro, Henri, 60
Castro County, 132
Castroville, Tex., 24
Catarina, Tex., 47
Catholics, 234
Catlett, Hellon, 129
Cat Spring, Tex., 57
cattle, 26–27, 28, 74, 86, 131, 132, 133, 207. *See also* ranching
cattle drives, 75
cattlemen, 76, 142, 144
Caucasians, 130
Cedar Grove, Tex., 52
cemeteries, 226
Central Texas, 131, 181–82, 183, 219, 220
Chambers, Thomas Jefferson, 39
Chambersea (later Anahuac), Tex., 39
change: in rural areas, 126, 134
Chapin, Edwin, 145
chemical industry, 81
Cherokee, Tex., 38
Cherokee Creek, 38
Cherry Springs, Tex., 52

Chicanos. *See* Mexican Americans
children, 227, 232
Childress, George W., 60
Childress County, 50
China Grove, Tex., 52
Chinese, 60, 64
Chittenden, Larry, 175
churches, 215, 226, 240
Cibolo, Tex., 39
"Cindy," 142
Civil War, 142, 174, 193
Clay County, 229, 230, 232, 236, 237
Cleek, Mauna Loa, 127, 132–33
Cleveland, Tex., 60
climate, 7, 17, 20, 23–24, 69, 93, 96, 104, 182
"Clinch Mountain," 151
Closner, John, 44
Clute, Tex., 64
coal, 80, 87
Coastal Plains, 93, 95
"Coffee Grows on White Oak Trees," 140–41
Coldwater Creek, 57
Coleman County, 41, 47, 58
Collin County, 59
Colorado County, 19, 40, 56
Colorado River, 25, 30, 177, 219
Colton, Walter, 57
Columbus, Tex., 19, 56
Comal County, 131
Comanche, Tex., 38, 46
Comanche County, 46, 55, 59
Comanche tribe, 5, 41, 143
Comfort, Tex., 58, 59
Commerce, Tex., 59
community, sense of, 209, 212
Concepcion, Tex., 46
Concho County, 40, 55, 133
conservation, 8, 10, 82
conservatism, 12
Constitution of 1876, 74
Corinth, Tex., 53
Corpus Christi, Tex., x, 57
Corpus Christi Bay, 41
Corsicana, Tex., 77
cotton, 204, 209–10; economic impact of, 109, 111; modern farming of, 85, 193; monoculture of, 79,

Index

253

cotton (cont.)
  111; and parity payments, 80; industries related to, 82, 85; and tenant farming, 109, 111, 193, 206
Cotton Belt Railroad, 77
Cotton Control (Bankhead) Act, 80
Cotulla, Simon, 70
Coupland, Tex., 61
courtship, 150–51, 213, 214
cowboys, 194. *See also* myth: of cowboy
Cox, Myrl, 131
Cox, Paris, 108
crawfish, 130, 134
Crèvecoeur, J. Hector St. John, 6
"Cripple Creek," 152
Crockett, David, 51
Crockett, Tex., 60
Crockett County, 133
Cross Timbers, 95, 142
Crystal City, Tex., 52
Cuero, Tex., 39, 47
Cuero Creek, 39
Cullinan, J. S., 77
cultural pluralism, 93
culture, 192–94, 219, 228
Czechs, 56

Daffan, Ted, 165
dairying, 132, 134
Dakota Freie Presse, 237
Dalhart, Vernon, 162
Dallas, George Mifflin, 60
Dallas, Tex., 60, 72, 73, 122, 132, 160, 165, 204, 243
Dallas County, 52, 58
Dalton, Hermann, 233
dancing, 152–54
Danes, 49
Danevang, Tex., x, 49
dating. *See* courtship
"The Daughter of Mendoza," 175
Dawson County, 133
Decatur, Stephen, 60
De Cordova, J., 19
Deep Creek, 100
Dees, Etta Rush, 126
DeLeon, Tex., 46
Del Rio, Tex., 43

Demmer, John, 45
Democratic party, 73, 74
depression, 81, 99, 111, 207
Devault family, 217
Dewees, W. B., 27–28
DeWitt, Bart, 45
Díaz, Porfirio, 47
Dilley, Tex., 196, 199, 200, 202
Dimmit County, 47, 70
Dinero, Tex., 51
discrimination, 205, 210, 222
Dixie, Tex., 59
Dixie Dewdrops, 3
Doak's Spring, Tex., 207
Dobie, J. Frank, 36, 175, 176, 177–79, 182, 185, 187
Donley County, 54
drama, 191
dress, 194, 196, 229, 236
drought, 10, 24, 90
Drummond, Thomas, 25
Duke, Cordia Sloan, 121
Dupree, Joe, 57
Dust Bowl, 12
Duster, Tex., 55
Duval, John Crittenden, 175
Duval County, 46, 47

Eagle Lake, Tex., 40
Eagle Pass, Tex., 19
Earth, Tex., 55
Eastland County, 54, 59
East Texas, 177, 204; cattle raising in, 74–75; entertainment in, 150, 160; housing in, 99, 101, 104; immigrants to, 95; rural women in, 129, 133, 134; steel production in, 88; timbering in, 88; writers from, 183
Ebenezer, Tex., 53
ecology, 169; transitions in, 24, 29, 30–32
economy, 67, 72, 77–78, 84, 86, 193; agriculture, 67, 69–71; cotton production, 69, 79, 84, 85; manufacturing, 67, 88; petrochemical industry, 76–77, 81, 87; railroads, 71–72; ranching, 74–76, 86
Ector County, 52

Edcouch, Tex., 62
Eden, Fred, 55
Eden, Tex., 37, 55
Edna, Tex., 62
Edom, Tex., 53
education, 129–34, 192, 198, 200, 205, 217, 240, 245
"Edward," 151
Edwards Plateau, 86, 95
El Campo, Tex., 50
Eldorado, Tex., 51
electricity, 130; introduction of, 126–27, 134
Ellis County, 56
Elm Grove, Tex., 52
El Paso, Tex., 2, 48, 88
El Paso County, 42, 43
Elysian Fields, Tex., 54
Encinal, Tex., 50, 130
Encino, Tex., 50
energy, 87, 245
Energy, Tex., 59
English, 5, 57, 226, 227, 228
Enon, Tex., 53
environment, 96, 105, 111, 169; protection of, 88. See also ecology
Eola, Tex., 40
Equal Rights Amendment (ERA), 128
Erath County, 131
Ernst, Friedrich, 5
Escandón, José de, 43, 44
Espinosa, Tex., 43
ethnic groups, 84, 92–116, 129–34. See also specific ethnic groups
ethnicity, 133, 245; discrimination and, 199, 204, 205, 206, 211, 222, 237, 238; language and, 200, 204, 219, 220–23, 224–28; life-styles and, 198, 204, 207, 212, 236, 238; pervasiveness of culture and, 193, 196, 228; religion and, 204, 213, 215–16, 219–20, 222, 224, 237. See also acculturation; assimilation; specific ethnic groups
Eulogy, Tex., 59
Eureka, Tex., 54
European immigrants, 219. See also specific ethnic groups
explorers, 5, 18–30

Fair Play, Tex., 59
Fairyland, Tex., 55
Falfurrias, Tex., 40
family, 162, 182, 204, 212–15
Fannin County, 51, 57, 58
Farm Bureau Federation, 80
farmers: cattlemen vs., 76
Farmers' Alliance, 72
Farmers' Alliance Exchange, 73
Farmers' Alliance Exchange of Texas, 72–73
Farmers Home Administration, 115
Farmers' Union, 74, 79, 80
farming, 29, 67, 69, 72, 84, 109, 131, 206, 207, 220, 231, 238
Farm-Labor Union, 80
farm-ranch economy, 229
farms: mortgages of, 79; size of, 112, 114, 129–34; tenancy and sharecropping on, 67, 71, 85, 109, 112, 193, 194, 207
Faulkner, William, 175
Fayette County, 19, 56
Federal Farm Board, 80
Fedor, Tex., 226
Fence-Cutting War, 76
fencing, 75, 109
festivals, 226
films, 244
Fincher, Suzan, 132
"Fire on the Mountain," 153
Fisher-Miller land grant, 38
floods, 24
flora and fauna, 17–34, 49, 52–53
Flores, Luciano, 43
Flores de Abryo, Francisco, 47
Floresville, Tex., 39, 47
Flour Bluff, Tex., 57
Flowering Judas, 179
Foley, Curtis, 153
Foley, Red, 153
folk groups. See ethnic groups
folklore, 138, 177, 194, 240
food processing, 88
foods, 129, 131, 148, 193, 194, 196, 236
football, 193
forests, 81, 88
Forsch, John, 236

Index

Fort, Fairy, 58
Fort Concho, 45
Fort Worth, Tex., 82, 122, 132, 172
Fort Worth and Denver Railroad, 107
Forward, Tex., 59
Franklin County, 129–30
Frantz, Joe B., 121
Fredericksburg, Tex., 56
Freeport, Tex., 81, 88
freight, 83
French, 5, 26, 130
Friendswood, Tex., 59–60
Frio County, 196
"Froggie Went a'Courtin," 149–50
From a Limestone Ledge, 187
frontier, 24, 29, 149–51, 169, 183, 193, 228
frontiersman, image of, 142
Frost, Robert, 172
Fruitland, Tex., 52
fruits, 85, 132, 133

Gail, Tex., 60
Gaines County, 133
Galilee, Tex., 53
Galveston, Tex., 24, 83, 107, 132
Galveston Bay, 40, 46
Galveston, Harrisburg and San Antonio Railway, 64
Galveston Island, 25
Gálvez, Bernardo de, 46
Garden City, Tex., 55
Garreau, Joel, 14
Garza, Felipe de la, 43
Garza Falcón, Blas María de la, 42
Gay, Thomas, 58
Gay Hill, Tex., 58
Gay's Mill, Tex., 55
General Land Office, 228
General Neighborhood Renewal Project, 197
geography, 3, 93
Georgetown, Tex., 123, 126, 131
Germans, 130, 131; architecture of, 104–105; founding of towns by, 45, 56, 58, 59; as immigrants, 5, 59, 95, 138; from Russia, 192, 228–38; Wendish, 220–28
Geronimo, Tex., 44

Gethsemene, Tex., 53
"The Gift Outright," 172
Gipson, Fred, 2, 183
Glensprings, Tex., 63
Glory, Tex., 55
goat and mohair production, 86, 133
Golden Triangle, 165
Goliad, Tex., 26
Gonzales County, 58
Goodbye to a River, 176, 187
Goodnight, Charlie, 175, 176, 177
Gospel Ridge (later Bells), Tex., 53
government, state, 78
Goyen, William, 2, 183
grain, 83, 85
Grand Bluff Road, 59
Grand Ole Opry, 162
Grand Prairie, Tex., 17, 184
Grange, 72, 73, 74
Grapevine, Tex., 52
"The Grave," 182
Graves, John, 10–11, 172, 176, 179, 185, 187, 189
Grayson County, 41, 53
The Great Frontier, 178
Great Plains, 143
The Great Plains, 177
Green, Frank, 217
Greenbacker Party, 72
Greene, A. C., 54
Greer County, 146–49
"The Greer County Bachelor" ("Irish Washerwoman"), 148
Gregg County, 58
Grider, Sylvia Ann, 182
Grit, Tex., 59
Growing Up in Texas, 175
Grulla, Tex., 50
Guadalupe County, 39, 44, 95
Guadalupe River, 25, 27
Guerra, Manuel, 50
Guide to the Life and Literature of the Southwest, 178–79
Gulf Coast, 87, 130
Gulf of Mexico, 48, 57

Hale County, 132
Haley, J. Evetts, 175, 176
Hamburg, Germany, 234

Index

Hamilton County, 58
Handbook of Texas, 39, 58
"Hangman's Tree," 151
Hardeman County, 41
Hard Scrabble, 187
"Hark! From the Tomb," 159–60
Harmony Hill, 59
Harris County, 19
Harrison County, 56, 59
Hartley, Marsden, 2
Hasinai tribe, 38
Hawkins, Tex., 57
Hays County, 29, 48, 53, 196, 203
"He," 181
Hebron, Tex., 53
Helotes, Tex., 40
Henrietta, Tex., 232
Henrietta *Independent*, 237
Herff, Ferdinand von, 20
Hewetson, James, 45, 47
Hickey, Dave, 171
Hicks, Ben, 44
Hidalgo County, 49
High Plains, 85, 90
highway system, 83
Hill, W. C., 58
Hill Country, 14, 24, 58, 95
Hilldale, Tex., 55
Hindman, Pete, 58
Hispanics. See Mexican Americans
Hockley County, 111
Hogg, James S., 74
Hohensee, Patricia, 133
holidays, 233
Honey Grove, Tex., 51
Hopkins County, 51, 55
Horner, J. E., 56
Horseman, Pass By, 185, 186
horses, 86
House, E. M., 78
houses, 194, 201, 229, 232, 236, 245; adobe, 92, 96; building materials for, 92–116; codes and standards for rural, 116; "dog-trot," 101; dugout, 92, 94, 105; *Fachwerk*, 92, 96, 105; farm, 92–116; frame, 99, 102, 105, 107–108; *jacal*, 92, 96–97, 98; living conditions in rural, 110–11, 112, 113, 114, 123, 127, 146–47, 197, 199;

houses (*cont.*)
log cabin, 92, 99–100, 101, 104; ownership of, 200–201, 202–203; site selection for, 104; size of, 110; sod, 105, 146, 148
Houston, Tex., 60, 83, 87, 107, 165, 168, 185, 204, 205, 243
Houston County, 27
Howard, V. C., 51
Howell, Joe, 54
Hoxey, Asa, 58
Hubbard, Richard, 60
Humboldt, Wilhelm von, 219
Humphrey, William, 183
Hungerford, Daniel E., 62
Hungerford, Tex., 62
Hurnville, Tex., 192, 228, 238
hurricanes, 24

Iago, Tex., 57
Ikin, Arthur, 18, 22
immigrants, illegal, 203
immigration, 220, 221
Impact, Tex., 57, 58
Independence, Tex., 57, 58
Indianola, Tex., 24
Indians. See native Americans
industrialization, 67, 77, 84, 86, 194
Industry, Tex., 59, 223, 224
Inez, Tex., 62
Inez, A Tale of the Alamo, 175
International and Great Northern Railway, 48
Interwoven, 175
Iowa Park, Tex., 55
Ireland, John, 60
"The Irish Washerwoman," 152
Italy, Tex., 56
Ivanhoe, Tex., 57

Jack Dobell: or A Boy's Adventures in Texas, 175
Jackson County, 42
Jacksonville, Tex., 60
Jefferson, Tex., 60
Jericho, Tex., 53, 54
Jewett, Tex., 207
Jim Hogg County, 130
Jim Wells County, 49

Index

Johnson City, 131
Johnson County, 51
Johnston, Eliza, 24
Jones, Anson, 60
Jones, Preston, 184
Jones County, 60
A Journey through Texas, 6
Juno, Tex., 48

Kapp, Ida, 7
Karankawa tribe, 3, 40
Karnack, Tex., 56
Katemcy, Tex., 41
Kaufman County, 129
Keechi, Tex., 38, 39
Kelton, Elmer, 176, 183, 185
Kemah, Tex., 40
Kendall County, 39, 58, 59
Kennedy, William, 18, 19
Kichai tribe, 39
Kickapoo, Tex., 38
Kilgore, Dan, 41
Kilian, John, 220, 222, 224
Kimble County, 58
King, Larry, 184
Kinney, Henry L., 42
Kiomatia, Tex., 40
Kiowa tribe, 143
Kiwanis Club, 199
Kleberg, Robert, 57
Kleberg County, 57
Knobb's Branch, 223
Kunetka, James, 2
Kuykendall, J. H., 29–30

labor, organized, 73, 86
Lagarto, Tex., 50
La Gloria, Tex., 196
La Grange, Tex., 177
La Grulla, Tex., 200, 202
Lamar, Mirabeau B., 175
Lamar County, 49, 55, 59
Lamb County, 55
Lamesa, Tex., 49
Lampasas, Tex., 49
Lampasas River, 49
land, 147–49, 170–71, 174, 192, 194, 240, 243; costs of, 75, 109; description of, 139–40; ownership

land (*cont.*)
of, 200–201; subdivisions of, 122
landscape, 3, 5, 7, 29–30, 39, 49, 52, 92, 93, 229, 232, 236–37, 238, 244
Langford, Georgia, 127
Langtry, Lillie, 60
language, 193, 194, 198, 200, 204, 211, 219, 221, 228, 233; bilingualism, 220, 224–25; trilingualism, 226
Laredo, Tex., 44, 131
La Salle County, 50
The Last Picture Show, 185, 186
Lavaca County, 55
Lavaca River, 43
law, attitude toward, 211
Lea, Tom, 183, 185
Leaving Cheyenne, 185, 186
Lee, Robert E., 60
Lee County, 56
Lehmann, Carolyn, 128
León, Alonso de, 42, 46
León, Martín de, 44, 47
Leon County, 39, 153
Levelland, Tex., 49
Lexington, Tex., 56
Liberty, Tex., 42
life-styles, 119, 196, 200, 204, 206, 219
Limestone County, 39, 47
Lipan, Tex., 38
Lipscomb County, 230
liquor, 214
literature, 57, 170–89, 192, 233; character types in, 181–82; of the Southwest, 178–79; urban vs. rural themes in, 185; about women, 121
———, types of: autobiography, 175; drama, 184; essay, 185; folklore, 178; novel, 185; poetry, 184; regionalism, 178
Little Hope, Tex., 52
"The Little Old Sod Shanty on My Claim" ("My Little Old Log Cabin in the Lane"), 146–47
Live Oak County, 50, 51
livestock, 134
Llano, Tex., 49
Llano Estacado, 32, 95

Index

Loco, Tex., 50
Locust Grove, Tex., 52
Lomax, John, 158
Lone Star Steel Company, 88
Long, Rhoda Ellen, 130
Long Point, Tex., 32
Longview, Tex., 130
Los Ebanos, Tex., 49
Los Fresnos, Tex., 49
"The Lost Frontier," 244
Louise, Tex., 62
Louisiana French, 130
Loving, Long Joe, 176
Lower Colorado River Authority, 90
Low Pinoak Creek, 223
Loyal Valley, Tex., 60
Lubbock, Tex., 53, 58, 132, 133, 185
Lucas, A. F., 77
Luckenbach, Tex., 3, 81–82, 168
Luling, Tex., 64
lumbering, 30
Lutherans, 222, 224, 225, 231, 234

McCulloch County, 41
McDonald, Walter, 185
Macedonia, Tex., 53
McGloin, James, 45
machinery, 127, 134
Mackay, J. W., 62
Mackay, Tex., 62
McMullen, John, 45
McMurtry, Larry, 171, 185–87
Macune, C. W., 72
Madero, Francisco, 42
Madisonville, Tex., 60
Major, Mabel, 174
Manchaca, Tex., 47
Marathon, Tex., 56
Marfa, Tex., 57
Marin, John, 2
Marion County, 129
marriage, 214, 233
Marshall, John, 60
Marshall, Tex., 60
Maryneal, Tex., 62
Mason County, 59, 60, 95
Massengill, Fred, 49
Matagorda, Tex., 49–50
Matagorda County, 56

Matthews, Sallie Reynolds, 175
maverick, 14
Maverick County, 19
meatpacking, 82
mechanization, 194
media and information, 126, 128–29
Medina, Pedro, 46
Medina, Tex., 45–46
Mekolik, Vlasta, 124
Menard, Michael B., 46
Menard County, 106
Menchaca, José Antonio, 47
Menchaca Spring, 47
Mencken, H. L., 174
Mennonites, 234
Mercedes, Tex., 47
Mesquite, Tex., 52
Methodists, 223
Meusebach, John O., 22, 41, 56
Mexía, Enrique Antonio Guillermo, 47
Mexia, Tex., 47
Mexican Americans, 95, 96, 99, 130, 132, 133, 134, 136, 192, 193, 194, 196–204, 245
Mexicans, 44, 48, 142
Michler, N., 25
Midland, Tex., 133
Midland County, 133
migrants, 194, 196, 199, 202, 203
migration, 206. *See also* immigration
Milam County, 131
Miller, Mrs. S. G., 30
Miller, Warren C., 184
Mills County, 131
minerals, 88
mining, 11, 31, 87
minstrelsy, 136
Mirando, Nicolas, 46
Mirando City, Tex., 46
Missouri Pacific Railroad, 47
mobility, 195, 196, 198, 200, 203–204; upward, 221
mohair, 86
Monclova, Tex., 44
Montague County, 41, 54
Montgomery, Cora, 19
Montgomery County, 59
Morris County, 88, 129

Index

mortgages, farm, 79
Mount Carmel, Tex., 53
Mount Moriah, Tex., 53
Mount Pisgah, Tex., 53
Mount Tabor, Tex., 53
Mount Zion, Tex., 53
movies, 191
Moving On, 186
music, 192, 194, 245; folk origins of, 137–38, 160, 168
———, types of: Austin sound, 165; black rhythm and blues, 160, 162; country and western, 136, 153, 160, 162, 167, 168; ethnic, 152, 157, 162; gospel, 160–61; hillbilly, 162; hymns, 215–16; jazz, 160, 162; modern rock, 160; play-party songs, 139; ragtime, 160; religious, 157–60; swing, 160; yodeling, 162
musical instruments, 152, 154, 160
"My Horses Ain't Hungry," 151
myth, 118, 137, 169, 186–87, 191, 194, 243, 244; of cowboy, 144–45, 176–77; denial of, 7, 23; of last frontier, 14; of promise, 7, 23; of rural scene, 93; of Texas, 2, 3, 6, 7, 8; of West, 52, 176–77

Nacogdoches, Tex., 26, 38, 76, 206
Nacogdoches tribe, 39
Nacona, Peta, 41
Nada, Tex., 56
National Industrial Recovery Act, 81
native Americans, 38, 47, 107, 142–43, 144, 177, 193, 228
natural gas, 81, 87, 133
natural resources, 82–83
Navarro County, 54
Navasota, Tex., 217
Navidad, Tex., 42
Navidad River, 42
Nazareth, Tex., 53, 54
Neff, Pat, 82
Nelson, Willie, 168
New Brandenburg (later Old Glory), Tex., 60
New Braunfels, Tex., 23, 28, 177
New Deal, 80, 83
New Deal, Tex., 57

New Hope, Tex., 52
New Jerusalem, Tex., 53
"New Morality," 213
newspapers, 172, 226, 237
New Ulm, Tex., 56, 223, 224
New York, Texas, and Mexican Railway, 62
Nielsen, George, 222
Nimrod, Tex., 53, 54
Nine Nations of North America, 14
Nineveh, Tex., 53
"Noon Wine," 181
"*Noon Wine*: The Sources," 179–80
Norse, Tex., 56
North Texas, 132, 238
Norwegians, 56, 241, 246
nostalgia, 2, 3, 11–12, 14–15, 55–56, 93, 119, 145, 168–69, 243, 246
Notla, Tex., 62
Notrees, Tex., 52
Nueces County, 42
Nueces Valley, 30, 45
Nugent, Thomas L., 74

Oak Grove, Tex., 52
occupations, changes in, 207
"The Ocean Burial" ("Bury Me Not on the Lone Prairie"), 145–46
Ochiltree County, 132
O'Connor, Flannery, 181
Odessa, 230, 231
"Ode to Texas," 175
Ogallala Aquifer, 79, 85
oil, 67, 76, 78, 80, 81, 84, 86–87, 90, 119, 133, 134, 183
Oilton, Tex., 131
O'Keefe, Georgia, 2
Oldenburg, Tex., 56
Old Glory, Tex., 60
"Old Joe Clark," 142, 154–56
"Old Mortality," 171, 182
Old Wire Road, 59
Olmsted, Frederick Law, 6, 7, 18, 23, 28, 172, 174, 177
Omega, Tex., 58
Oncken, Johann Gerhart, 234
Onion Creek, 24, 29
Onstott, A. H., 51
Orange, Tex., 82

Index

Orange County, 130
Oster, Adolph, 236
Ozona, Tex., 48

Pages, Pierre, 27
Palatinate, 231
Palestine, Tex., 53
Palito Blanco, Tex., 49
Paluxy River, 187
Pampa, Tex., 49
Pandora, Tex., 57
Panhandle, 48, 75, 81, 85, 132
panic of 1893, 74
Panna Maria, Tex., 45
Panola County, 59
Paradise, Tex., 54
Parker, Cynthia Ann, 41
Parker, Quanah, 41
Parker County, 41
Parrilla, Diego, 41
Pawnee, Tex., 39
Peach Creek, 27
Pearce, T. M., 174
Pearland, Tex., 52
Pecan Gap, Tex., 52
Pecos and Northern Texas Railroad, 50
Peerless, Tex., 55
Peneteka tribe, 41
Penn, Gabriel J., 56
Pep, Tex., 59
Permanent School Fund, 76
Perry, George Sessions, 183
Perry, Henry, 39
Perry's Point (later Anahuac), Tex., 39
A Personal Country, 54
petrochemical industry, 87
Petrolia, Tex., 236
Petronila, Tex., 42
phonographs, 162
Pierce, Shanghai, 62
Pierce's Station, 64
Pilkington, Tom, 178
Pine Grove, Tex., 52
Piñeda, Alonzo Álvarez de, 41
"Piney Woods," 93
Pipeline Act, 81
Placedo Junction, 47
place names, 36–65, 223; Anglo-

place names (*cont.*)
  American, 51; etymology of, 41, 51, 57, 65; Hispanic, 41–51; native American, 38–41; opposition to, 64
Place Names of Northeast Texas, 53
Plains, Tex., 49
Plano, Tex., 49
Pleasant Grove, Tex., 52
Pluck, Tex., 59
Plum, Tex., 52
Poles, 45
politics, 72–73, 74, 119, 198, 204, 205, 233
Polk County, 59
poll tax, 205
Pope, John, 25
population, 183, 198, 243; dispersal of, 138, 142, 168; distribution of, 112, 114, 115–16, 122; shifts in, 84
Populists, 73, 74, 77
Porter, Katherine Ann, 171, 179–82, 186, 187
Port Lavaca, Tex., 50
Porvenir, Tex., 51
Potter, R. M., 175
Potter County, 45
poultry, 86
poverty. *See* wealth, distribution of
Power, James, 45, 47
Praha, Tex., 56
prairie, 17–22, 32, 34, 144; defined, 22
Prairie Creek, Tex., 17, 18
Prairie Hill, Tex., 17
Prairie View, Tex., 17
Presidio County, 47, 51, 57
Progress, Tex., 59
Progressives, 74
Prosper, Tex., 59
Providence, Tex., 53
Prussia, 222
public lands, 76
public services, 246
Purgatory Creek, 53

Quail, Tex., 53
Quanah, Tex., 41
Quitaque, Tex., 39

Index

Rabb's Creek, 223
radios, 162
Ragtime (later Amarillo), Tex., 48
Railroad Commission, 81
railroads, 69, 72, 73, 75, 76, 83, 95, 107, 109, 130, 201. *See also specific railroads*
Ramón, Domingo, 43
ranching, 27–28, 86, 130, 131, 133
Ransom, Harry, 37
Raymondville, Tex., 130
Reagan County, 45
Reconstruction, 174, 217
Red River, 40, 52, 146–47, 228, 229, 238
Red River County, 40, 56
Reformed Protestants, 234
Refugio, Tex., 45
Refugio County, 47
regions, 14. *See also specific regions in Texas*
Reichsdeutsche, 236, 237
Reklaw, Tex., 62
religion, 194, 233–34, 240; of immigrants, 204, 219–20, 222, 227, 229; and music, 136, 154, 157–60; in place names, 41, 53, 59–60; as reason for migration, 230; in rural black community, 215–16
Remember the Alamo, 175
Remlig, Tex., 62
Republic of Texas, 204
resources, 22–23, 105
revivals, 157
Richardson, Tex., 58
Rio Grande, 27, 44, 48, 49, 51, 79, 85, 95, 190, 199, 200
Rio Grande City, Tex., 200
Rio Hondo, Tex., 196
Rising Star, Tex., 59
Riviera, Tex., 57
Roans Prairie, Tex., 17
Robertson, Eck, 153
Robertson County, 28
Rodgers, Jimmie, 162, 168
Roemer, Ferdinand, 18, 22
Rogers, Polly Ann, 38
Rohrbach/Odessa, Russia, 232, 238
romanticism, 3, 11. *See also* nostalgia

Roosevelt, Franklin D., 80
Roosevelt, Tex., 60
Ropesville Farms, 111
Rosenbusch, Joyce, 123–24, 126
Ross, Lawrence S., 76
Rotary Club, 199
Rusk, Thomas J., 60
Rusk County, 59
Russia, 229, 231, 232, 233, 237

Sabine River, 205
Sacred Harp, 157
Sacul, Tex., 62
Saint Francis, Tex., 45
Saint Hedwig, Tex., 45
Saint Jo, Tex., 54
Salado, Tex., 49
Salado Creek, 49
"Sally Goodin," 153
Saltillo, Tex., 51
Samnorwood, Tex., 62
San Angelo, Tex., 133
San Antonio, Tex., 14, 26, 28, 40, 42, 45, 96, 98, 131, 198, 203
San Antonio and Aransas Pass Railroad, 47, 55
San Antonio River, 39, 45
San Augustine, Tex., 43–44, 206
San Augustine County, 18
San Benito, Tex., 44, 97
San Elizario, Tex., 43
San Isidro, Tex., 44
San Juan, Tex., 44
San Marcos, Tex., 18, 196, 197, 199, 200, 202, 203
San Marcos Baptist Academy, 203
San Marcos River, 43
San Patricio, Tex., 45
San Saba, Tex., 22, 43
San Saba County, 38
San Saba River, 43
Santa Anna, Antonio López de, 51
Santa Anna, Tex., 41
Santa Fe Railroad, 107
Santa Maria, Tex., 43
Santa Rita, Tex., 45
Santa Rosa, Tex., 196
San Ygnacio, Tex., 43

Index

Sardis, Tex., 53
sawmills, 82
Scarborough, Dorothy, 182
Schaffner, Heinrich, 236
Schleicher County, 51
Schmidt, J. F., 60
schools, 193, 198, 200, 226
school tax, 78
Scotch-Irish, 138
Sealsfield, Charles [Karl Anton Postl], 5, 6, 7
Security, Tex., 59
segregation, 196, 198–99, 205
Seguin, Juan N., 46
Seguin, Tex., 46
Seminole tribe, 38, 39
Seminole Wells, Tex., 39
Serbin, Tex., 220, 223, 224, 225, 226, 227, 228
Setag, Tex., 62
Shackelford County, 77
Shady Grove, Tex., 52
sharecroppers, 193, 206, 209, 217
sheep and wool production, 28–29, 73, 86
Shelby County, 41
Shepherd, Albion E., 56
Sherman, Tex., 132
Sherman County, 57
Shiloh, Tex., 53
shipping, 83
"Shoot the Buffalo," 139–40
Shrake, Bud, 183
Sinton, Tex., 45
slavery, 174, 193, 204, 205, 207, 209, 217, 240
Slide, Tex., 53, 57
A Small Town Is Best for Waiting, 184
Smith, Edward, 54
Smith, Henry Nash, 6
Smyrna, Tex., 53
social relationships, 207, 208–12
Somebody's Darling, 186
Sour Lake, Tex., 52, 80
Southern Literary Messenger, 145
Southern Pacific Railroad, 56, 107
South Texas, 96, 99, 133, 192, 194, 196, 197, 199, 200

Southwest, 146, 152, 165, 177, 193, 196
Southwestern University, 126, 131
Southwest Texas State University, 197, 203
Spaniards, 40, 41, 45, 53
Spanish, 5, 26, 38, 48, 49, 50, 193, 198, 199
Spindletop, 77, 78, 80
Stamps-Baxter Music Company, 160, 165
Stamps Quartet, 160
Starr, Belle, 121
Starr County, 44, 50, 200
Stephens County, 127
Stephenville, 131
Sterling, Ross, 81
Sterne, Adolphus, 25
Stiff, Edward, 19
Stock Raisers' Association of North West Texas, 75
Stonewall County, 60
Stratford, Tex., 57
Stratton, Nathan, 46
Streiber, Whitley, 2
String Prairie, Tex., 17
Stringtown, Tex., 53
Sublime, Tex., 55
Sulphur Creek, 39
Sunbelt, 86, 132
"Sweet Rivers," 159
Sweetwater, Tex., 52, 182

Taft, Tex., 60
Tahoka Lake, 40
Talon, Pierre and Jean Baptiste, 26
Tanner, Gid, 162
Tarpley, Fred, 37, 53, 56
Tarrant County, 122
Tawakoni tribe, 39
taxes, 78
technology, 109, 207, 240; changes caused by, 126–27, 134
Tehuacana, Tex., 38, 39
Telegraph, Tex., 58
Telephone, Tex., 58
Telfener, Joseph, 62
Telferner, Tex., 62

Index

tenant farming. *See* sharecroppers; farms
Teneha, Tex., 41
Tennessee Colony, Tex., 56
Tennyson, Tex., 57
Terán, Domingo de, 42
Terlingua, Tex., 56
Terms of Endearment, 186
Terry County, 133
Texas: origin of name, 38
Texas Agricultural Extension Service, 122
Texas Almanac, 32
Texas and New Orleans Railroad, 47, 50, 60
Texas and Pacific Railroad, 53, 54, 107
Texas Board of Water Engineers, 10
"Texas Boys," 141–42
Texas Cattle Raisers' Association, 76
Texas Co-operative Association, 73
Texas Cooperative Forest Management Act, 88
Texas Forest Service, 10
Texas legislature, 73, 76
Texas Observer, 171
Texas Planning Board, 83
Texas Railroad Commission, 74
Texas Rangers, 204
Texas State Land Board, 76
Texas Trilogy, 184
Texas Water Conservation Association, 10
Texas Water Plan, 90
textiles, 69, 88
Throckmorton, James, 60
Tinrag, Tex., 62
Tioga, Tex., 41
Titus County, 130
Tom Bean, Tex., 62
Tom Green County, 45
Tonkawa tribe, 5
towns: layout of, 198–99, 201, 232
Trammel's Trace, 59
transportation, 83, 196, 204; changes caused by, 126, 134. *See also* railroads
Travis County, 47
Treviño, Jesús, 43

Trickham, Tex., 58
Trinity, Tex., 42
Trinity Bay, 83
Trinity River, 39, 42, 90, 190, 204
Tulia, Tex., 49
Turkey, Tex., 53
Turner, Frederick Jackson, 176
Tyler, Tex., 60, 132

Ugalde, Juan de, 46
Uncertain, Tex., 37, 59
United States Post Office Department: role of, in naming towns, 42, 43, 45, 50, 54, 55, 56, 57, 58, 59
Unity, Tex., 59
University of Texas, 76, 124, 192
urbanization, 31, 77, 86, 238, 240, 243, 245, 246
Utopia, 54
Uvalde, Tex., 46
Uvalde County, 46, 54

values, 123, 170–72, 191, 207, 209, 228
Val Verde County, 43, 48
A Vaquero of the Brush Country, 177
Vega, Tex., 49
Viboras, Tex., 50
Victoria, Tex., 44, 62
Victoria County, 47
Vidaurri, José Jesús, 47
Vidaurri, Tex., 47
Vietnamese, 130
villages, 194, 202
Vliet, R. G., 183

Waco, Tex., 38, 72
Walnut Grove, Tex., 52
Wamba, Tex., 58
Warren, Robert Penn, 175
Washington, Tex., 58, 60
Washington County, 58, 95, 237
water, 5, 8, 10, 27, 29–30, 40–41, 49, 52, 79, 82, 90, 246
Waverley, Tex., 57
Waxahachie, Tex., 39
Waxahachie Creek, 39
wealth, distribution of, 8, 116, 162, 200–201

weather, 146, 243
Webb, Walter Prescott, 177–78, 187
Webb County, 46, 52, 130
Weesatche, Tex., 47
Weimar, Tex., 56
Weir, Esther, 124
Welcome, Tex., 59–60
Welfare, Tex., 58, 215, 216
Wends (Serbs), 192, 220–28
West, myth of. *See* myth: of West
West Texas, 83, 85, 95, 96, 107, 129, 130, 133, 134, 182, 183, 184, 244, 246
Wharton County, 49, 50, 57
White, B. F., 157
White, James P., 184
White, Theodore, 12
White Deer, Tex., 53
whites, 207, 210, 217
Whitman, Walt, 36
Whon, Tex., 47
Wichita County, 56
Wichita Falls, Tex., 38, 229, 232
Wier, Allen, 183
Wiest (Wüst), George, 236
Wilhelm, Johanna, 106
Willacy County, 130
Williams, Hank, 165, 168
Williamson County, 131
Wilson, Augusta E., 175
Wilson County, 57
The Wind, 182
windmills, 75, 93, 130
Windthorst, Tex., 236
Wise County, 54, 132
Wohlgemuth, Fred, 236
women, 7, 118–34, 150, 183, 191, 200, 245
Wood, George T., 60
Wood County, 52
Woodville, Tex., 60
wool, 28–29, 73, 86
World War I, 79, 226, 237
World War II, 80, 84, 85, 90, 115, 165, 168, 179, 196, 227
Worster, Donald, 12
Wrede, Friedrich von, 24
Württemberg, 231

XIT Ranch, 50, 121

Yoakum County, 133
York's Creek, 53
Ysleta, Tex., 42

Zapata, Antonio, 46
Zapata, Tex., 46, 196
Zapata County, 43, 46
Zavalla, Tex., 46
Zephyr, Tex., 55